SOUND

Edited by Terry Jones

A - K

100
CONTEMPORARY
FASHION
DESIGNERS

TASCHEN

100 zeitgenössische Modedesigner
100 créateurs de mode contemporains

PHOTOGRAPHY TERRY JONES. RAF SIMONS. AUTUMN/WINTER 2002.

PHOTOGRAPHY TERRY JONES. YOHJI YAMAMOTO.

**Volume I
A - K**

PHOTOGRAPHY TERRY JONES. JOHN GALLIANO AUTUMN/WINTER 2004.

Volume II
L - Z

100 CONTEMPORARY FASHION DESIGNERS

When Benedikt Taschen first proposed this idea – to make a two-volume encyclopedic selection from the highly successful 'Fashion Now' editions, my first reaction was uncertainty. The nature of fashion and the business that naturally changes every season flagged up various problems. Designers move about, some go out of business. Fashion is constantly reinvented. But on reflection, I realised that after three decades of promoting creativity and ideas, this book selection from the pages of i-D since 2000 would serve as an inspiration for a new generation. The potential of fashion is to create work and jobs in which many people find self-expression. As we approach 2010, the challenges that face the industry are to research fabrics and dyes and improve production techniques in a sustainable way and also to maintain traditional crafts and skills in an increasingly competitive market. In editing these books from the original 160 to 100 designers, we have tried to keep a cross section, from the revered titans in the industry to the exciting new talent that are constantly striving to survive. Every season is a new challenge and the global recession, which has hit the fashion industry hard, is forcing re-evaluation, reinvention and the reinterpretation of luxury through necessity. I always thought fashion communicates who we are. Human priorities are shelter, food and clothing. Clothing is often an expression of your life. After any hardship, whatever war or natural disaster, people have found different ways to express survival. Whether fashion is frivolous, fabulous or functional, the designers' task is to surprise and entertain. Recession is for the brave heart. Ideas are the currency for success along with value for money, innovation not imitation, authenticity and a new ethical awareness. With fashion today the choice is massive: from laser to hand-cut, from stitch to weld, from man-made to nature-made, organic or chemical, sustainability is the new byword, which could see us all recycling our wardrobe within the next decade. Share-ware could be the next chic. Travel light – toothbrush and panties in your bum bag and your wardrobe arranged over the internet with 'fashion family friends' or share-ware by clubbing together to buy a fabulous couture creation and time share. It's not so far removed from borrowing Wellingtons and raincoats when visiting friends in their country home or renting ski boots while on holiday! 2008 saw many collections inspired by resourceful ideas. From Prada and Comme des Garçons to Rodarte and Ralph Lauren, we saw patches, overstitch or over-dying. The designers' skill is to exploit every idea and retain their individuality, which gives them a sustainable credibility not to be lost or their name depends on it. A decade in fashion is a history within the game to create an illusion of change. Look in your wardrobe and the odds are you will be mixing that Spring 2000 piece with an Autumn 2005 with a hot-in-the-shop bargain or another find on eBay.

Fashion has never before produced so much stuff and the current crunch has forced us all to re-evaluate our spending habits. A well-known fashion collector with a banker husband confided in me this spring that he had told her to be more careful. But why, she asked. Her purchases are of more value than the interest she might get from money in the bank. She might buy less Comme des Garçons or Margiela but is interested in Christopher Kane or Antonio Marras at Kenzo. Fashion continues to be variable art for many and placing your bets on the future is a demanding challenge for every retail fashion buyer. Their survival depends on their nose for the zeitgeist. People don't just want to replace something they already have in their wardrobe. They want to have a fresh input – something unique – and that is what gets these designers out of bed each day.

TERRY JONES

100 ZEITGENÖSSISCHE MODEDESIGNER

Als Benedikt Taschen vorschlug, aus den überaus erfolgreichen Ausgaben von ‚Fashion Now‘ eine zweibändige Enzyklopädie zu machen, war ich mir zunächst nicht sicher, was ich davon halten sollte. Die Mode an sich und das Geschäft mit ihr bringt es mit sich, dass jede Saison Veränderung bedeutet, was für zahlreiche Probleme sorgt. Designer suchen sich andere Herausforderungen, manche ziehen sich ganz aus dem Geschäft zurück. Mode erfindet sich ständig neu. Als ich länger darüber nachdachte, wurde mir jedoch klar, dass die Auswahl für dieses Buch aus den Seiten von i-D seit 2000 nach drei Jahrzehnten, in denen ich Kreativität und Ideen gefördert habe, einer neuen Generation als Inspiration dienen könnte. Mode bietet die Möglichkeit, Jobs zu schaffen, in denen viele Menschen sich selbst verwirklichen können. Jetzt, wo wir auf das Jahr 2010 zusteuern, sind die Herausforderungen, denen die Textilindustrie sich stellen muss, die Entwicklung von nachhaltigen Materialien, Farben und Produktionstechniken, aber auch die Bewahrung traditioneller Handwerkstechniken in einem immer stärker umkämpften Markt. Bei der Auswahl der 100 Designer für die vorliegenden Bücher aus ursprünglich 160 Namen haben wir versucht, einen Querschnitt zu bieten – von hochverehrten Titanen der Branche bis hin zu aufregenden neuen Talenten, die noch permanent ums Überleben kämpfen. Jede Saison bedeutet eine neue Herausforderung, und die weltweite Rezession, die die Modebranche hart getroffen hat, zwingt zur Neubewertung, Neuerfindung und zu einer neuen Interpretation von Luxus im Verhältnis zur puren Notwendigkeit. Ich war schon immer der Überzeugung, dass Mode unsere Umgebung wissen lässt, wer wir sind. Unterkunft, Nahrung und Kleidung sind menschliche Grundbedürfnisse. Kleidung ist oft Ausdruck unseres Lebensstils. Nach Entbehrungen aller Art, ob durch Krieg oder Naturkatastrophen, haben die Menschen schon immer Wege gefunden, ihr Überleben auszudrücken. Ob frivol, fabelhaft oder funktional – der Designer hat die Aufgabe, uns mit seiner Mode zu überraschen und zu unterhalten. Eine Rezession ist etwas für Kämpfernaturen. Ideen sind die Währung des Erfolgs, dazu Wertigkeit, Innovation statt Imitation, Authentizität und ein neues ethisches Bewusstsein. In der gegenwärtigen Mode ist die Auswahl überwältigend, ob per Laser oder von Hand zugeschnitten, ob genäht oder geschweißt, ob von Menschenhand gemacht oder natürlich gewachsen, organisch oder chemisch. Nachhaltigkeit lautet das neue Schlagwort, das dafür sorgen könnte, dass wir im nächsten Jahrzehnt alle unsere Garderobe recyceln. Shareware könnte der künftige Trend sein. Unbeschwert reisen – mit Zahnbürste und Unterhosen in der Gürteltasche, während man sich die Garderobe via Internet über ‚fashion family friends‘ organisiert. Oder Shareware, bei der man sich zusammentut, um eine fantastische Couture-Kreation zu erstehen, die man sich dann nach dem Prinzip Timesharing teilt. Das ist schließlich nicht so viel anders, als sich beim Besuch von Freunden auf dem Land Gummistiefel und Regenmäntel auszuleihen oder in den Ferien Skischuhe zu mieten. 2008 waren viele Kollektionen von erfinderischen Ideen geprägt. Angefangen bei Prada und Comme des Garçons bis hin zu Rodarte und Ralph Lauren sahen wir Flicken, Gestopftes oder Umgefärbtes. Hier zählt die Fähigkeit der Designer, jede Idee auszunutzen und so ihre Individualität zu bewahren, um sich die nötige Glaubwürdigkeit in Sachen Nachhaltigkeit zu verschaffen, auf die inzwischen kein Markenname mehr verzichten kann. Ein Jahrzehnt entspricht in der Mode einer Epoche in dem Spiel, bei dem es darum geht, die Illusion von Veränderung zu erzeugen. Wenn Sie in Ihren eigenen Schrank schauen, stehen die Chancen gut, dass Sie ein Teil aus dem Frühling 2000 mit einem anderen aus dem Herbst 2005, einem aktuellen Schnäppchen sowie einer Entdeckung bei eBay kombinieren.

Die Mode hat noch nie so viel produziert wie heute, und die aktuelle Wirtschaftskrise hat uns alle gezwungen, unsere Ausgabenpolitik zu überdenken. Eine bekannte Sammlerin von Mode mit einem Banker als Ehemann gestand mir dieses Frühjahr, dass er ihr geraten hätte, zurückhaltender zu sein. Warum?, fragte sie. Denn die von ihr erworbenen Stücke verzeichnen wahrscheinlich mehr Wertzuwachs, als sie im Moment an Zinsen für ihr Geld auf der Bank bekommt. Vielleicht kauft sie weniger Comme des Garçons oder Margiela, interessiert sich aber für Christopher Kane oder Antonio Marras bei Kenzo. Denn Mode gilt weiterhin vielen als veränderliche Kunst, und auf künftige Trends zu setzen ist selbst für den Einkäufer im Einzelhandel eine gehörige Herausforderung. Da hängt das Überleben vom Gespür für den Zeitgeist ab. Die Menschen wollen schließlich nicht einfach nur etwas ersetzen, das sich bereits in ihrem Kleiderschrank befindet. Sie wünschen sich frischen Input – etwas Einzigartiges, und genau das lässt diese Designer jeden Tag aufs Neue motiviert ans Werk gehen.

TERRY JONES

100 CRÉATEURS DE MODE CONTEMPORAINS

La première fois que Benedikt Tachen m'a fait part de son idée, c'est-à-dire réaliser une sélection encyclopédique en deux volumes à partir des deux éditions ‹Fashion Now› à succès, je ne savais pas trop quoi en penser. La nature même de la mode, avec son marché qui change à chaque saison, soulevait divers problèmes. Certains créateurs font faillite, d'autres changent de maison. La mode ne cesse de se réinventer. Après mûre réflexion, je me suis pourtant rendu compte qu'avec trois décennies au service de la créativité et des idées, ce livre réunissant une sélection des pages d'i-D depuis l'an 2000 pourrait servir de source d'inspiration à toute une nouvelle génération. La mode a le potentiel de créer des emplois où de nombreuses personnes auront la possibilité de s'exprimer. Alors que l'année 2010 approche, l'industrie fait face à plusieurs défis : innover dans le domaine des tissus et des teintures, améliorer les techniques de production dans le respect du développement durable, préserver le savoir-faire artisanal et la tradition au sein d'un marché de plus en plus concurrentiel. En réduisant le nombre de créateurs de mode de 160 à 100, nous avons cherché à garder un échantillon représentatif de ce métier, entre les géants adulés déjà bien établis et les nouveaux talents prometteurs qui luttent constamment pour survivre. Chaque saison représente un nouvel enjeu et, nécessité oblige, la crise mondiale qui frappe l'industrie de la mode de plein fouet la contraint à réévaluer, réinventer et réinterpréter le concept de luxe. J'ai toujours pensé que la mode nous permettait d'exprimer qui nous sommes. L'être humain a en priorité besoin d'un toit, de nourriture et de vêtements. La façon dont on s'habille est souvent le reflet d'un style de vie. Après une épreuve, qu'il s'agisse d'une guerre ou d'une catastrophe naturelle, les gens trouvent toujours différentes façons d'exprimer leur idée de la survie. La mode est frivole, la mode est merveilleuse ; fonctionnelle ou fantastique, la mission du créateur consiste à surprendre et à divertir. Seuls les plus courageux survivront à la récession. Les idées sont la condition du succès, tout comme le rapport qualité-prix, l'innovation et non l'imitation, l'authenticité et une nouvelle conscience éthique. La mode d'aujourd'hui nous offre l'embarras du choix ; coupe à la main ou au laser, couture ou soudure, synthétique ou naturel, bio ou chimique, la durabilité est le nouveau maître mot qui, peut-être, nous incitera tous à recycler le contenu de nos placards au cours des dix prochaines années. La culture du partage pourrait devenir le nouveau chic : voyager léger – brosse à dents et culottes dans votre banane – composer sa garde-robe sur Internet avec les « amis de l a famille de la mode », se cotiser à plusieurs pour acheter de fabuleuses créations haute couture et se les partager. En somme, ce n'est pas si différent que d'emprunter bottes de pluie et imperméables quand on part en week-end dans la maison de campagne de ses amis, ou de louer des chaussures de ski pour les vacances à la montagne ! En 2008, de nombreuses collections reposaient sur des idées ingénieuses. Chez Prada, Comme des Garçons, Rodarte et Ralph Lauren, on a vu des patchs, des surpiqûres ou des surteintures. Le talent des créateurs dépend de leur capacité à exploiter la moindre idée tout en conservant la personnalité qui pérennise leur crédibilité ou leur nom. Une décennie de mode, c'est une tranche d'histoire dans le jeu qui consiste à créer l'illusion du changement. En ouvrant votre armoire, il y a de fortes chances que vous combiniez une pièce du printemps 2000 et une de l'automne 2005 avec une bonne affaire ultra tendance ou quelque trouvaille faite sur eBay.

La mode n'a encore jamais produit autant de choses, et les difficultés actuelles nous forcent tous à réévaluer le budget que nous y consacrons. Au printemps dernier, une célèbre collectionneuse de vêtements mariée à un banquier m'a confié que ce dernier lui avait demandé de faire plus attention. Elle ne comprenait pas pourquoi. Ses achats représentent plus d'argent que tous les intérêts qu'elle pourrait gagner en plaçant de l'argent à la banque. Elle achète peut-être moins de Comme des Garçons ou de Margiela, mais s'intéresse à Christopher Kane ou à ce que fait Antonio Marras chez Kenzo. Pour beaucoup, la mode reste un art variable, et miser sur l'avenir représente un risque pour toutes les boutiques. Leur survie dépend de leur flair à capter l'air du temps. Les gens ne veulent pas seulement remplacer un vêtement par un autre. Ils ont besoin de nouveauté, de quelque chose d'unique. Et c'est justement cela qui donne envie aux créateurs de se lever chaque matin.

TERRY JONES

RUFFO RESEARCH BY HAIDER ACKERMANN. SPRING/SUMMER 2003.

"You can only design what you know"
HAIDER ACKERMANN

One of Antwerp's brightest young stars, Haider Ackermann has seen many more ports than the one fronting the town in which he now lives and works. Born in Santa Fe de Bogotá, Colombia, in 1971, he was adopted by a French family. Due to his father's business obligations, he spent his childhood moving around the globe. After living in Ethiopia, Chad, France, Algeria and the Netherlands, he decided fashion was his vocation. High school finished, he left home in 1994 and headed for Belgium to study at the fashion department of Antwerp's Royal Academy. During his three-year stay (he left the four-year course prematurely because of financial difficulties), he also worked as an intern at John Galliano's Paris office. Taking a job as an assistant to his former academy teacher Wim Neels in 1998, he worked on both the men's and womenswear collections of the Belgian designer. After saving money and taking encouragement from his friends and acquaintances – among them Raf Simons – Ackermann finally took the plunge and presented his first, self-financed women's collection in Paris for autumn/winter 2002. His subtle, dignified and sensuous clothes immediately struck a chord with buyers and editors, as they did with Italian leather manufacturer Ruffo. Just two weeks after his debut show, Ackermann was hired as the head designer for Ruffo Research and commissioned to create two collections (spring/summer and autumn/winter 2003), while continuing to produce his own line. Ackermann is now receiving even wider acclaim, not least in the form of the prestigious Swiss Textiles Award at the 2004 Grand Fashion Festival. Ackermann's sensitivity with drape and textures shows through in every collection. His autumn/winter 2009 collection showed his mastery of leather and heavy metal chainmail. These are modern clothes for strong women who love the subtle colour palette that adds to Ackermann's seasonal collections.

Haider Ackermann gilt als einer der viel versprechenden Jungstars von Antwerpen und hat schon einiges mehr von der Welt gesehen als nur die Stadt, in der er jetzt lebt und arbeitet. Geboren wurde er 1971 im kolumbianischen Santa Fe de Bogotá und kurz darauf von einer französischen Familie adoptiert. Aufgrund der geschäftlichen Verpflichtungen seines Vaters kam er schon als Kind in der ganzen Welt herum. Nachdem er in Äthiopien, dem Tschad, Frankreich, Algerien und den Niederlanden gelebt hatte, erkannte er in der Mode seine Berufung. Als er 1994 die Schule abgeschlossen hatte, machte er sich auf den Weg nach Belgien, um an der Königlichen Akademie in Antwerpen zu studieren. Während seines dreijährigen Aufenthalts (er musste die an sich vierjährige Ausbildung wegen finanzieller Schwierigkeiten vorzeitig abbrechen) jobbte Ackermann bereits als Praktikant im Pariser Atelier von John Galliano. Nachdem er 1998 eine Assistentenstelle bei seinem ehemaligen Dozenten Wim Neels bekommen hatte, arbeitete er sowohl an Herren- wie an Damenkollektionen des belgischen Designers mit. Als er etwas Geld gespart hatte, wagte er mit Unterstützung seiner Freunde und Bekannten – darunter Leute wie Raf Simons – schließlich den Sprung ins kalte

Wasser. In Paris präsentierte Ackermann seine erste selbst finanzierte Damenkollektion, und zwar für Herbst/Winter 2002. Seine raffinierten, würdevollen und sinnlichen Kreationen kamen bei Einkäufern und Journalisten wie auch beim italienischen Lederwarenhersteller Ruffo auf Anhieb gut an. So wurde Ackermann nur zwei Wochen nach seinem Debüt Chefdesigner von Ruffo Research und erhielt den Auftrag für zwei Kollektionen (Frühjahr/Sommer und Herbst/Winter 2003). Nebenbei entwarf der Designer noch für seine eigene Linie. Heute erhält er mehr Zuspruch denn je, nicht zuletzt 2004 mit dem angesehenen Swiss Textiles Award im Rahmen des Grand Fashion Festival. Ackermanns Gespür für Drapierungen und Texturen ist in jeder einzelnen Kollektion sichtbar. Die Kreationen für Herbst/Winter 2009 zeigten sein meisterhaftes Geschick mit Leder und schweren Kettenhemden aus Metall. Dabei handelt es sich um moderne Kleider für starke Frauen, die die dezente Farbpalette lieben, die Ackermann für seine saisonalen Kollektionen verwendet.

Célébré comme l'une des étoiles montantes d'Anvers, Haider Ackermann a fait étape dans bien d'autres ports que celui qui borde la ville dans laquelle il travaille et vit aujourd'hui. Adopté par une famille française, il est en fait né en 1971 à Santa Fe de Bogota en Colombie. En raison des obligations professionnelles de son père, il passe son enfance à parcourir le monde. Après avoir vécu en Ethiopie, au Tchad, en France, en Algérie et aux Pays-Bas, il se rend compte que la mode est sa véritable vocation. En 1994, il termine le lycée et part pour la Belgique afin d'étudier la mode à l'Académie Royale d'Anvers. Pendant son cursus de trois ans (il abandonnera prématurément la quatrième année en raison de problèmes financiers), il fait un stage dans les bureaux parisiens de John Galliano. En 1998, il devient l'assistant de son ancien professeur à l'Académie, le styliste belge Wim Neels, travaillant sur les collections pour homme et pour femme. Il réussit sagement à mettre de l'argent de côté et, encouragé par ses amis et relations, parmi lesquels Raf Simons, Ackermann fait finalement le grand plongeon et présente une première collection féminine autofinancée aux défilés parisiens automne-hiver 2002. Grâce à leur style subtil et voluptueux néanmoins empreint de dignité, ses vêtements séduisent immédiatement les acheteurs et les rédacteurs de mode, ainsi que le maroquinier italien Ruffo qui, deux semaines après son premier défilé, nomme Ackermann styliste principal de Ruffo Research et lui demande de créer deux collections (printemps-été et automne-hiver 2003) tout en lui permettant de continuer à travailler sous sa propre griffe. Aujourd'hui, la réputation d'Ackermann n'est plus à faire. Il a notamment reçu le prestigieux Swiss Textiles Award décerné au Grand Fashion Festival en 2004. Toutes ses collections témoignent d'un grand sens du drapé et de la texture. Son défilé automne/hiver 2009 affiche sa maîtrise du cuir et de la cotte de mailles revisitée « heavy metal » : autant de vêtements modernes destinés aux femmes de caractère qui adorent la palette de couleurs subtile de chaque collection d'Ackermann.

PETER DE POTTER

What are your signature designs? I can't define that, it would be up to others, but besides that, I guess it is still too early to talk about a certain signature. There are elements, there is a constant search. There are muted non-colours, the smock, the timelessness, the masculinity… **What is your favourite piece from any of your collections?** I am still waiting for that feeling of a favourite. Still chasing that moment… **What's your ultimate goal?** To find the right balance **What inspires you?** The contrast **Can fashion still have a political ambition?** It somehow always reflects the time and all aspects of the life we live **Who do you have in mind when you design?** It is getting more abstract with time. A gesture, a mood, an attitude, a passerby **Is the idea of creative collaboration important to you?** Yes it is, though the difficulty is allowing yourself to be lost in the trust of the other. **Who has been the greatest influence on your career?** My friends for their encouragment and support! **How have your own experiences affected your work as a designer?** You can only design what you know… there is no distinction between you and your memories, your experiences and your daily life. And that all is attached to my work **Is designing difficult for you? If so, what drives you to continue?** Yes… it puts me in doubt, in a situation where you are not confident with yourself, but it challenges me and I am driven by the unknown, the dissatisfaction **Have you ever been influenced or moved by the reaction to your designs?** Impossible not to be **What's your definition of beauty?** The intriguing thing that makes your heart beat **What's your philosophy?** Never stop challenging yourself! Never lose enthusiasm! **What is the most important lesson you've learned?** The richness of friendship.

"Perfection is never achieved, so you need to go on working"
AZZEDINE ALAÏA

Azzedine Alaïa's place in the design hall of fame is guaranteed – his signature being the second skin that he creates when challenging the boundaries of flesh and fabric. Alaïa was born in Tunisia in the '40s to wheat-farming parents. A French friend of his mother's fed Alaïa's instinctive creativity with copies of 'Vogue' and lied about his age to get him into the local Ecole des Beaux-Arts to study sculpture – a discipline in which he didn't excel, but that he would put to good use in the future. After spotting an ad for a vacancy at a dressmaker's, Alaïa's sister taught him to sew and he started making copies of couture dresses for neighbours. Soon afterwards, he went to Paris to work for Christian Dior, but managed only five days of sewing labels before being fired. Alaïa moved to Guy Laroche, where for two seasons he learned his craft while earning his keep as housekeeper to the Marquise de Mazan. In 1960, the Blegiers family snapped up Alaïa, and for the next five years he was both housekeeper and dressmaker to the Countess and her friends, mixing with glamorous Paris society: His first ready-to-wear collection for Charles Jourdan in the '70s was not well received, but eventually fashion editors tuned in to Alaïa's modern elegance. Worldwide success followed with exhibitions, awards, supermodel disciples and the power to command an audience outside of the catwalk schedule: Alaïa shows when he wants, regardless of the round of timetabled international fashion weeks, and editors never miss it. In 1998, he published a book of photographs of his creations, entitled 'Alaïa'. In 2000, he was honoured with a solo exhibition at the New York Guggenheim. In October 2004, he opened his own hotel (5 rue de Moussy) adjoining the Alaïa headquarters in Paris. The headquarters also house an exhibition space that has been showing work by fashion and furniture designers such as Paul Poiret and Shiro Kuramata as well as several photo exhibitions since 2004. After a seven-year-long successful and positive partnership with the Prada group, Alaïa joined forces with the Richemont group in 2007.

Ein Platz in der Hall of Fame der Designer ist Azzedine Alaïa bereits sicher – dank seines Markenzeichens, der zweiten Haut, mit der er die Grenzen zwischen Körper und Stoff aufzuheben scheint. Geboren wurde der tunesische Bauernsohn in den 1940er Jahren. Eine französische Freundin seiner Mutter förderte seine angeborene Kreativität mit Ausgaben der Vogue und mogelte bei seinem Alter, um ihn an der Kunstakademie von Tunis im Fach Bildhauerei unterzubringen. Er erwies sich zwar nicht als überragender Student, doch sollte ihm diese Ausbildung in der Zukunft noch von Nutzen sein. Weil ihn die Anzeige für eine freie Stelle in einer Schneiderei interessierte, ließ er sich von seiner Schwester das Nähen beibringen und kopierte schon bald Haute-Couture-Kleider für die Frauen der Nachbarschaft. Kurz darauf ging er nach Paris, um für Christian Dior zu arbeiten, dort nähte er allerdings gerade mal fünf Tage lang Etiketten ein, bevor man ihn feuerte. Daraufhin wechselte Alaïa zu Guy Laroche, wo er zwei Saisons lang sein Handwerk lernte und sich seinen Lebensunterhalt als Haushälter der Marquise de Mazan verdiente. 1960 engagierte ihn die Familie Blegiers, bei der er fünf Jahre lang Haushälter und Hausschneider für die Comtesse und ihre Freundinnen sein sollte und auch Zugang zur Glamour-Gesellschaft von Paris fand. Seine erste Prêt-à-porter-Kollektion für Charles Jourdan in den 1970er Jahren kam nicht besonders gut an, doch irgendwann hatten sich die Modejournalisten an Alaïas moderne Eleganz gewöhnt. Der weltweite Erfolg wurde von Ausstellungen, Preisen, treu ergebenen Supermodels und der Macht begleitet, ein Publikum auch abseits des offiziellen Modenschau-Kalenders zu finden. Alaïa präsentiert seine Entwürfe, wann es ihm passt, und ignoriert einfach die exakt terminierten internationalen Modewochen. Die Journalisten sind trotzdem immer da. 1998 veröffentlichte der Designer einen Band mit Fotos seiner Kreationen unter dem Titel „Alaïa". Im Jahr 2000 begab er sich unter die Fittiche des Prada-Konzerns. Im selben Jahr ehrte das New Yorker Guggenheim Museum ihn mit einer Einzelausstellung. Sein Hotel in der Pariser Rue de Moussy Nummer 5, gleich neben der Alaïa-Zentrale, wurde im Oktober 2004 eröffnet. Der Firmensitz umfasst auch eine Austellungsfläche, wo seit 2004 Arbeiten von Mode- und Möbeldesignern wie Paul Poiret und Shiro Kuramata sowie einige Fotoschauen präsentiert wurden. Nach einer siebenjährigen erfolgreichen und einvernehmlichen Partnerschaft mit der Prada-Gruppe schloss Alaïa sich 2007 dem Richemont-Konzern an.

Défiant les frontières qui séparent la chair du tissu, les créations « seconde peau » qui distinguent le travail d'Azzedine Alaïa lui garantissent une place de choix dans l'Olympe de la mode. Alaïa est né dans les années 40 en Tunisie de parents cultivateurs de blé. Sa créativité instinctive se nourrit des exemplaires de Vogue d'une amie française de sa mère, qui mentira sur son âge pour le faire entrer à l'Ecole des Beaux-Arts de Tunis. Il y étudie la sculpture, discipline dans laquelle il n'excelle pas particulièrement mais qu'il utilisera à bon escient par la suite. Après avoir repéré une offre d'emploi chez un couturier, la sœur d'Alaïa lui apprend à coudre et il commence à copier les robes haute couture pour ses voisines. Peu de temps après, il s'installe à Paris pour travailler chez Christian Dior, mais se fait mettre à la porte après cinq jours passés à coudre des étiquettes. Alaïa travaille ensuite pour Guy Laroche, chez qui il se forme au métier pendant deux saisons tout en gagnant sa vie en tant qu'intendant de la marquise de Mazan. En 1960, la famille Blegiers embauche Alaïa et pendant cinq ans, il est à la fois l'intendant et le couturier de la comtesse et de ses amis, se mêlant à la haute société parisienne. Dans les années 70, sa première collection de prêt-à-porter pour Charles Jourdan n'est pas bien accueillie, mais les journalistes de mode s'intéressent tout de même à l'élégance moderne d'Alaïa. Le succès mondial s'ensuit grâce à des expositions, des récompenses, le soutien des plus grands top models et le pouvoir de séduire le public même en dehors du calendrier officiel : Alaïa présente ses collections sans se soucier de l'agenda mondial des semaines de la mode, et la presse ne rate pas un seul de ses défilés. En 1998, il sort un livre de photos de ses créations intitulé « Alaïa », puis en 2000, il s'associe au Groupe Prada. La même année, le musée Guggenheim de New York lui consacre toute une exposition. En octobre 2004, il ouvre son propre hôtel (5, rue de Moussy), juste à côté du siège social parisien d'Alaïa. Son quartier général abrite aussi un espace d'exposition qui présente depuis 2004 les œuvres de couturiers et de designers tels que Paul Poiret et Shiro Kuramata, ainsi que plusieurs expositions de photographie. En 2007, après sept années d'un partenariat très réussi avec le groupe Prada, Alaïa s'associe au groupe Richemont. JAMIE HUCKBODY

What is your favourite piece from any of your collections? I'm still waiting for that feeling. I always doubt **How would you describe your work?** It's not me but only journalists who can describe my work **What's your ultimate goal?** Only the future will tell us **What inspires you?** Women **What do you have in mind when you design?** How and when shall I finish it **Is the idea of creative collaboration important to you?** Always **What has been the greatest influence on your career?** Art, sculpture, design, paintings **Which is more important in your work: the process or the product?** The process **Is the designing difficult for you? If so, what drives you to continue?** What drives me to continue is the pleasure to keep on learning. In other words, perfection is never achieved, so you need to go on working **Have you ever been influenced or moved by the reaction to your designs?** Always – emotion is very important **What's your philosophy?** Overall integrity.

"I have realised over time that I have to take responsibility for my actions and beliefs"
GIORGIO ARMANI

Now in his fifth decade of working in fashion, Giorgio Armani is more than just a designer – he's an institution, an icon and a multinational, billion-dollar brand. Armani was born in 1934 in Piacenza, Northern Italy. He spent his formative years not in fashion but studying medicine at university and completing his national service. After working as a buyer for Milanese department store La Rinascente, he scored his first break in 1964, when he was hired by Nino Cerruti to design a menswear line, Hitman. Several years as a successful freelance designer followed, but it was in 1975 that the Giorgio Armani label was set up, with the help of his then business partner Sergio Galeotti. Armani's signature 'unstructured' jackets for both men and women (a womenswear line was established in 1976) knocked the stuffing out of traditional tailoring and, from the late '70s, his clothes became a uniform for the upwardly mobile. Men loved his relaxed suits and muted colour palette of neutral beiges and greys. His designs for women, meanwhile, were admired for an androgynous and modern elegance. Richard Gere's suits in American Gigolo (1980) were a landmark for the designer, as was featuring on the cover of 'Time' magazine in 1982. The brand now encompasses six major fashion lines and has diversified into bedlinen, chocolates and even hotels. From 2000, his designs have been exhibited in a major retrospective show that has travelled worldwide. Armani has also picked up a dedicated Hollywood following, and January 2005 saw the launch in Paris of 'Giorgio Armani Privé', an haute couture-like collection. In February 2009, Armani opened a flagship store on Fifth Avenue, New York, at the height of a global recession. With David Beckham sporting Armani undies on a billboard near you, it's a safe bet that the world of Armani, from bedroom to beyond, will continue to increase its global stature with quiet confidence, which in turn helps his personal projects for disadvantaged children in the global AIDS campaign.

Er arbeitet inzwischen seit fast 50 Jahren in der Modebranche und ist viel mehr als „nur" ein Designer. Giorgio Armani ist eine Institution, eine Ikone und ein internationales, milliardenschweres Markenzeichen. Geboren wurde er 1934 im norditalienischen Piacenza. Die ersten Jahre als Erwachsener verbrachte Armani jedoch nicht in der Modeszene, sondern beim Medizinstudium an der Universität und beim Militär. Nach einer Anstellung als Einkäufer für das Mailänder Kaufhaus La Rinascente landete er 1964 seinen ersten Coup, nachdem Nino Cerruti ihn mit dem Entwurf einer Herrenlinie namens Hitman beauftragt hatte. Es folgten einige Jahre als gefragter freischaffender Designer, bis 1975 mit der Gründung des Labels Giorgio Armani die Weichen für die Zukunft der Mode neu gestellt wurden. Daran beteiligt war damals auch Armanis Geschäftspartner Sergio Galeotti. Markenzeichen waren die „unstrukturierten" Jacketts für Männer wie Frauen (eine Damenlinie wurde 1976 gegründet), die im Unterschied zu traditionell geschneiderten Modellen ganz ohne Polster auskamen. Ab Ende der 1970er galt seine Mode als eine Art Uniform für Leute, die Karriere machten. Männer liebten seine legeren Anzüge und gedämpften Beige- und Grautöne. Dagegen fanden die Entwürfe für Frauen wegen ihrer Androgynität und modernen Eleganz großen Zuspruch. Richard Geres Anzüge in „American Gigolo" (1980) waren ein Meilenstein für den Modemacher, ebenso das Time-Cover von

1982. Heute umfasst die Marke Armani sechs große Modelinien, aber auch Bereiche wie Bettwäsche, Schokolade und sogar Hotels. 2000 wurden seine Entwürfe im Rahmen einer großen Retrospektive weltweit gezeigt. Armani hat sich aber auch eine treue Anhängerschaft in Hollywood aufgebaut. Vielleicht eines seiner ambitioniertesten Projekte war die Präsentation von „Giorgio Armani Privé" im Januar 2005 in Paris, eine Kollektion im Stil der Haute Couture. Im Februar 2009, auf dem Höhepunkt der weltweiten Rezession, eröffnete Armani einen Flagship-Store an der New Yorker Fifth Avenue. Solange David Beckham auf einer Plakatwand in Armani-Slips posiert, kann man wohl ziemlich sicher davon ausgehen, dass die Welt von Armani, angefangen im Schlafzimmer, aber auch weit darüber hinaus, ihren Ruf in der Welt mit ruhiger Selbstverständlichkeit kontinuierlich steigern wird. Das nützt auf der anderen Seite auch den persönlichen Hilfsprojekten des Designers zugunsten unterprivilegierter Kinder in der weltweiten Kampagne gegen Aids.

Avec cinquante ans de métier derrière lui, Giorgio Armani est bien plus qu'un couturier : c'est une véritable institution, une icône et une multinationale qui pèse plusieurs milliards de dollars. Armani est né en 1934 à Piacenza dans le nord de l'Italie. Il suit d'abord des études de médecine à l'université avant de faire son service militaire. Après avoir travaillé comme acheteur pour La Rinascente, le grand magasin milanais, il se lance dans la mode en 1964 quand Nino Cerruti le recrute pour dessiner une ligne pour homme, Hitman. Les années suivantes, il rencontre un grand succès en tant que styliste free-lance mais il faut attendre 1975 pour voir l'avenir de la mode se transformer grâce à la création de la griffe Giorgio Armani, qu'il fonde avec l'aide de Sergio Galeotti, son partenaire en affaires de l'époque. Les vestes « déstructurées » pour homme et pour femme devenues la signature d'Armani (une ligne pour femme sera lancée en 1976) bouleversent les codes et dès la fin des années 70, ses créations s'imposent comme l'uniforme des ambitieux aux dents longues. Les hommes adorent ses costumes décontractés et sa palette de beiges et de gris neutres, tandis que ses vêtements pour femme séduisent grâce à leur élégance androgyne et moderne. Les costumes dessinés pour le personnage de Richard Gere dans « American Gigolo » (1980) marquent un tournant dans la carrière du créateur, qui connaît la consécration en 1982 en faisant la couverture du magazine Time. La marque, qui regroupe aujourd'hui six grandes lignes de mode, s'est aussi diversifiée dans des domaines tels que la literie, les chocolats et même les hôtels. En l'an 2000, son travail a fait l'objet d'une grande rétrospective qui a voyagé dans les musées du monde entier. Armani revendique aussi des fans parmi l'élite d'Hollywood. Son projet le plus ambitieux à ce jour a été révélé en janvier 2005 à Paris, théâtre du lancement de « Giorgio Armani Privé », collection de haute couture de coupe traditionnelle. En février 2009, la marque a ouvert une immense boutique sur la Cinquième Avenue de New York en pleine crise mondiale. Alors qu'il est impossible d'échapper aux affiches de David Beckham posant en sous-vêtements Armani, on peut être certain que l'univers Armani poursuivra tranquillement mais sûrement son expansion internationale au-delà des chambres à coucher. En retour, ce succès profite aux initiatives personnelles de Giorgio Armani pour les enfants défavorisés dans le cadre de la campagne mondiale de lutte contre le sida. LAUREN COCHRANE

GIORGIO ARMANI

PHOTOGRAPHY KAYT JONES. STYLING PIPPA VOSPER. MODELS BAR RAFAELI AND JACK HUSTON. SEPTEMBER 2008.

PHOTOGRAPHY TESH. FASHION DIRECTOR EDWARD ENNINFUL. MODEL GISELE BÜNDCHEN. FEBRUARY 2002.

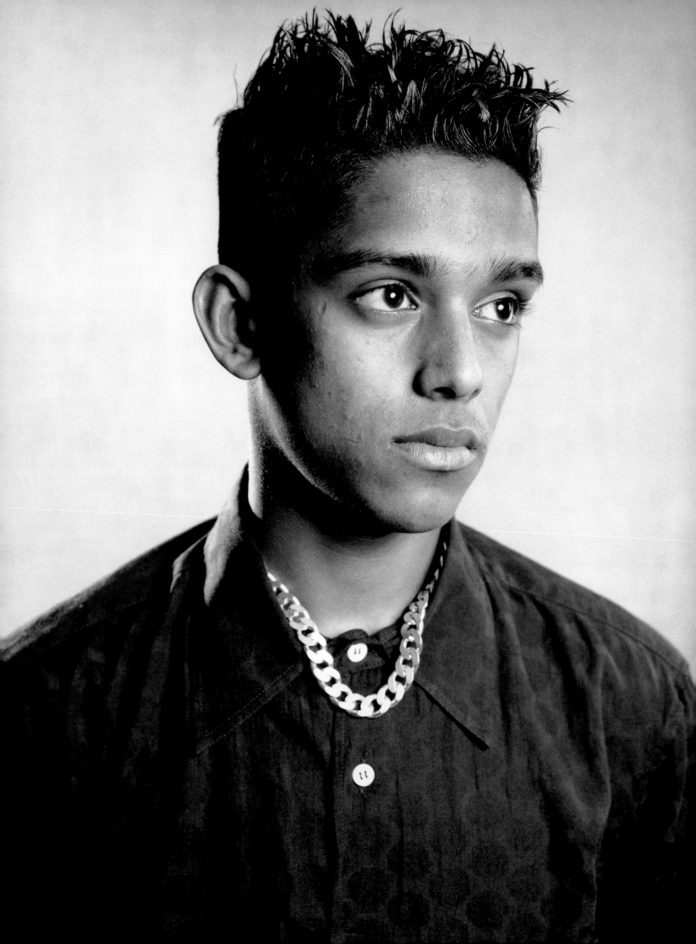

What are your signature designs? I would say that I am best known for my deconstructed jackets, for men and for women **What is your favourite piece from any of your collections?** I would have to say 'the Jacket'. In early years, it was the deconstructed style, and most recently the close-fitting cardigan-style 'Beckham' jacket **How would you describe your work?** Maybe that I strive to keep the world of fashion personal **What's your ultimate goal?** I like to think that I can introduce people to the idea of simplicity and elegance **What inspires you?** I am a great people-watcher, and I suppose they are my greatest inspiration – the way people behave, move, dress this is what really interests me **Can fashion still have a political ambition?** Yes, of course. My notions of deconstruction were political inasmuch as I was advocating a change to the status quo – and I still believe that people should be allowed to be themselves where their clothes are concerned **Who do you have in mind when you design?** I sometimes might base a design on a specific person. But mostly I design without actual people in mind – more a notion of a certain type of person who will understand and appreciate my aesthetic **Is the idea of creative collaboration important to you?** Absolutely. I have found my experience working in film, for example, extremely stimulating. I find that any creative dialogue you enter into with another person or another medium (furniture, for example) is bound to push you and make you grow. If you are the kind of fashion designer who looks no further than the runway, you will never really progress **Who has been the greatest influence on your career?** There have been several influential people in my working life, but perhaps the greatest was my first business partner, Sergio Galeotti. It was Sergio who saw what I was capable of and encouraged me to start a label that bore my name. It was Sergio who through his irrepressible flair got me to believe that anything was possible **How have your own experiences affected your work as a designer?** All experiences can have an influence on your work – both major and minor. When I was a kid, I was severely burnt during the Second World War when an unexploded shell I was playing with went off. It killed my friend and I spent weeks in hospital in a vat of alcohol recovering. I lost my sight for about ten days – I thought I was blind. Something like that doesn't leave you, but if you come through it, the chances are you will be a survivor. Then there's the less serious stuff, like when I bought a boat a couple of years ago. I decided to design the interior myself and I also looked at the way I could make the hull more suited to my tastes. The experience clearly had an influence on my next collection, which contained the colours of the ocean and naval details and fastenings **Which is more important in your work: the process or the product?** I think for many designers the process is the important thing, and they consider the product more important for the customer than for themselves. But without customers you have nothing, so for me both process and product are critical **Is designing difficult for you? If so, what drives you to continue?** No, I am lucky in that I find designing relatively easy. It is running the business that is difficult **Have you ever been influenced or moved by the reaction to your designs?** I used to take great interest in what the press had to say, which to begin with was a real problem as my first collections were regarded by many as a type of heresy **What's your definition of beauty?** A natural, clean, effortless quality. Beautiful people are not necessarily the best looking – more the ones with poise, and self-confidence **What's your philosophy?** Be true to what you believe in and follow your passions **What is the most important lesson you've learned?** To trust my own instincts. I have realised over time that I have to take responsibility for my actions and beliefs. In terms of fashion, this means that I stand by what I do. If others don't like it, then that's fair enough. But I have to be consistent, and create what I believe in. Otherwise I have nothing.

"The reward in seeing a garment being worn brings me endless pleasure"
KRIS VAN ASSCHE + DIOR HOMME

Born in Belgium in 1976, Kris Van Assche is a tall and gentle figure. His choice to have a humming bird tattoo on his arm because the tiny bird has the biggest heart is symbolic of the man. Treading a considered path through menswear from the start, Van Assche followed in the footsteps of his Belgian fashion designer predecessors, studying at the Royal Academy in Antwerp, becoming the youngest graduate of the school. Moving to Paris in 1998, Van Assche soon took up an internship at Yves Saint Laurent under the direction of Hedi Slimane. In 2000, Van Assche followed Slimane to Dior, where, as first assistant, he helped the menswear maverick transform the French label into Dior Homme, reinventing the contemporary menswear silhouette. In September 2004, the Kris Van Assche label was established. The debut autumn/winter 2005/6 collection was met with instant critical and public success, as Van Assche presented a refined take on simple tailored classics. Collaborating with American photographer Jeff Burton on a set of distinctive campaigns, Van Assche soon established the label as a one to watch. In 2007, Van Assche introduced womenswear, playing again with loose silhouettes and beautiful fabrics. In the same year, Van Assche also elected to return to Dior Homme as artistic director after Hedi Slimane's departure, bringing with him his relaxed contemporary tailoring and Latino casting that he had established so well with his own label. As well as designing for his own label and Dior Homme, Van Assche continues to collaborate with a wide artistic circle, including taking guest editorship of 'A Magazine', 'issue 7' and working with Nan Goldin on a special backstage project for Dior Homme's spring/summer 2009 collection.

Der 1976 in Belgien geborene Kris Van Assche ist eine große, sanftmütige Erscheinung. Seine Entscheidung, sich einen Kolibri auf den Arm tätowieren zu lassen, weil der winzige Vogel das größte Herz besitzt, ist typisch für diesen Mann. Von Beginn an schlug er einen wohlüberlegten Weg durch die Herrenmode ein und trat dabei in die Fußstapfen seiner Vorgänger unter den belgischen Modedesignern, indem er an der Royal Academy of Fine Arts in Antwerpen studierte und dort als bislang jüngster Student seinen Abschluss machte. Nachdem er 1998 nach Paris gezogen war, begann er schon bald ein Praktikum bei Yves Saint Laurent unter dem damaligen Chef Hedi Slimane. Im Jahr 2000 folgte er Slimane zu Dior, wo er als erster Assistent dem Rebell der Männermode half, das französische Label in Dior Homme zu verwandeln und dabei eine zeitgemäße Silhouette der Menswear zu erfinden. Im September 2004 wurde das Label Kris Van Assche gegründet. Die Debütkollektion für Herbst/Winter 2005/06 stieß auf unmittelbare Zustimmung bei Kritikern und Publikum, nachdem Van

Assche eine verfeinerte Version schlicht geschneiderter Klassiker präsentierte. Durch seine Zusammenarbeit mit dem amerikanischen Fotografen Jeff Burton in einer Reihe außergewöhnlicher Kampagnen etablierte sich Van Assche rasch als ein Label, das es zu beachten galt. 2007 stellte Van Assche erstmals Damenmode vor und spielte dabei erneut mit lockeren Silhouetten und wunderbaren Stoffen. Im selben Jahr entschloss sich der Designer auch, zu Dior Homme zurückzukehren, wo er als Nachfolger von Hedi Slimane Artistic Director wurde. Er brachte dabei sein lässig modernes Verständnis von Schneiderei mit, das er bei seinem eigenen Label so erfolgreich etabliert hatte. Neben den Entwürfen für seine eigene Marke und Dior Homme arbeitet Van Assche weiterhin mit einem großen Kreis von Künstlern zusammen, etwa als Gast-Herausgeber der Ausgabe 7 von A Magazine oder mit Nan Goldin für ein besonderes Backstage-Projekt anlässlich der Kollektion Frühjahr/Sommer 2009 von Dior Homme.

Né en Belgique en 1976, Kris Van Assche est un homme grand et doux, comme le prouve le colibri qu'il a choisi de se faire tatouer sur le bras parce que ce minuscule volatile possède le plus gros cœur de tous les oiseaux. Évoluant de façon réfléchie dans la mode pour homme dès ses débuts, Van Assche marche sur les pas de ses prédécesseurs belges en suivant des études de mode à l'Académie Royale d'Anvers, dont il est d'ailleurs le plus jeune diplômé. Lorsqu'il s'installe à Paris en 1998, Van Assche décroche rapidement un stage chez Yves Saint Laurent sous la direction d'Hedi Slimane. En l'an 2000, il suit Slimane chez Dior où, en tant que premier assistant, il aide le dissident du menswear à transformer la griffe française en Dior Homme et à réinventer la silhouette masculine contemporaine. En septembre 2004, il fonde la marque Kris Van Assche. Sa première collection, pour la saison automne/hiver 2005–2006, séduit d'emblée la critique et le public, car Van Assche présente une vision raffinée des costumes simples et classiques. En travaillant avec le photographe américain Jeff Burton sur une série de campagnes de pub originales, Van Assche s'impose rapidement comme un créateur à suivre de près. En 2007, il se lance dans la mode pour femme en jouant à nouveau sur les silhouettes amples et les beaux tissus. La même année, il choisit aussi de revenir chez Dior Homme en tant que directeur artistique après le départ d'Hedi Slimane, apportant avec lui les coupes contemporaines décontractées et le style latino déjà bien établi par sa propre griffe. Outre sa collection éponyme et son travail chez Dior Homme, Van Assche poursuit ses collaborations dans des domaines artistiques très divers : il a notamment dirigé le n° 7 d'A Magazine et conçu un projet photo avec Nan Goldin pour les coulisses du défilé Dior Homme printemps/été 2009. MAX PEARMAIN

PHOTOGRAPHY NAN GOLDIN. COURTESY DIOR HOMME. OCTOBER 2008.

What are your signature designs? A man with natural elegance. With class but without stiffness. A discreet modernity, removed from any caricature. Men do not obey the dictatorship of imposed virility anymore. The 'armour-like clothes' have been replaced by an individual and subtle search which has nothing to do with any feminisation. Today this mutation is essential **What is your favourite piece from any of your collections?** The street. The youth has taken back the white shirt. It's a classic which is coming back into favour, a renewed symbol for entry into adulthood. I like to shake it up and reinvent it **How would you describe your work?** Obsession with elegance. Invention of details. A will to seduce, always **What's your ultimate goal?** Find the balance which escapes rationality: the perfect silhouette. **What inspires you?** The person you love **Can fashion still have a political ambition?** I don't ask myself the question. I find it too arrogant **Who do you have in mind when you design?** It depends. It can be a piece of music, a film. Sometimes, absolutely nothing. Just a detail, the lapel of a jacket or the shape of a button can be the starting point of a new story. Each collection is a tale that guides me. People I know have an impact. Whether they are young or not, they have a significant influence **Is the idea of creative collaboration important to you?** It is fundamental for me to collaborate regularly with artists who are free from the commercial constraints of fashion. Nan Goldin, Andrea Mastrovito are friends of mine who often play a part in my work. Those collaborations are fulfilling. As such, the experience I've had as 'A Magazine' editor has been amazing. I have been able to gather round me all the artists that influence me: a real identity mosaic **Who has been the greatest influence on your career?** My grandmother taught me that you can make anything beautiful, that you can enhance everyday life. This is priceless **How have your own experiences affected your work as a designer?** South America and Brazil are places that attract and 'feed' me. My travels have taken me away from the North and led me towards the Latin world, which is essential to my work **Which is more important in your work: the process or the product?** Both. Stress during elaboration is productive, stimulating. The reward in seeing a garment being worn brings me endless pleasure **Is designing difficult for you? If so, what drives you to continue?** Managing my own brand as well as being artistic director for Dior Homme. I create four men's collections and two women's collections for KVA. It's a lot of work. However, this hyperactivity allows me to remain in a permanent state of creativity.

"I love to meet someone who shows me his jacket and says: "'Look at it, it's all worn, I have been wearing it for six years!'" AGNÈS B.

Believing that things do not have to be complicated to be beautiful, agnès b. designs clothes, simply, rather than high fashion. Shying away from global business practices, her outlook is alluringly fresh. Her style might be summed up as modern, crisp and definite. Born in Versailles (1941) as Agnès Trouble, she studied at Paris's Ecole Nationale Supérieure des Beaux-Arts before starting work as a junior editor for French 'Elle'. From here she assisted the designer Dorothée Bis as a stylist and worked as a freelance designer before opening her own Parisian boutique in 1975. A tonic for any wardrobe, agnès b. designs are intended to make one feel good in one's own skin. Her tailoring creates an air of unadulterated elegance, while her simple angular cuts ensure timelessness. A true lover of people rather than fashion, she neither shops nor attends catwalk shows, choosing instead to find inspiration in 'people watching', a trait she describes as very French. From her popular snap cardigan to her press-studded cotton jackets, there's something resolutely personal in agnès b. designs. She'll remake a piece from a past season if a customer requests it, reiterating her belief that people are more important than the clothes. With over 200 boutiques and concessions around the world, agnès b.'s business has grown without advertising. Her collections include clothes and accessories for all – maternity, babies and teenagers included. She is also a photographer, film producer and avid art collector. With two art galleries, a modern-art magazine and a cinema production company of her own, agnès b. has got her finger on the pulse of the creative world.

Gemäß der Überzeugung, dass etwas nicht kompliziert sein muss, um schön zu sein, entwirft agnès b. lieber schlichte Sachen als Haute Couture. Abseits internationaler Geschäftspraktiken, verfolgt sie einen verlockend unorthodoxen Ansatz. Man könnte ihren Stil als modern, frisch und zielstrebig charakterisieren. Unter dem Namen Agnès Trouble 1941 in Versailles geboren, studierte sie an der Pariser Ecole Nationale Supérieure des Beaux-Arts, bevor sie bei der französischen Elle als Jungredakteurin begann. Von dieser Position aus assistierte sie der Designerin Dorothée Bis als Stylistin und arbeitete als freie Designerin, bevor sie 1975 ihre eigene Boutique in Paris eröffnete. Ihre Kleider sind das reinste Tonikum für jede Garderobe, denn die Entwürfe sind so gestaltet, dass man sich in seiner eigenen Haut wohl fühlt. Sie erzeugen ein Flair unverfälschter Eleganz, die schlichten eckigen Schnitte garantieren Zeitlosigkeit. Die Designerin macht sich mehr aus Menschen als aus Mode und geht daher weder shoppen noch besucht sie Modenschauen. Ihre Inspirationen holt sie sich lieber beim „Menschen beobachten", einer Passion, die sie als typisch französisch

empfindet. Angefangen bei ihrer beliebten Jacke mit Druckknöpfen (Cardigan pression) bis hin zu nietenbesetzten Baumwolljacken haben die Kreationen von agnès b. etwas absolut Persönliches. Und wenn ein Kunde es wünscht, fertigt sie auch ein Stück aus einer älteren Kollektion noch einmal. Mit über 200 Filialen und Lizenzen in aller Welt ist das Geschäft von agnès b. ohne jegliche Werbung beträchtlich gewachsen. Ihre Kollektionen umfassen Kleider und Accessoires vom Baby bis zum Teenager. Die Modeschöpferin ist außerdem als Fotografin, Filmproduzentin und leidenschaftliche Kunstsammlerin tätig. Mit zwei Galerien, einer Zeitschrift für moderne Kunst und einer eigenen Filmproduktionsfirma hat agnès b. ihre Finger wahrlich am Puls der Kreativität.

Convaincue que les choses n'ont pas besoin d'être compliquées pour être belles, agnès b. dessine des vêtements, tout simplement, plutôt que des créations d'avant-garde. Elle fuit les grands groupes mondiaux et propose une vision qui séduit par sa fraîcheur. Son style peut être considéré comme moderne, précis et univoque. Née à Versailles (1941) sous le nom d'Agnès Trouble, elle étudie à l'Ecole Nationale Supérieure des Beaux-Arts de Paris avant de travailler comme journaliste junior pour le Elle français. Ensuite, elle assiste Dorothée Bis en tant que styliste et travaille comme créatrice free-lance avant d'ouvrir sa propre boutique parisienne en 1975. Tel un tonique énergisant pour toute garde-robe, les créations agnès b. sont conçues pour que ceux qui les portent se sentent bien dans leur peau. Ses tailleurs dégagent une impression d'élégance pure, avec des coupes simples et angulaires qui ne sont pas près de se démoder. Aimant plus les gens que la mode, elle ne fait pas les boutiques et n'assiste à aucun défilé, préférant puiser son inspiration dans «l'observation des autres», une attitude qu'elle considère comme très française. De son célèbre cardigan à ses vestes de coton à boutons-pression, on distingue quelque chose de résolument personnel dans ses créations. Si un client le lui demande, elle n'hésitera pas à reproduire une pièce d'une saison passée, réitérant sa conviction selon laquelle les personnes comptent plus que les vêtements. Avec plus de 200 boutiques et franchises à travers le monde, l'entreprise d'agnès b. s'est développée sans publicité. Ses collections proposent des vêtements et des accessoires pour tous, y compris les femmes enceintes, les bébés et les adolescents. Elle est également photographe, productrice de films et une avide collectionneuse d'art. Avec deux galeries d'art, un magazine d'art moderne et sa propre société de production cinématographique, agnès b. a toujours le doigt sur le pouls du monde créatif.

HOLLY SHACKLETON

What are your signature designs? The 'snap cardigan' created in 1979, the 'fifre' leather jacket, the wrinkled cotton voile petticoat or skirt **What is your favourite piece from any of your collections?** The one I just did **How would you describe your work?** Exciting, amusing, light, heavy, intense, too much, too cool and never-ending! **What is your ultimate goal?** To be where I am, doing my best for love and peace **What inspires you?** I like to watch people in the street, because people astonish me and it can be positive and negative **Can fashion still have a political ambition?** How could it have? But T-shirts have always been and still are a great medium for affirming art, humour and political ideas **Who do you have in mind when you design?** A lot of people! It can be Marilyn or Jackie Kennedy, peasants or artists, Cocteau or my friends **Is the idea of creative collaboration important to you?** I design everything myself, I don't have a studio, but I like very much to collaborate with my team and with the artists on their agnès b. T-shirts **Who has been the greatest influence on your career?** The many people around me with their happiness to be alive, their courage and their good humour **How have your own experiences affected your work as a designer?** I can put myself in any of the times of my life and I think it's great luck! I think I am working with all these feelings. I have very clear memories from the age of two **Which is more important in your work: the process or the product?** The product depends on the process, you can't separate them, and of course it's important to succeed in creation **Is designing difficult for you? If so, what drives you to continue?** I don't have and never had creative difficulties. I enjoy doing my work and I am quick! Dressing the models for the show is for me like playing with dolls (for men and women), which is the finale of the designs for the season **Have you ever been influenced or moved by the reaction to your designs?** I love to meet someone I don't know who shows me his jacket and says: "Look at it, it's all worn, I have been wearing it for six years!" **What's your definition of beauty?** From the encyclopédie Diderot et d'Alembert – completed in the 18th century, "la beauté est une sensation de rapports agréables…": beauty is a sensation of agreeable rapports… **What's your philosophy?** Love them all! **What is the most important lesson you've learned?** Caring for others, and I keep learning.

"I'm a very down-to-earth designer"
CHRISTOPHER BAILEY • BURBERRY

Yorkshire-born Christopher Bailey has become something of a household name, thanks to his sterling work as creative director of Burberry, the British company he joined back in 2001. Yet Bailey (born 1971) is far from an overnight sensation, having previously notched up impressive fashion credentials. On completing a Master's degree at the Royal College of Art in London (1994), Bailey worked in New York for Donna Karan from 1994 to 1996, before being hired by Tom Ford as a senior designer of womenswear at Gucci in Milan, from 1996 to 2001. At Burberry, Bailey is responsible for the direction of all product lines, as well as the definition of the company's overall image and seasonal advertising concepts. His flagship collection is the forward-thinking Prorsum lines for men and women that are presented in Milan to consistently rave reviews and from which he has banished almost all trace of the hallmark Burberry check. An unerring eye for clear, bright colour and subtle innovations in tailoring have emerged as key to both menswear and womenswear collections. Developing his codes gradually, Bailey is concerned with longevity, rather than resting on the corporate laurels. Nonetheless, the designs he has produced respectfully acknowledge the Burberry heritage (the company was founded in 1856). For example, he has made no secret of his admiration for their classic gabardine trenchcoat, which for autumn/winter 2004 he abbreviated into capes, for both men and women. Renowned for his hands-on approach to design and an enthusiasm for details, he continues to propel the brand into the 21st century with his customary passion, enthusiasm and cheerful demeanour. In acknowledgement of his many successes, the Royal College of Art awarded Bailey an Honorary Fellowship in 2003. He was also twice awarded Menswear Designer of the Year by the British Fashion Awards (2007 and 2008).

Der aus Yorkshire stammende Christopher Bailey ist inzwischen selbst zu einer Art Markenzeichen avanciert. Zu verdanken hat er das seiner soliden Arbeit als Creative Director für das britische Modehaus Burberry, in das er 2001 eintrat. Bailey (Jahrgang 1971) wurde jedoch keineswegs über Nacht zum Star, sondern erwarb sich zunächst eindrucksvolle Referenzen. Nachdem er 1994 sein Studium am Londoner Royal College of Art mit dem Mastertitel abgeschlossen hatte, arbeitete er bis 1996 für Donna Karan in New York. Dann warb ihn Tom Ford als Senior Designer für die Damenmode bei Gucci ab, so dass er von 1996 bis 2001 in Mailand tätig war. Bei Burberry ist Bailey für die Leitung aller Produktlinien ebenso verantwortlich wie für das Image der Marke und die Werbekonzepte der jeweiligen Saison. Seine Flagschiffkollektion ist die zukunftsorientierte Prorsum-Linie für Damen und Herren. Wenn diese in Mailand präsentiert wird, erntet er regelmäßig hymnische Kritiken. Das typische Burberry-Karo ist daraus übrigens fast vollständig verbannt. Sein unfehlbarer Blick für klare, leuchtende Farben und raffinierte handwerkliche Innovationen hat sich als Erfolgskriterium für die Herren- wie für die Damenkollektionen herauskristallisiert. Bailey, der seine Stile schrittweise entwickelt, hat eher die Langlebigkeit seiner Entwürfe im Sinn, anstatt sich auf den Lorbeeren seines Hauses auszuruhen. Dennoch spricht aus seinen Kreationen die respektvolle Anerkennung des Vermächtnisses von Burberry (die Firma wurde bereits 1856 gegründet). So macht er kein Geheimnis aus seiner Bewunderung für den klassischen Trenchcoat aus Gabardine, den er für die Kollektion Herbst/Winter 2004 zu Capes für Damen und Herren abwandelte. Bailey ist bekannt für seine pragmatische Einstellung zum Thema Design und für seine Detailversessenheit. So führt er die Traditionsmarke weiter ins 21. Jahrhundert – mit gewohnter Leidenschaft, Enthusiasmus und einer optimistischen Grundhaltung. Als Anerkennung für seine diversen Leistungen wurde Bailey 2003 vom Royal College of Art ein Honorary Fellowship verliehen. Zweimal (2007 und 2008) wurde er bei den British Fashion Awards zum Menswear Designer of the Year gekürt.

Né en 1971 dans le Yorkshire, Christopher Bailey est aujourd'hui un nom connu de tous les Anglais grâce au travail remarquable qu'il a accompli à la direction de la création de Burberry, maison britannique qu'il a rejointe en 2001. Pourtant, Bailey n'a rien d'une star éphémère dans la mesure où son CV affichait déjà d'impressionnantes références dans le domaine de la mode. Après avoir décroché son Master au Royal College of Art de Londres (1994), Bailey travaille à New York pour Donna Karan entre 1994 et 1996, avant d'être embauché par Tom Ford chez Gucci à Milan, où il occupera le poste de styliste senior des collections pour femme de 1996 à 2001. Chez Burberry, Bailey ne se contente pas de superviser toutes les lignes de produits, il développe également l'image de la maison et ses concepts publicitaires saisonniers. Sa collection phare inclut les lignes visionnaires Prorsum pour homme et femme qu'il a entièrement dépouillées des fameux carreaux Burberry, un travail salué par une critique unanime lors de chaque défilé milanais. Son œil aiguisé pour les couleurs claires et vives et ses innovations subtiles en matière de coupe distinguent aujourd'hui ses collections pour homme comme pour femme. Bien que Bailey impose progressivement ses propres codes, il cherche aussi à faire durer la marque Burberry sans se reposer sur ses lauriers. Ses créations rendent néanmoins un respectueux hommage à l'héritage de cette maison fondée en 1856. Par exemple, il n'a jamais caché son admiration pour le fameux trenchcoat Burberry, un classique qu'il a raccourci sous forme de cape pour homme et femme lors de la saison automne/hiver 2004. Réputé pour son approche pratique de la création et pour sa passion du détail, il continue à propulser Burberry dans le XXᵉ siècle, animé d'une passion et d'un enthousiasme qui sont aujourd'hui devenus sa marque de fabrique. En reconnaissance de ses nombreux succès, le Royal College of Art lui a décerné un doctorat honorifique en 2003. Il a également reçu deux fois le prix de Menswear Designer of the Year aux British Fashion Awards (en 2007 et en 2008).

JAMES ANDERSON

What are your signature designs? I'm a very down-to-earth designer in the sense that I love that mix of really classic, traditional, historical design with real fashion. I love fashion for its throwaway, of-the-moment value, but I enjoy mixing it with something that's really thought about. That's what makes my role at Burberry particularly exciting **What's your favourite piece from any of your collections?** In terms of this company, without it sounding clichéd, I really love the trenchcoat. Obviously it's not something I designed, but it's an incredible piece: completely genderless, crossing all the different age groups and inspiring so many people and designers. It's a classic staple. Anything that I have designed I'm bored of; anything that is a trenchcoat for me is good **How would you describe your work?** It's very considered. I hate anything slapdash **What's your ultimate goal?** To always enjoy my work. I dread boredom. If I ever sensed that I was getting bored of my job, it would just be the end for me **What**

inspires you? It comes in so many guises that it's impossible to say. I love architecture, I love design, I love art, I love people and I love eating. For me, inspiration is really about keeping your mind open and never getting jaded **Who do you have in mind when you design?** I don't have one particular person. It's much more about an attitude and a spirit and character than an actual person. It's nice if you can find somebody – it's my dream to discover a muse. I would love an ideal person who personifies everything I'm thinking, but I don't think that person will ever exist **Is the idea of creative collaboration important to you?** I love working with people who share my sense of passion – I'm a very upbeat person and my natural spirit is cheerful. For me it's a pleasure working with enthusiastic, passionate, happy people. I also like working with people who have a very strong will and strong mind, because it's a challenge – but it's a huge frustration as well **Who has been the greatest influence on your career?**

The little person inside my body who tells me what to do. Whenever I've made any major decisions, I've always completely relied on that little voice. Even when I decided to leave Gucci and everybody without fail told me I was crazy, that little voice kept saying "it's time, you need to move on". I was going to nothing and I certainly didn't have this role here, but I did it anyway **Which is more important in your work: the process or the product?** The process – once you've got to the product, you're kind of over it **Is designing difficult for you? If so, what drives you to continue?** The actual process of designing isn't difficult, but the process of designing something that fulfils all the criteria it needs to fulfil is very difficult. Fashion is functional, practical, emotional, commercial and aesthetic: there are so many things to take into consideration. Also, I have two agendas – my personal agenda when designing and then the company's one as well **Have you ever been influenced or moved by the**

reaction to your designs? I guess every time and never. It's always a great feeling when someone tells you that they love it and it's always depressing when someone doesn't like what you've done. It's important in both instances to say okay, that was then and now we're on other things **What's your definition of beauty?** It's got nothing to do with fashion or clothes. It's really somebody's inner self. For me, a beautiful person is someone with kindness and happiness, a good spirit and a good soul **What's your philosophy?** Enjoy everything that you do. It's important to be happy. If tomorrow I became jaded and bored in this job and wanted to go back to filling shelves in a supermarket, which I used to do and loved, then I would do that… Listen to me sounding like I want to work at Tesco! **What is the most important lesson you've learned?** Listen to your heart. It's never wrong.

"It's good to listen, to discuss, but it has to be your own conviction that makes each decision"
NEIL BARRETT

With his own Milan-based label, a host of celebrity clients and a stint as an MTV presenter, Neil Barrett has come a long way from his Devonshire roots. Known for clothes that focus on detail and cut, Barrett's is an approach underpinned by an extensive knowledge of fabric production, which he employs to rejuvenate classic designs. With subdued colours and restrained tailoring, Barrett's menswear range is avowedly masculine – a factor that has contributed to its widespread appeal. Born in 1965, Barrett graduated in 1986 from Central Saint Martins, and received an MA from the Royal College of Art in 1989. Within a year, he was made senior menswear designer at Gucci in Florence, where he worked until 1994 – a period in which the brand underwent an important revival, both creatively and financially. Success at Gucci enabled Barrett to approach Prada with a proposal for a menswear line. Prada accepted his offer and he began work as the company's menswear design director. He remained at Prada until 1998, when he launched his first self-named menswear collection. This was an immediate success that was snapped up by over 100 designer stores across the world. The following year, Barrett set up White, his own Prada-produced label, which was invited to open the Pitti Immagine Uomo Fair in 2000, where he also introduced his first womenswear collection. The next few years saw Barrett sign a footwear deal with Puma and in 2004 he redesigned the Italian national football team's strip for the European Championship – an honour for a non-Italian and a testament to the worldwide success of his label. In 2006, the Italians won the world cup wearing the kit designed by Barrett, reinforcing his collaboration with Puma. This was the year he also launched his Indigo jean collection and showed his autumn/winter 2006, collection for the first time, in New York. His 'A-list' group of actors and musicians continues to grow from Tokyo, Seoul to West Coast Hollywood. Fans of Barrett love his sharp sartorial tailoring learnt from his great-grandfather and grandfather and fused with classic British street-style genres.

Ein eigenes Label mit Sitz in Mailand, eine Schar prominenter Kunden und ein Job als Moderator bei MTV – Neil Barrett, dessen Wurzeln in Devonshire liegen, hat es zweifellos weit gebracht. Er ist bekannt für den Detailreichtum und Schnitt seiner Kleider, dazu kommt noch sein umfangreiches Wissen über die Stoffproduktion, das er nutzt, um klassische Designs zu verjüngen. Mit gedämpften Farben und schlichten Schnitten ist Barretts Herrenlinie dezidiert maskulin – was zu seiner großen Beliebtheit sicher beigetragen hat. Der 1965 geborene Designer machte 1986 seinen Abschluss am Central Saint Martins und 1989 seinen Master am Royal College of Art. Innerhalb eines Jahres brachte er es dann zum Chefdesigner der Herrenmode bei Gucci in Florenz, wo er bis 1994 tätig war – in dieser Zeit erfuhr die Marke eine wichtige Renaissance, sowohl im kreativen wie im wirtschaftlichen Sinne. Der Erfolg bei Gucci versetzte Barrett in die Lage, Prada eine eigene Herrenlinie anzubieten. Dort ging man auf sein Angebot ein, und Barrett fing als Design Director der Herrenmode an. Bis 1998 blieb er bei Prada und präsentierte dann seine erste Herrenkollektion unter eigenem Namen. Der Erfolg stellte sich unmittelbar ein – über hundert Designläden in aller Welt sicherten sich seine Entwürfe. Ein Jahr später gründete Barrett White sein eigenes, bei Prada produziertes Label. 2000 wurde er eingela-

den, die Messe Pitti Immagine Uomo zu eröffnen. Dort lancierte Barrett dann seine erste Damenkollektion. In den folgenden Jahren unterzeichnete Barrett u. a. einen Kooperationsvertrag mit Puma über eine Schuhkollektion und entwarf 2004 anlässlich der Europameisterschaft ein neues Dress für die italienische Fußballnationalmannschaft. Das war zum einen eine Auszeichnung für den Nicht-Italiener, zum anderen ein Beleg für den weltweiten Erfolg seines Labels. 2006 wurden die Italiener in dem Fußballdress Weltmeister, das Barrett entworfen hatte, was seine Zusammenarbeit mit Puma natürlich stärkte. Im selben Jahr präsentierte der Designer auch seine Jeanskollektion Indigo und zeigte seine Kreationen für Herbst/Winter 2006 erstmals in New York. Seine Kontakte zu den Stars der Schauspiel- und Musikszene reichen von Tokio und Seoul bis nach West Coast Hollywood, und ständig kommen neue hinzu. Seine Anhänger lieben Barretts messerscharfe Schnitte, die er von Großvater und Urgroßvater gelernt hat und mit den Genres des klassischen britischen Street-Style kombiniert.

Avec sa propre griffe à Milan, une profusion de clients célèbres et un job de présentateur sur MTV, on peut dire que Neil Barrett a fait du chemin depuis son Devon natal. Réputé pour des vêtements qui font la part belle aux détails et à la coupe, Barrett adopte une approche étayée par sa grande connaissance de la production de tissus, qu'il exploite pour rajeunir les classiques. Marquée par des couleurs sobres et des coupes maîtrisées, la mode pour homme de Barrett est, de son propre aveu, très masculine : un aspect qui contribuera à son immense succès. Né en 1965, Neil Barrett sort diplômé de Central Saint Martins en 1986 avant d'obtenir un MA du Royal College of Art en 1989. Un an plus tard, il devient styliste senior de la ligne masculine de Gucci à Florence, où il travaille jusqu'en 1994 : pendant cette période, la marque connaît un véritable renouveau, tant sur le plan créatif que financier. Son succès chez Gucci lui permet d'approcher Prada en proposant la création d'une ligne pour homme. Prada accepte son offre et le nomme directeur de la création pour homme. Il quittera Prada en 1998 pour lancer sa première collection éponyme de vêtements masculins. Il remporte un succès immédiat et ses créations sont achetées par plus de 100 boutiques de créateurs à travers le monde. L'année suivante, Barrett crée White, sa propre griffe produite par Prada, et il est invité à faire l'ouverture du salon professionnel Pitti Immagine Uomo en l'an 2000, à l'occasion duquel il lance également sa première collection pour femme. Les années suivantes, Puma lui commande une collection de chaussures, puis en 2004 il redessine la tenue officielle de l'équipe nationale de football d'Italie pour l'Euro 2004 : un véritable honneur pour un « étranger » et une reconnaissance du succès mondial de sa griffe. En 2006, les Italiens remportent la Coupe du Monde habillés en Barrett, ce qui consolide la collaboration du créateur avec Puma. La même année, il lance une collection de jeans baptisée Indigo et défile pour la première fois à New York lors de la saison automne/hiver 2006. Sa clientèle élitiste de stars de cinéma et de la musique ne cesse de s'agrandir, que ce soit à Tokyo, Séoul, Hollywood ou le reste de la Côte ouest. Les fans de Barrett raffolent des coupes précises que lui ont léguées son arrière-grand-père et son grand-père, et qu'il réinterprète dans des modèles typiques du « street style » britannique.

DAVID VASCOTT

What are your signature designs? Hybrids of (reworked) 'iconic' menswear **What is your favourite piece from any of your collections?** Spring/summer 2005, the hand-polished fine pinstripe jacket – autumn/winter 2004, the waxed denim jeans – spring/summer 2004, the worn-in shrunken cotton blue blazer – autumn/winter 2003, the hobnail, Dickensian boots, etc… all of these I continue to wear today… together **Who do you have in mind when you design?** Me in the body of different people **Is the idea of creative collaboration important to you?** Yes, it's good to listen, to discuss, but it has to be your own conviction that makes each decision **Who has been the greatest influence on your career?** For personal inspiration, it's definitely my mother. For creative influence, it's seeing my clothes on clients and in stores worldwide and wanting to do more **How have your own experiences affected your work as a designer?** All personal experiences, good or bad, contribute to your work, both driving you and inspiring you **Which is more important in your work: the process or the product?** The product of course, the final garment on the body: this is my goal, the process just happens to be the enjoyable (or not!) means to this end **Is designing difficult for you? If so, what drives you to continue?** No, it's straightforward, your instinct dictates what is right or wrong **Have you ever been influenced or moved by the reaction to your designs?** Of course, it's when the final customer understands and gets your design that the satisfaction is greatest **What's your definition of beauty?** When the inner goodness is visible **What's your philosophy?** Follow your instinct **What is the most important lesson you've learned?** Never take anything for granted and no matter what you do, learn from the past, live for the present and dream of your future.

"You can have it all, it's just really hard work"
LUELLA BARTLEY

Born in Stratford-upon-Avon, Luella Bartley has in the past said her success can be partly attributed to not being born in London. For every ounce of humility, she matches in talent – which was recently recognised (November 2008) at the British Fashion Awards with a Designer of the Year award. Her whimsical English designs laced with a dark edge have won her a loyal following internationally. The Luella brand currently has 120 stockists in 50 countries. Bartley's first brush with the fashion world after graduating from Central Saint Martins was as a fashion journalist. She worked for Vogue and the Evening Standard before swapping pen and paper for needle and thread. In 1999, with the support of her close friends like Katie Grand, Bartley presented her first collection, entitled 'Daddy I Want a Pony' in her friend Steve Mackey's (bassist from Pulp) flat. The following season was followed by 'Daddy Who Are The Clash' (with the band present) modelled by Kate Moss. In 2002, Bartley designed the Gisele bag for Mulberry, which proved a turning point for her. Mulberry, backed by the Singapore-based Club 21, saw the potential in Bartley and signed a license agreement with Bartley for bags (2003) followed by ready-to-wear (2005). The company now has two flagship stores, in London and Hong Kong. In September 2008, her first full 'Luella by Georgina Goodman' shoe collection was launched. Bartley currently shows at London Fashion Week and lives in Cornwall with the photographer David Sims and their three children.

Die in Stratford-upon-Avon geborene Luella Bartley hat einmal von sich selbst behauptet, ihr Erfolg hänge teilweise damit zusammen, dass sie keine geborene Londonerin sei. Die Designerin bringt ebensoviel Talent wie Demut mit – was erst kürzlich (im November 2008) bei den British Fashion Awards anerkannt wurde, wo man sie als Designer of the Year auszeichnete. Ihre skurril englischen Kreationen, die sie mit einem düsteren Touch versieht, haben ihr eine treue internationale Fangemeinde beschert. Gegenwärtig ist die Marke Luella bei 120 Händlern in 50 Ländern vertreten. Ihre ersten Kontakte zur Modewelt knüpfte Bartley nach ihrem Abschluss am Central Saint Martins College of Art and Design als Modejournalistin. Sie schrieb für Vogue und Evening Standard, bevor sie Stift und Papier gegen Nadel und Faden eintauschte. 1999 präsentierte sie, unterstützt von engen Freunden wie Katie Grand, ihre erste Kollektion unter dem Titel „Daddy I Want a Pony" in der Wohnung ihres Freundes Steve Mackey

(Bassist von Pulp). In der nächsten Saison folgte „Daddy Who Are The Clash" (in Anwesenheit der Band), gemodelt von Kate Moss. 2002 entwarf Bartley eine Tasche namens Gisele für Mulberry, was einen Wendepunkt für die Designerin bedeutete. Mulberry, das von Club 21 mit Sitz in Singapur finanziert wird, erkannte Bartleys Potenzial und schloss einen Lizenzvertrag für Taschen (2003), gefolgt von der Prêt-à-porter (2005). Inzwischen betreibt das Unternehmen je einen Flagship Store in London und Hongkong. Im September 2008 kam ihre erste komplette Schuhkollektion „Luella by Georgina Goodman" auf den Markt. Gegenwärtig präsentiert Luella Bartley auf der London Fashion Week. Sie lebt mit dem Fotografen David Sims und drei gemeinsamen Kindern in Cornwall.

Née à Stratford-upon-Avon, Luella Bartley a déclaré par le passé que son succès était en partie dû au fait de ne pas être une vraie Londonienne. Aussi modeste que talentueuse, elle a récemment reçu (novembre 2008) le prix de Designer of the Year aux British Fashion Awards. Ses créations fantasques, typiquement anglaises, qui lorgnent du «côté sombre», lui ont valu des fans fidèles dans le monde entier. La griffe Luella est actuellement distribuée par 120 distribuuteurs dans 50 pays. Diplômée du Central Saint Martins College of Art and Design, Luella Bartley fait ses premiers pas dans la mode en tant que journaliste. Elle travaille d'abord pour Vogue et l'Evening Standard avant d'abandonner stylo et carnet de notes au profit du fil et de l'aiguille. En 1999, avec le soutien d'amies proches telles que Katie Grand, elle présente une première collection baptisée « Daddy I Want a Pony » dans l'appartement de son copain Steve Mackey (le bassiste de Pulp), tandis que Kate Moss défile pour sa collection suivante intitulée « Daddy Who Are The Clash ? » (le groupe assiste d'ailleurs au défilé). En 2002, la carrière de Luella Bartley prend tout son élan quand elle conçoit le sac Gisele pour Mulberry. Consciente du grand potentiel de la créatrice, la marque lui fait signer un accord de licence pour les sacs (2003) puis pour le prêt-à-porter (2005), avec le soutien financier du Club 21 de Singapour. L'entreprise possède actuellement deux boutiques phares à Londres et à Hong Kong. En septembre 2008, Luella Bartley lance « Luella by Georgina Goodman », sa première collection de chaussures complète. Elle continue de présenter ses collections à la London Fashion Week et vit à Cornwall avec le photographe David Sims et leurs trois enfants.

KAREN LEONG

What are your signature designs? A short frilly cocktail dress, a school boy blazer and skinny trousers with frilly waistband, a tweed skirt suit, a school boy shirt, a lamp shade skirt, Gisele bag, flower bag **What is your favourite piece from any of your collections?** A wonky, frilly tea dress from Spring/Summer with pleated panels and jersey straps, a pink frilly shift with a diamante belt, a sequin striped blazer and the Carmen biker bag. **How would you describe your work?** Traditional, wonky, irreverent, playful, English with minor rebellions, spirited, well made and cute **What's your ultimate goal?** To have a healthy balance between work and home — to clone myself to become a full time mother and full time fashion designer and to build my brand into something unique, thought

provoking and fun **What inspires you?** Everything; personal things, silly things, small things, English things, odd things **Can fashion still have a political ambition?** Yes I think so, fashion should have a social and cultural view point if not be overtly political **Who do you have in mind when you design?** A fictional character that goes by the name of Luella. She's a very interesting girl that touches the hearts of many a girl and woman. I like her **Is the idea of creative collaboration important to you?** The main reason I started designing instead of writing was because I found writing such a lonely process. I love collaborating with people who have a similar spirit, I love having a good old fashioned chat about the stuff I love and come out of it with surprising, impos-

sible and life changing ideas (or at least that's how it seemed down the pub) **Who has been the greatest influence on your career?** It would have to be the work of Barbara Hulanicki who said of her work, "the art of creating every day things that can change your life". That travels with me a lot. Also, everyone I have worked with and continue to work with, the everyday people that change my life **How have your own experiences affected your work as designer?** As soon as I had kids I found the confidence to be more experimental. It gave me the perspective to take a few risks and have more fun without the crippling effects of trying to be cool. What happens? People suddenly think your cool. It's funny **Which is more important in your work: the process or the**

product? The process is the fun bit, the product hopefully reflects that and then passes it on **Is designing difficult for you? If so, what drives you to continue?** I don't find designing difficult, but it can bring up a lot of crap at the time **What's your definition of beauty?** Individuality, something very natural **What's your philosophy?** It changes on a very regular basis, at the moment it is putting into practice all those silly ideas I have, whether it's a childrens circus in Cornwall, or a new collection. Don't let ideas go wasted. And of course, to have fun and be mindful. I have stolen that last one from Barbara too **What is the most important lesson you've learned?** That everything you do affects other people. You can have it all, it's just really hard work.

"My goal is to change the boundaries of fashion"
WALTER VAN BEIRENDONCK

If Walter Van Beirendonck were in a band, it would play a fusion of punk, folk, trash, pop, techno and chamber music. One of Belgium's most prolific fashion designers, Van Beirendonck places his sense of humour to the fore of his creations in an approach that humanises the sexuality that is often woven into his garments as patterns and graphics. Safe sex is a common thematic thread, as are literary, cinematic and folkloric references. Knitwear also plays a large part in Van Beirendonck's repertoire, but no prim twin sets or crewnecks for him – his jumpers are likely to come with matching balaclavas bearing garish cartoon faces, bold messages or sexual motifs. Born in Belgium in 1957, Van Beirendonck studied at Antwerp's Royal Academy. Part of the legendary Antwerp Six who brought Belgian fashion to greater public consciousness with their 1987 London show, Van Beirendonck – along with Dirk Van Saene, Dries Van Noten, Dirk Bikkembergs, Marina Yee and Ann Demeulemeester – was responsible for moving fashion towards a new rationale. From 1993 to 1999, he created the cyberpunk label that was W&LT (Wild and Lethal Trash), after which he relaunched his eponymous line, Walter Van Beirendonck. A second line, Aestheticterrorists, was founded in 1999. He has taught at the Royal Academy since 1985 and has designed costumes for stage, film and for bands such as U2 and The Avalanches. He has curated exhibitions in the world's top galleries and has illustrated books, created his own comic and won numerous awards. In March 1998, the book 'Mutilate' was dedicated to Van Beirendonck's first ten years in fashion, and in September 1998, he opened his own store, Walter, in Antwerp. Van Beirendonck could be described as the industry's blue-sky thinker, for both his visionary perspective, and his constantly optimistic outlook.

Wenn Walter van Beirendonck Mitglied einer Band wäre, würde die vermutlich eine Mischung aus Punk, Folk, Trash, Pop, Techno und Kammermusik spielen. Als einer der produktivsten Modedesigner Belgiens stellt er seinen Sinn für Humor in den Vordergrund seiner Kreationen. Das nimmt der Sexualität, die oft in Form von Mustern in seine Kleidung eingewoben ist, etwas von ihrer Schärfe. Safer Sex ist ein häufiges Thema, ebenso wie literarische, filmische und folkloristische Bezüge. Stricksachen spielen ebenfalls eine große Rolle in van Beirendoncks Repertoire, allerdings keine braven Twin Sets oder Matrosenkragen, seine Pullis kommen eher mit passenden wollenen Kopfschützern daher, auf denen grelle Comicgrimassen, forsche Botschaften oder sexuelle Motive zu sehen sind. Der 1957 in Belgien geborene van Beirendonck studierte an der Königlichen Akademie von Antwerpen und war einer der legendären Antwerp Six, die 1987 mit ihrer Schau in London der belgischen Mode die Aufmerksamkeit eines breiteren Publikums sicherten. Zusammen mit Dirk van Saene, Dries van Noten, Dirk Bikkembergs, Marina Yee und Ann Demeulemeester brachte er

eine neue Form von Rationalität in die Mode. Zwischen 1993 und 1999 lancierte er das Cyberpunk-Label W&LT (Wild and Lethal Trash) und kümmerte sich anschließend um den Relaunch der nach ihm benannten Linie Walter van Beirendonck. Mit Aestheticterrorists wurde 1999 die zweite Linie gegründet. Seit 1985 lehrt der Designer an der Königlichen Akademie und entwirft außerdem Kostüme für Theater und Film sowie für Bands wie U2 und Avalanches. Er hat als Kurator Ausstellungen in den besten Museen der Welt konzipiert, Bücher illustriert, einen eigenen Comic kreiert und zahlreiche Auszeichnungen gewonnen. Im März 1998 erschien das Buch „Mutilate", das sich van Beirendoncks ersten zehn Jahren in der Modebranche widmet. Im September desselben Jahres eröffnete der Modemacher seinen ersten eigenen Laden namens ,Walter' in Antwerpen. Man könnte van Beirendonck mit seinen visionären Perspektiven einen unverbesserlichen Optimisten der Branche nennen.

Si Walter Van Beirendonck était membre d'un groupe, il jouerait une fusion de punk, de folk, de trash, de pop, de techno et de musique de chambre. Créateur parmi les plus prolifiques de Belgique, Van Beirendonck place son sens de l'humour au cœur de ses créations en adoptant une approche qui humanise la sexualité, souvent intégrée à ses vêtements sous forme de motifs et de graphiques. Le « safe sex » apparaît comme le fil rouge de son travail, à côté des références littéraires, cinématographiques et folkloriques. La maille joue également un grand rôle dans le répertoire de Van Beirendonck, mais point de twin-sets guindés, ni de convenables pulls à col rond chez lui : ses pulls s'accompagnent plutôt de passe-montagnes ornés de messages osés, de motifs sexuels ou de visages criards de bande dessinée. Né en 1957 en Belgique, Van Beirendonck étudie à l'Académie Royale d'Anvers. Membre des légendaires Antwerp Six qui ont fait connaître la mode belge lors de leur défilé londonien en 1987, Walter Van Beirendonck, aux côtés de Dirk Van Saene, Dries Van Noten, Dirk Bikkembergs, Marina Yee et Ann Demeulemeester, a contribué à faire avancer la mode vers une nouvelle logique. Entre 1993 et 1999, il crée une griffe cyberpunk baptisée W&LT (Wild and Lethal Trash) avant de relancer sa ligne éponyme, Walter Van Beirendonck, ainsi qu'une autre gamme, Aestheticterrorists, en 1999. Depuis 1985, il enseigne la mode à l'Académie Royale et dessine des costumes de théâtre, de cinéma et de scène, notamment pour les groupes U2 et les Avalanches. Walter van Beirendonck a illustré des livres et organisé des expositions dans les plus grands musées d'art du monde, créé sa propre bande dessinée et remporté de nombreux prix. En mars 1998, le livre « Mutilate » retrace les 10 premières années de sa carrière et en septembre de la même année, il ouvre sa propre boutique, Walter, à Anvers. Van Beirendonck peut être considéré comme l'insouciant de la mode, tant pour sa perspective visionnaire que pour son indéfectible optimisme.

LIZ HANCOCK

What are your signature designs? Experiments I did in every collection, designs to underline the silhouettes or statements of that particular collection **How would you describe your work?** A continuing challenge to create collections and clothes to reflect my personal vision and style independent of fashion trends and movements **What's your ultimate goal?** To change the boundaries of fashion and to achieve personal satisfaction **What inspires you?** The world, my world, love… **Can fashion still have a political ambition?** Yes – fashion statements are still important, despite the fact that not many designers are thinking in that direction **Who do you have in mind when you design?** Nobody in particular. Gender, physique and age aren't important for my customers. It is more about being sensitive to my style, colours and forms **Is the idea of creative collaboration important to you?** Yes, very important. My most fascinating co-operations were with Stephen Jones, Bono, Mr Pearl, Mondino, Juergen Teller, Marc Newson, Paul Boudens **Who has been the greatest influence on your career?** My friend and colleague Dirk Van Saene **How have your own experiences affected your work as a designer?** I am still learning every day, but feel more mature than 20 years ago **Which is more important in your work: the process or the product?** Process and result are important. I do enjoy the process a lot **Is designing difficult for you? If so, what drives you to continue?** I love it and despite the fact that it is a permanent (financial) struggle, I have never thought of giving it up **Have you ever been influenced or moved by the reaction to your designs?** Every reaction, good or bad, lets you think about what you are doing **What's your definition of beauty?** Rethink beauty! **What is your philosophy?** Think and dream **What is the most important lesson you've learned?** To stick to my own personality, style and ideas. A necessity in this fashion world.

"I'm inspired by the inner complexity of a woman"
VÉRONIQUE BRANQUINHO

Véronique Branquinho doesn't design attention-seeking clothes. Instead, she prefers to create beautiful garments whose desirability is only enhanced by their functionality. Born in 1973 in the Belgian town of Vilvoorde, Branquinho studied modern languages and then painting, switching to fashion in 1991 at Antwerp's Royal Academy. She graduated in 1995 and began working for some of Belgium's top commercial labels, but always maintained the desire to create her own line. In October 1997, she presented her first fashion collection at an art gallery in Paris. The show drew the attention of the international press and retailers, allowing her to launch the following season onto the official fashion calendar. With a discreet sexuality, her clothing uses a muted palette of colours, mannish tailoring and street references in order to temper the femininity of fabrics such as lace, satin and chiffon. Through her garments, she acknowledges the duality of female fashion identity – a constant seesaw between the masculine and feminine, the girl and the woman. For spring/summer 2005, she was inspired by '70s soft-core porn icon Emmanuelle; the long-line skirts and tailoring that actually appeared on Branquinho's runway however were as subtle as ever. Now central to Belgium's formidable fashion community, Branquinho has exhibited at Florence's Biennale Della Moda, Colette in Paris, New York's Fashion Institute of Technology and Walter Van Beirendonck's 2001 'Landed' exhibition in Antwerp. She received the 1998 VH1 Fashion Award for best new designer, the Moët & Chandon Fashion Award in 2000 and was chosen by Ruffo Research to create their spring/summer and autumn/winter 1999 collections. In 2003, Branquinho launched her first men's collection, in Paris, and opened her first flagship store, in Antwerp. Recently appointed artistic director of luxury-goods house Delvaux, Branquinho continues to win over legions of fans by mixing sharp yet feminine tailoring and chic proportions to create a look that is all about laidback grown-up cool.

Véronique Branquinho entwirft keine Aufsehen erregende Mode. Stattdessen kreiert sie lieber Kleidungsstücke, deren Reiz nur noch von ihrer Funktionalität übertroffen wird. Die 1973 im belgischen Vilvoorde geborene Branquinho studierte zunächst Philologie, dann Malerei und wechselte 1991 zur Mode an der Königliche Akademie von Antwerpen. Dort machte sie 1995 ihr Examen und war im Anschluss für einige der kommerziellen belgischen Spitzenlabels tätig. Schon damals hegte sie jedoch den Wunsch nach einer eigenen Linie. Im Oktober 1997 präsentierte sie schließlich ihre erste Kollektion in einer Pariser Galerie und erzielte damit bei der Presse und den Einkäufern aus aller Welt solchen Erfolg, dass sie bereits in der darauf folgenden Saison im offiziellen Kalender der Mode-schauen erschien. Ihre diskrete Erotik verdanken ihre Kleider einer gedämpften Farbpalette, maskulinen Schnitten und Zitaten aus der Streetwear, die feminine Materialien wie Spitze, Satin und Chiffon ausgleichen. Die Designerin themati-siert in ihren Entwürfen den Dualismus weiblicher Identität in der Mode – das permanente Schwanken zwischen männlich und weiblich, zwischen dem Mäd-chenhaften und dem Fraulichen. Für die Kollektion Frühjahr/Sommer 2005 ließ sie sich von der Softporno-Ikone Emmanuelle aus den 1970er Jahren inspirieren.

Die langen Röcke und Kostüme, die Branquinho dann letztlich bei ihrer Schau präsentierte, waren jedoch so raffiniert wie eh und je. Als wichtiges Mitglied der geachteten belgischen Fashion Community hat die Designerin bereits bei der Biennale Della Moda in Florenz, bei Colette in Paris, am New Yorker Fashion Insti-tute of Technology sowie 2001 im Rahmen von Walter van Beirendoncks Projekt „Landed" in Antwerpen ausgestellt. 1998 erhielt sie den VH1 Fashion Award als beste neue Designerin, 2000 den Moët & Chandon Fashion Award. Ruffo Research erteilte ihr den Auftrag, die Kollektionen für Frühjahr/Sommer und Herbst/Winter 1999 zu entwerfen. 2003 zeigte Branquinho ihre erste Herrenkollektion in Paris und eröffnete den ersten Flagship Store ihres Labels in Antwerpen. Seit sie kürzlich Art Director der Luxusmarke Delvaux wurde, wächst ihre Fangemeinde rasend schnell, denn Branquinho versteht es, glasklare und den-noch feminine Schnitte mit schicken Proportionen zu kombinieren und so einen Look zu kreieren, der perfekt zu lässig-coolen erwachsenen Frauen passt.

Les vêtements dessinés par Véronique Branquinho ne cherchent pas à attirer l'attention. Au contraire, la créatrice préfère proposer de belles pièces qui seront d'autant plus désirables grâce à leur côté fonctionnel. Née en 1973 à Vilvoorde en Belgique, Véronique Branquinho étudie d'abord les langues modernes et la peinture avant d'entamer une formation en mode à l'Académie Royale d'Anvers en 1991. Diplômée en 1995, elle commence à travailler pour certaines des plus grandes marques commerciales de Belgique, mais envisage néanmoins de créer sa propre ligne. En octobre 1997, elle présente sa première collection de vêtements dans une galerie d'art à Paris. L'exposition attire l'attention de la presse inter-nationale et des acheteurs, lui permettant de se lancer dès la saison suivante dans le calendrier officiel des défilés de mode. Affichant une sensualité discrète, ses vêtements utilisent une palette de couleurs neutres, des coupes masculines et des références streetwear afin d'atténuer la féminité évidente des tissus tels que la dentelle, le satin et la mousseline de soie. A travers ses créations, elle reconnaît la dualité de l'identité féminine dans la mode : une oscillation constante entre le masculin et le féminin, la fille et la femme. Pour la saison printemps/été 2005, elle s'inspire d'Emmanuelle, l'icône érotique des années 70, mais ses jupes longues et ses tailleurs restent pourtant toujours aussi subtils. Membre désormais in-contournable de la formidable scène fashion belge, Véronique Branquinho a exposé son travail à la Biennale Della Moda de Florence, à la boutique Colette de Paris, au Fashion Institute of Technology de New York, ainsi qu'à l'occasion de l'exposition «Landed» organisée par Walter Van Beirendonck en 2001 à Anvers. En 1998, elle a reçu le prix de Best New Designer décerné par la chaîne VH1, puis le Moët & Chandon Fashion Award en l'an 2000. On lui doit également les collections printemps/été et automne/hiver 1999 de Ruffo Research. En 2003, Véronique Branquinho a lancé sa première collection pour homme à Paris et ouvert sa toute première boutique à Anvers. Récemment nommée directrice artistique du maroquinier de luxe Delvaux, Véronique Branquinho continue à séduire des lé-gions de fans en conjuguant des coupes strictes mais féminines avec des propor-tions élégantes pour créer un look cool, adulte et décontracté.   LIZ HANCOCK

PHOTOGRAPHY YANINA SORRENTI. STYLING JOHN HULLUM. SEPTEMBER 2001.

What are your signature designs? All my designs have my signature **What is your favourite piece from any of your collections?** The pants called 'Poison'. They have been in the collection since I started. And I don't see the point of changing them every six months just because there is a new fashion season **What's your ultimate goal?** To have the liberty to decide what I will be doing next **What inspires you?** People, their emotions as well what they can create **Who do you have in mind when you design?** I do not have a particular person in mind when I design. It's not about physique or features. It's more abstract. About a certain mood or state of mind. I'm inspired by the inner complexity of a woman. About the struggle she has with ambiguous feelings. About the attraction and rejection of those feelings, looking for harmony between them **Is the idea of creative collaboration important to you?** It is very rare, but if successful, it really opens up new horizons **How have your own experiences affected your work as a designer?** I see my collections as a personal diary. They are very close to me. In a way, they reflect my feelings **Which is more important in your work: the process or the product?** I cannot see process apart from product. It's about continuity. That makes them both equally important. It's a circle **Is designing difficult for you? If so, what drives you to continue?** I design very intuitively. It comes very naturally to express myself through my collections, so in a way it's not difficult **Have you ever been influenced or moved by the reaction to your designs?** More moved than influenced **What's your definition of beauty?** I don't want to define beauty. It's part of beauty that it can move you where you wouldn't expect it **What's your philosophy?** Freedom **What is the most important lesson you've learned?** That life and work become more interesting and satisfying when you have caring people around you.

"I like to provoke people to rethink about what can be done with menswear"
THOM BROWNE

There is no mistaking a Thom Browne suit. Narrow lapels, cropped jackets and trousers the cornerstones of a Browne design, Browne's ankle-skimming trousers revolutionised menswear and redefined the wardrobe of the modern man. Born in 1965, Browne was a one-time actor before landing himself a job as a salesman in Giorgio Armani's showroom in New York in 1997. At the Ralph Lauren-owned Club Monaco, Lauren noticed Browne's creative flair and promptly installed Browne – who has no formal fashion training – in their design and merchandising departments. In 2001, Browne left to start work on his self-named fashion house. Way before launching his own label the designer would buy old Brooks Brothers' suits from thrift stores and cut them down to resemble the aesthetic he is known for today. Along with his precise approach, Browne was perfect contender for Brooks Brothers' Black Fleece concept (a 50-piece men and women's high-end collection) in 2006. So successful was the collaboration that Brooks Brothers decided to carry on with Black Fleece until 2011. Launched in the UK last November (2007), Black Fleece is the first capsule collection for the 190-year-old brand by a guest designer. Browne received the 2006 CFDA Menswear Designer of the Year, a finalist for the National Design Award from the Cooper-Hewitt National Design Museum for 2006 and 2008, the Rising Star Award for Menswear by Fashion Group International for 2005 and the runner-up prize of the 2005 CFDA Vogue Fund. Browne has also added a men's jewellery line to his credentials, launched in 2007. In January 2009, Browne unveiled his men's collection for Moncler during Men's Fashion Week in Milan.

Ein Anzug von Thom Browne ist unverkennbar. Schmale Revers, kurze Jacken und Hosen bilden die Eckpfeiler des Browne-Designs. Seine die Knöchel zeigenden Hosen revolutionierten die Herrenmode und haben die Gaderobe des modernen Mannes neu definiert. Der 1965 geborene Browne war ursprünglich Schauspieler, bevor er sich 1997 einen Job als Verkäufer in Giorgio Armanis Showroom in New York besorgte. Im Club Monaco, der Ralph Lauren gehört, fiel Lauren Brownes kreative Ausstrahlung auf und er holte ihn – obwohl er keinerlei reguläre Ausbildung im Bereich Mode hat – in seine Abteilungen für Design und Verkauf. 2001 ging Browne von dort weg, um ein Modehaus unter eigenem Namen zu starten. Lange bevor er sein eigenes Label präsentierte, kaufte der Designer in Second-Hand-Läden alte Anzüge von Brooks Brothers zusammen und schnitt sie nach den ästhetischen Vorstellungen zurecht, für die er heute bekannt ist. Mit seiner korrekten Art war Browne der perfekte Anwärter für das Konzept Black Fleece von Brooks Brothers (eine hochwertige 50-teilige Herren- und Damenkollektion) im Jahr 2006. Die Zusammenarbeit war sogar derart erfolgreich, dass Brooks Brothers entschied, Black Fleece bis 2011 fortzusetzen. Die im November 2007 in Großbritannien präsentierte Kollektion ist die erste Sonderkollektion eines Gastdesigners bei der 190 Jahre alten Marke. 2006 war Browne Menswear Designer of the Year der CFDA, Finalist beim National Design Award des Cooper-Hewitt National Design Museum (wie auch 2008). Den Rising Star Award for Menswear der Fashion Group International erhielt er 2005, im selben Jahr belegte er den zweiten Platz beim CFDA Vogue Fund. Zu den Tätigkeitsnachweisen, die er 2007 erbrachte, zählt auch eine Schmuck-Kollektion für Herren. Im Januar 2009 stellte Browne im Rahmen der Men's Fashion Week in Mailand seine Herrenkollektion für Moncler vor.

Impossible de confondre un costume Thom Browne avec un autre. Caractérisées par des revers étroits, des vestes courtes et des pantalons qui laissent voir les chevilles, les créations de Browne ont révolutionné la mode masculine et redéfini la garderobe de l'homme moderne. Né en 1965, l'ex-acteur Thom Browne décroche un job de vendeur dans le showroom Giorgio Armani à New York en 1997, puis travaille pour la marque Club Monaco de Ralph Lauren. Ce dernier repère sa grande créativité et lui trouve rapidement une place de choix dans ses départements de création et de merchandising, alors que Browne ne possède aucune formation officielle dans ces domaines. En 2001, il quitte la maison Ralph Lauren pour travailler sur sa propre griffe. Bien avant de lancer sa collection, il achetait déjà de vieux costumes Brooks Brothers dans les boutiques d'occasion et les refaçonnait dans le style qui a depuis fait sa réputation. En ajoutant à cela son amour de la précision, Browne devient en 2006 le prétendant idéal au titre de styliste du concept Black Fleece de Brooks Brothers (une collection haut de gamme de 50 pièces pour homme et pour femme). Cette collaboration remporte un tel succès que Brooks Brothers décide de poursuivre la collection Black Fleece jusqu'en 2011. Lancée au Royaume-Uni en novembre 2007, Black Fleece est la première mini-collection que cette vénérable maison de 190 ans confie à un styliste invité. Lauréat du Menswear Designer of the Year du CFDA en 2006, Thom Browne était aussi finaliste pour le National Design Award du Cooper-Hewitt National Design Museum en 2006 et en 2008, le Rising Star Award for Menswear du Fashion Group International en 2005 et le CFDA Vogue Fund en 2005. Browne a étendu sa collection avec une ligne de bijoux pour homme lancée en 2007. En janvier 2009, il a présenté sa collection masculine pour Moncler pendant la Semaine de la mode pour homme de Milan. KAREN LEONG

What are your signature designs? My collection is based on the handmade tailored suit, with a shorter jacket, higher-armhole, high-waisted shorter trouser silhouette **What is your favourite piece from any of your collections?** Isn't that like asking to say who is your favourite child? I love all my collections **How would you describe your work?** Fundamentally, it's about introducing a new idea, the handmade tailored suit to men who already wear suits but want to wear something different or a younger person who thinks suits are for their fathers and/or grandfathers. But to further that idea, I like to provoke people to rethink about what can be done with menswear **What's your ultimate goal?** Keep reminding people that anything is possible **What inspires you?** Real people and fantasy **Who do you have in mind when you design?** A confident, true individual **Is the idea of creative collaboration important to you?** Not necessarily **How have your own experiences affected your work as a designer?** I think that being comfortable with who I am, being an individual, has affected my work as a designer **Which is more important in your work: the process or the product?** They are equally important to me **Is designing difficult for you? If so, what drives you to continue?** No, the designing part is not difficult **Have you ever been influenced or moved by the reaction to your designs?** I am influenced when I see my collection live during the show **What's your definition of beauty?** My definition of beauty is something unique **What's your philosophy?** Historically and culturally speaking, there is a higher expectation in innovation in design and unique usage of fabrics in womenswear, and I want to show that this can be done with menswear while keeping it masculine **What is the most important lesson you've learned?** The most important lesson I've learned is to just stay true to yourself.

"In every collection there are pieces with which I literally fall in love"
CONSUELO CASTIGLIONI · MARNI

In little more than fifteen years Consuelo Castiglioni's label Marni has become a byword for innovative Italian design, charming its way into fashion folklore with an eclectic vision of femininity. What began as a stint of fashion consulting for her husband's fur and leather company, Ciwi Furs, has developed into a business that has produced some of the most cultish items of the last few years – ponyskin clogs, corsages, charm-embellished bags, the cropped jacket – and a look that has helped define contemporary notions of prettiness. Marni was launched in 1994 with an experimental collection produced through Ciwi Furs (supplier to Prada and Moschino). Treating fur like a fabric, Castiglioni removed the lining, and with it the bulkiness, of the usual rich-bitch fur coat. With each collection she gradually introduced new fabrics, mixing fur with perfectly-cut leathers and suedes, and by 1999 Marni had become an established line independent from its furrier origins. The arts and crafts richness of the Marni look comes from a considered mismatching of print, cut and texture. The Marni girl wears a veritable haberdashery of luxurious and love-worn fabrics which are layered across the body and nipped in at the waist with a decorative belt. The Marni print – from faded florals and mattress ticking stripes to '50s retro and block prints – may have become an influential motif, but one that can distract from the slick couture finish that adds to the creatively haphazard look. Since 2000 Marni has undergone giddying retail expansion, opening 38 boutiques around the world, designed either by architecture firm Future Systems or Sybarite, and selling menswear, childrenswear and homeware alongside a successful line of accessories.

In wenig mehr als 15 Jahren ist Consuelo Castiglionis Label Marni zum Synonym für innovatives italienisches Design geworden. Mit einer eklektischen Vision von Weiblichkeit hat sich die Marke ihren Weg in die folkloristisch angehauchte Mode gebahnt. Begonnen hat es mit einem Job als Fashion Consultant für den Kürschnerbetrieb Ciwi Furs, der Castiglionis Mann gehört. Doch bald entwickelte sich das Ganze zu einem eigenständigen Geschäft, das einige der kultigsten Produkte der letzten Jahre hervorbrachte – Ponyfell-Clogs, Bandschleifen-Corsagen, mit Glücksbringern verzierte Taschen, Boleros. Der Marni-Look hat das gegenwärtige Verständnis von Schönheit mitbestimmt. Gegründet wurde Marni 1994 mit einer Versuchskollektion, die bei Ciwi Furs (u. a. Zulieferer von Prada und Moschino) produziert wurde. Castiglioni verarbeitete Pelz wie Stoff, verzichtete auf das Futter und reduzierte so das Volumen des traditionell protzigen Pelzmantels. Mit jeder Kollektion führte sie neue Materialien ein, mixte Pelz mit perfekt geschnittenem Leder und Wildleder, so dass Marni sich ab 1999 als eine von ihren pelzigen Ursprüngen unabhängige, eigenständige Marke etabliert hatte. Der bohemienhafte Marni-Look verdankt sich den absichtlichen Gegensätzen von Muster, Schnitt und Textur. So trägt das typische

Marni-Girl einen veritablen Mischmasch aus luxuriösen und abgetragenen Stoffen, die sich schichtweise um ihren Körper legen, in der Taille von einem dekorativen Gürtel zusammengehalten werden und eine organische Silhouette erzeugen. Das Marni-Muster – ob verblichen-floral, gestreift wie Matratzendrillich, 50er-Jahre-Retro oder Blockstreifen – mag ein wichtiges Motiv sein, kann jedoch nicht vom raffinierten Couture-Finish ablenken, das unverzichtbar für den bewusst kreierten, aber zufällig wirkenden Look ist. Seit dem Jahr 2000 hat Marni im Einzelhandel auf geradezu schwindelerregende Weise expandiert und 38 Boutiquen in aller Welt eröffnet, die von den Architekturbüros Future Systems oder Sybarite entworfen wurden. Dort verkauft man Herren- und Kindermode, Wohnbedarf sowie ein erfolgreiches Sortiment von Accessoires.

En un peu moins de 15 ans, la griffe Marni de Consuelo Castiglioni est devenue synonyme d'innovation à l'italienne, se frayant un chemin dans la mode aux accents folkloriques grâce à sa vision éclectique de la féminité. Ce qui a commencé par un job de consultante pour Ciwi Furs, fabricant de cuirs et de fourrures dirigé par son mari, s'est transformé en une grande entreprise qui produit certaines des pièces les plus cultes de ces dernières années : sabots en vachette, corsages, sacs ornés de grigris porte-bonheur, vestes tondues... pour un look qui a contribué à définir les canons contemporains de la beauté. Consuelo Castiglioni lance sa griffe Marni en 1994 avec une collection expérimentale produite par le biais de Ciwi Furs (fournisseur de Prada et Moschino). Travaillant la fourrure comme du tissu, elle en retire la doublure, et avec elle la lourdeur généralement associée au manteau de fourreur tape-à-l'œil. Au fil des collections, elle introduit progressivement de nouvelles matières, coordonnant la fourrure à des cuirs et des daims parfaitement coupés ; en 1999, la griffe devient entièrement indépendante de ses origines de fourreur. La richesse artistique et artisanale du style Marni naît d'un assortiment d'imprimés, de coupes et de textures volontairement dépareillé. La fille Marni arbore donc avec amour tout un arsenal de tissus luxueux superposés sur le corps et pincés à la taille à l'aide d'une ceinture décorative pour produire une silhouette organique. Des floraux passés aux rayures matelas, des motifs rétro années 50 aux impressions à la planche, les imprimés Marni exercent certes beaucoup d'influence sur la mode, mais ils réussissent toujours à détourner l'attention du fini haute couture irréprochable qui caractérise ce look délibérément aléatoire. Depuis l'an 2000, les ventes de Marni connaissent une ascension vertigineuse : la marque a ouvert 38 boutiques à travers le monde, conçues par les cabinets d'architecture Future Systems ou Sybarite. Elles proposent des vêtements pour homme, une ligne pour enfant et des meubles, ainsi qu'une ligne d'accessoires à succès.

AIMEE FARRELL

What do you consider your signature designs? My signature characteristics are: prints, combinations of fabrics, colours and lengths, details, luxury and ease **What is your favourite piece from any of your collections?** In every collection there are pieces with which I literally fall in love **How would you describe your work?** Free from formal constraints. It's dressing with patchworks of fragments, shreds, tinkers of style **What is your ultimate goal?** The fashion world is now becoming extremely competitive. Our ultimate goal as a company is to control all the value chain, from design up to retail and distribution. My personal objective is to continue to design and produce collections

in which every item receives special attention. This has always been for me a focus and a privilege **What inspires you?** Memories and passions, fashions and costumes, arts and techniques **Can fashion still have a political ambition?** In a strict sense, I do not feel it ever has **Who do you have in mind when you design?** When I design, I do not have a particular woman in mind. I merge different elements which I like. My inspiration comes from a combination of emotions **Is the idea of creative collaboration important to you?** Creative collaboration means to me the people who surround me in my daily work. At Marni, the family approach is important. I do not only

work for myself, I work for them and they for me **Who or what has been the greatest influence on your career?** Every single person who has believed in the Marni project, giving us the chance to develop it, from the fabric companies to the editors worldwide **How have your own experiences affected your work as a designer?** My personal experiences, feelings and moods constantly affect my design **Which is more important to you in your work: the process or the product?** In my work, the product really depends on the process: at the beginning it's always a fabric or a print which stimulates my creativity. Then I start mixing and matching **Is designing difficult to you?**

If so what drives you to continue? For the moment, designing is still a pleasure for me and the mere fact that I enjoy it so much drives me to continue **Have you ever been influenced or moved by the reaction to your designs?** Obviously a positive response encourages you to put increasing effort in your work **What's your definition of beauty?** Beauty does not have age or sex, I see it as a combination of qualities from within, which are projected to the exterior **What's your philosophy?** Creating timeless pieces **What is the most important lesson you've learned?** I feel that I am constantly learning. I strongly believe it is important to keep an open mind towards different stimuli.

"We're inspired by things that are normally not fashionable"
DEAN & DAN CATEN • DSQUARED

Dean and Dan Caten of Dsquared know a thing or two about mixing and matching. Not only did the now 40-year-old identical twins leave their native Canada in 1991 for Italy, the homeland of their paternal grandmother (Caten is short for Catenacci, while the maternal side is English), they've managed to turn the fashion world on its head with a ballsy blend of American pop culture and superior Italian tailoring. The Milan debut of their men's line in 1994 garnered fans such as Lenny Kravitz, Justin Timberlake and Ricky Martin for its cheeky, MTV-ready ebullience paired with precision craftsmanship. Soon thereafter, the duo further solidified their fashion credibility by creating the costumes for Madonna's 'Don't Tell Me' video and the cowboy segment of her 2002 Drowned World Tour, as well as the outfits for Christina Aguilera's 2003 Stripped Tour (the diminutive diva was later recruited to walk the catwalk for the spring/summer 2005 men's collection). The launch of a women's line in 2003 saw supermodels Naomi Campbell, Eva Herzigova, Karolina Kurkova and Fernanda Tavares saunter out of a pink private jet in unapologetically sex-charged regalia. For autumn/winter 2005, the brothers, who spent their childhoods as born-again Christians, looked to a higher power with skinny ties stitched with 'John 3:16', caps and T-shirts printed with the word 'Angel' and sweaters emblazoned with 'Jesus Loves Me' or, on one notable cardigan, 'Jesus Loves Even Me'. Apparently, even fashion designers know God is in the details, a well-worn principle that, along with backing from the Italian conglomerate Diesel, has shot sales for the erstwhile party boys into the heavens. In the last few years, Dsquared have raised their game even further. Since shooting their autumn/winter 2005 campaign with photographers Mert & Marcus, they have gone on to collaborate with Steven Meisel. In 2007, their long-awaited 5,400 sq ft Milan store was opened and they also launched their first fragrance.

Dean und Dan Caten von Dsquared verstehen einiges von Mixing und Matching. 1991 verließen die heute 40-jährigen eineiigen Zwillinge ihr kanadisches Zuhause, um nach Italien zu ziehen, in die Heimat ihrer Großmutter väterlicherseits (Caten ist die Abkürzung von Catenacci; die Familie mütterlicherseits hat englische Wurzeln). Mit einer gewagten Mixtur aus amerikanischer Popkultur und anspruchsvoller italienischer Schneiderkunst ist es ihnen gelungen, die Modewelt auf den Kopf zu stellen. Nach ihrem Mailänder Debüt der Herrenlinie 1994 zählten dank des frechen, mit handwerklicher Präzision gepaarten Überschwangs Lenny Kravitz, Justin Timberlake und Ricky Martin zu ihren Fans. Bald danach untermauerte das Duo seine modische Glaubwürdigkeit durch Madonnas Kostüme für das Video zu „Don't Tell Me" und die Cowboy-Outfits ihrer Drowned World Tour 2002. Es folgte die Ausstattung von Christina Aguilera bei ihrer Tour Stripped 2003 (die kleine Diva wurde später anlässlich der Herrenkollektion Frühjahr/Sommer 2005 für den Catwalk verpflichtet). Bei der Präsentation der Damenlinie im Jahr 2003 sah man die Supermodels Naomi Campbell, Eva Herzigova, Karolina Kurkova und Fernanda Tavares mit eindeutig zweideutigen Insignien

einem pinkfarbenen Privatjet entsteigen. Für die Kollektion Herbst/Winter 2005 orientierten sich die Brüder, die ihre Kindheit in einer Gemeinde wiedergeborener Christen verbrachten, an einer höheren Macht und bestickten schmale Krawatten mit „Johannes 3.16", bedruckten Baseballcaps und T-Shirts mit dem Wort „Angel" und verzierten Pullover mit „Jesus Loves Me" sowie eine Strickjacke mit dem bemerkenswerten „Jesus Loves Even Me". Offenbar wissen selbst Modedesigner, dass Gott sich im Detail verbirgt. Dieses kluge Prinzip sorgte neben der Unterstützung durch den italienischen Diesel-Konzern dafür, dass die Verkaufszahlen der einstigen Partyboys in himmlische Höhen schossen. In den letzten Jahren hat Dsquared sogar noch weiter zugelegt. Nach der Herbst/Winter-Kampagne 2005/06 mit den Fotografen Mert & Marcus setzte man die Zusammenarbeit mit Steven Meisel fort. 2007 wurde schließlich der langersehnte 500 m² große Store in Mailand eröffnet. Außerdem kam der erste eigene Duft auf den Markt.

On peut dire que Dean et Dan Caten de Dsquared s'y connaissent en métissage des styles. Ces vrais jumeaux, aujourd'hui âgés de 40 ans, quittent leur Canada natal en 1991 pour l'Italie, patrie de leur grand-mère paternelle (Caten est une abréviation de Catenacci tandis qu'ils sont d'origine anglaise du côté de leur mère), et réussissent à bouleverser l'univers de la mode avec leur fusion osée entre pop culture américaine et coupe virtuose à l'italienne. En 1994, les débuts milanais de leur ligne pour homme ravissent des fans tels que Lenny Kravitz, Justin Timberlake et Ricky Martin grâce à leur exubérante insolence formatée pour MTV mais conjuguée à un savoir-faire de précision. Peu de temps après, le duo assoie sa crédibilité en créant les costumes du clip « Don't Tell Me » de Madonna et les tenues de cow-boy de sa Drowned World Tour en 2002, sans oublier les costumes de la tournée Stripped de Christina Aguilera en 2003 (la mini-diva sera plus tard recrutée pour défiler lors de leur collection pour homme printemps/été 2005). Le lancement d'une ligne pour femme en 2003 voit les top models Naomi Campbell, Eva Herzigova, Karolina Kurkova et Fernanda Tavares sortir d'un jet privé rose, vêtues d'insignes sexuellement explicites. Pour l'automne/hiver 2005, les frères jumeaux élevés dans la doctrine évangélique des Born-Again Christians semblent retrouver la foi avec des cravates étroites cousues de l'inscription « Jean 3.16 », des casquettes et des T-shirts imprimés du mot « Angel » et des pulls proclamant « Jesus Loves Me » ou, sur un certain cardigan, « Jesus Loves Even Me ». Apparemment, même les créateurs de mode savent que Dieu se cache dans les détails, un principe éprouvé qui, allié au soutien financier du conglomérat italien Diesel, propulse les ventes de ces anciens fêtards au firmament. Depuis ces dernières années, les jumeaux de Dsquared visent encore plus haut. Ils ont confié leur campagne automne/hiver 2005–2006 aux photographes Mert & Marcus et collaboré avec Steven Meisel. En 2007, ils ont ouvert la boutique milanaise de 500 mètres carrés que tout le monde attendait et lancé leur tout premier parfum. LEE CARTER

PHOTOGRAPHY ELLEN VON UNWERTH. STYLING MARK MORRISON. MODEL, OMAHYRA. AUGUST 2004.

What are your signature designs? Super sexy, super low-cut trousers **What is your favourite piece from any of your collections?** Our brown leather 'chiodo' pant with quilted knees and gold snaps **How would you describe your work?** Honest and real **What's your ultimate goal?** To contribute to the fashion industry with something real and be respected for it **What inspires you?** Our lives, our pasts, things we've done and things we haven't! We're inspired by things that are normally not fashionable, making a negative into a positive, everyday people **Can fashion still have a political ambition?** We don't get political in anything! **Who do you have in mind when you design?** Ourselves, be it men or women… we can get into anything **Is the idea of creative collaboration important to you?** We're a design team, 'per forza' collaboration is second nature to us **Who has been the greatest influence on your career?** The man who gave us the chance at 19 to design, Mr Luke Tanabe, our maestro who taught us discipline and sensibility and fine-tuned our eye **How have your own experiences affected your work as designers?** In every sense, our work is a product of our lives and the experiences that surround us **Which is more important in your work: the process or the product?** They go hand in hand, the product is the consequence of the procedure **Is designing difficult for you? If so, what drives you to continue?** Difficult or not, it's the challenge to come up with new ideas that drives us to continue **Have you ever been influenced or moved by the reaction to your designs?** We are moved by the incredible loyal following we have. It stimulates us to keep them smiling **What's your definition of beauty?** Something that can evoke a positive personal reaction: you absorb it, it warms you and makes you feel good. Beauty is so subjective… **What's your philosophy?** Free to be and do as you please **What is the most important lesson you've learned?** Go with your gut and stay true to your heart and always believe in yourself.

> ## "Nature is my main source of inspiration –
> ## I will never stop taking hints from what I call 'the greatest artist'"
> # ROBERTO CAVALLI

Roberto Cavalli (born 1940, Florence) designs some of the most glamorous clothes in fashion: baroque combinations of exotic feathers, overblown florals, animal prints and incredibly lightweight leathers comprise the signature Cavalli look for day or night, which is always shown on his Milan runway atop the highest heels and with the biggest, blow-dried hair in the city. In winter collections, fur – the more extravagant the better – is dominant. And to think it all started on a ping-pong table. This is where, as a student at Florence's Academy of Art, Cavalli began to experiment with printing on leather, later patenting a similar technique. The son of a tailor and the grandson of a revered painter (of the Macchiaioli movement), Cavalli is an expert embellisher and decorator of textiles. After founding his own fashion company in the early '60s, Cavalli was one of the first to put leather on a catwalk, patchworking it together for his debut show in 1972, which was staged at the Palazzo Pitti in Florence. Cavalli was an outsider to high fashion during the '80s, but staged a remarkable comeback in the '90s. In this renaissance period, Cavalli has become the label of choice among the R&B aristocracy, not to mention any starlet with both the bravado and the body to carry off one of his attention-seeking frocks. Assisted by his second wife, Eva Düringer, a former Miss Universe, Cavalli brought his distinctive look – a unique combination of thrusting sex appeal, artisanal prints and frankly eccentric themes and catwalk shows – to the Milan collections, where press and clients alike received him with open arms. The collections bearing his name now include Just Cavalli, a menswear line, a childrenswear line and perfume licences, among others. In 2003, his company scored a turnover of € 289 million and its collections are distributed in more than 50 countries. Cavalli also owns one of Italy's best racehorse stud farms.

Der 1940 in Florenz geborene Roberto Cavalli entwirft einige der glamourösesten Modekreationen überhaupt: Barocke Kombinationen aus exotischen Federn, schwülstigen Blumenmustern, Raubtier-Prints und unglaublich leichten Ledersorten ergeben zusammen den typischen Cavalli-Look für den Tag und den Abend. Präsentiert wird dieser ausschließlich auf dem Mailänder Catwalk des Designers, mit allerhöchsten Absätzen und den voluminösesten Fönfrisuren der ganzen Stadt. In den Winterkollektionen dominiert Pelz – je extravaganter desto besser. Kaum zu glauben, dass das alles auf einer Tischtennisplatte angefangen hat. Doch genau dort begann Cavalli als Student der florentinischen Kunstakademie mit dem Bedrucken von Leder zu experimentieren. Später ließ er sich diese Technik sogar patentieren. Als Sohn eines Schneiders und Enkel eines geachteten Malers (aus der Macchiaioli-Schule) ist Cavalli ein begnadeter Verschönerer und Dekorateur von Textilien. Nachdem er in den frühen 1960er Jahren seine eigene Modefirma gegründet hatte, war er einer der Ersten, der Leder auf den Laufsteg brachte. Für seine Debütschau von 1972 im Palazzo Pitti in Florenz nähte er es im Patchworkstil zusammen. Die 1980er-Jahre erlebte er als Außenseiter der Haute Couture, in den 1990er-Jahren gelang ihm jedoch ein beachtliches Comeback. Im Zuge dieser Renaissance avancierte Cavalli zum Lieblingslabel der R&B-Stars, gar nicht zu reden von den zahlreichen Starlets, die die Courage und den Körper besaßen, eines von seinen Aufsehen erregenden Kleidern zu tragen. Unterstützt von seiner zweiten Frau, der ehemaligen Miss Universum Eva Düringer, brachte Cavalli seinen unverwechselbaren Look – eine Kombination aus offensivem Sexappeal, künstlerischen Mustern sowie exzentrischen Themen – in Mailand heraus, wo ihn Presse und Publikum mit offenen Armen empfingen. Zu den Labels unter seinem Namen zählen inzwischen u. a. Just Cavalli, eine Herrenlinie, eine Kinderkollektion und eine Parfümlizenz. 2003 machte das Unternehmen 289 Millionen Euro Umsatz mit dem Vertrieb der Kollektionen in mehr als 50 Ländern. Cavalli besitzt übrigens auch eines der besten italienischen Gestüte für Rennpferde.

Roberto Cavalli (né en 1940 à Florence) dessine certains des vêtements les plus glamour de la mode: combinaisons baroques de plumes exotiques, motifs de fleurs géantes, imprimés d'animaux et cuirs incroyablement légers composent son look signature pour le jour ou le soir, toujours présenté sur les podiums milanais par des mannequins haut perchées sur leurs talons et coiffées des brushings les plus flamboyants de la ville. Ses collections d'hiver font la part belle à la fourrure, toujours plus extravagante. Tout a commencé sur la table de ping-pong où l'étudiant de l'Académie des Beaux-Arts de Florence s'essayait à l'impression sur cuir, une technique qu'il finira par faire breveter. Fils de tailleur et petit-fils d'un illustre peintre (du mouvement Macchiaioli), Roberto Cavalli excelle dans l'embellissement et la décoration des textiles. Après la création de sa propre griffe au début des années 60, Cavalli fait figure de précurseur en proposant du cuir travaillé en patchworks pour son premier défilé donné au Palazzo Pitti de Florence en 1972. Pendant les années 80, Cavalli se marginalise un peu par rapport à la mode haut de gamme, mais fait un retour remarqué dans les années 90. Pendant cette période de renaissance, Cavalli devient la griffe de prédilection des stars du R&B, sans oublier toutes les starlettes assez courageuses et bien roulées pour oser porter ses robes scandaleuses. Epaulé par sa seconde épouse Eva Düringer, une ex-Miss Univers, Cavalli présente son look original (une combinaison unique entre sex-appeal explosif, imprimés artisanaux, thématiques et défilés franchement excentriques) aux collections milanaises, où la presse comme les acheteurs l'accueillent à bras ouverts. Les collections qu'il signe de son nom incluent désormais Just Cavalli, une ligne pour homme, une ligne pour enfant et des licences de parfums, entre autres. En 2003, son entreprise a réalisé un chiffre d'affaires de 289 millions d'euros, avec des collections distribuées dans plus de 50 pays à travers le monde. Cavalli possède également l'un des plus beaux haras de chevaux de course d'Italie.

SUSIE RUSHTON

ROBERTO CAVALLI

ROBERTO CAVALLI

What are your signature designs? It is a skilful mixture of innovation, technology, cheerful fantasies and well-fitted cuts. My experiments on prints together with Eva's ability in setting them off with the right cut made Roberto Cavalli well known for its feminine, elegant, unique fashion **What is your favourite piece from any of your collections?** It is really difficult to choose. If I have to select, I am particularly attached to the first patchwork jeans I designed, an experiment that led to a big success. As I started matching denim with leather, I could say I will always consider them my favourite materials **How would you describe your work?** Highly creative, elaborate, innovative, one of its kind **What's your ultimate goal?** I will keep on expanding my commercial network following the openings of recent months… an early 18th-century edifice at the corner of rue Cambon and St Honoré in Paris, dedicated to innovative fashion: a Roberto Cavalli Palazzo in the heart of haute couture! I will also produce, together with Dino De Laurentiis, a film. An ambitious venture based on a masterpeace of Italian literature: Giovanni Boccaccio's Decameron **What inspires you?** Nature is the main source of inspiration with its multicoloured animal coats, flowers, landscapes… I will never stop taking hints from what I call 'the greatest artist'. Also Eva is my muse. She is my wife, the mother of my children and she is the only person able to interpret my dreams and my ideas **Can fashion still have a political ambition?** I believe that fashion has partially lost its political ambition. Just think about the difference between the folk fashion in the '70s and the ethnic trend of the last period: while in the past it meant a radical rebellion against the institution, nowadays it represents a charming journey towards unexplored territories in search of new vibes **Who do you have in mind when you design?** When I design, I have in mind sunny people: that love life, nature and love; women or men who like to express their strong personality through my colours and my prints **Is the idea of creative collaboration important to you?** Yes, it is very important, but at the same time very difficult to reach. I thank my lucky stars that I met my wife, Eva: we have a wonderful mutual understanding in both, our private and professional life **Who has been the greatest influence on your career?** Painting has been one of the greatest influences in my career. Following in my grandfather's path, I attended the Academy of Art… in a sense, my way was already marked out **How have your own experiences affected your work as a designer?** In fact, my devotion to my job was from a personal defeat: my first girlfriend's parents rejected me because I was neither rich nor attending university. I was really in love with her and this hurt me deeply. Therefore I decided I would demonstrate to them what a big mistake they made! **Which is more important in your work: the process or the product?** It is very difficult to choose. While creating, I am completely absorbed by the process: testing new prints, designing original cuts, searching for fabrics. But I don't leave the final product out of consideration: if I am not satisfied with it, even though I have experimented with new, fabulous techniques, I step back and start again **Is designing difficult for you? If so, what drives you to continue?** Fortunately not: it comes spontaneously **Have you ever been influenced or moved by the reaction to your designs?** No, I have never been influenced by the reaction to my designs. Fashion is my way of translating art: I cannot think of market rules directing my creative process **What's your definition of beauty?** Beauty is something coming from the inside; it is a reflection of the personality. This is the reason why, unlike good looks, it does not grow old **What's your philosophy?** My philosophy is to live day by day **What is the most important lesson you've learned?** I have learned that somehow you have to adapt yourself to the circumstances. I am a Scorpio: if I had not been so stubborn, I probably would have been successful 20 years ago. At that time, I did not feel like being a personality and attending parties all the time: maybe because I refused to wear a tuxedo… or maybe because I was too shy. Afterwards, I realised that people expect a designer to be recognisable: his face, the story of his life, his opinions are as important as his creations. I have started to organise beautiful parties and I have taken a liking to it: I really enjoy the idea that people have a good time! But you know what? Now I am criticised because my parties are 'too much'. Sometimes life is funny!

"My inspiration comes from anthropology, genetic anthropology, migration, history, social prejudice, politics, displacement, science fiction and, I guess, my own cultural background"
HUSSEIN CHALAYAN

Hussein Chalayan pushes clothing into sculpture, furniture, performance, art and beyond. Since his graduate collection at Central Saint Martins in 1993 he has confirmed his reputation as one of the most original designers working anywhere in the world today. Chalayan is famed for his spectacular shows in which anything could happen, from coffee tables turning into dresses to the use of confessional boxes and trampolines as catwalk props. At the same time, the designer's attention to technical detail, structure and stitching is exceptional. His collections have often focused on cultural displacement, something that Chalayan himself has experienced; his spring/summer 2003 collection 'Kinship Journey', for example, was inspired by Viking, Byzantine, Georgian and Armenian cultures following a DNA test taken by the designer. Aside from his eponymous label, Chalayan has during his career worked for cashmere brand TSE and was appointed creative director of Asprey in 2001, leaving the company in 2004. His creative touchstones are science and new technology. He is a twice-crowned British Designer of the Year, having picked up the prize in 1999 and 2000. 2004 saw Chalayan open his first store in Tokyo, to complement his existing womenswear and menswear collections; in 2005, he also launched a younger line, 'Chalayan'. Chalayan's career has continued on the upward trajectory. He was awarded an MBE in the Queen's Birthday Honours List 2006 for his services to the fashion industry, and the prestigious Design Star Honoree by The Fashion Group International in 2007. In 2008, Chalayan was appointed Creative Director of German sportswear label Puma, where his passion for technology and forward-thinking design continues to breathe new life into the 80-year-old brand. Chalayan's retrospective at the Design Museum in London (2009) celebrated 15 years of ground-breaking experimental design and explored the inspirations and themes that continue to influence the designer, in particular issues of cultural identity, displacement and migration.

Hussein Chalayan überwindet mit seiner Kleidung die Grenzen zu Bildhauerei, Möbelherstellung, Performance und Kunst. Seit seiner Abschlusskollektion am Central Saint Martins im Jahr 1993 gelang es ihm, seinen Ruf als einer der originellsten Designer der Gegenwart weiter zu festigen. Chalayan ist berühmt für seine spektakulären Modenschauen, bei denen alles Mögliche passieren kann, von Kaffeetischen, die sich in Kleider verwandeln, bis zu Beichtstühlen und Trampolinen als Requisiten auf dem Laufsteg. Dazu kommt die außergewöhnliche Sorgfalt des Designers hinsichtlich technischer Details, Strukturen und Nähte. Oft stehen kulturelle Verschiebungen, die Chalayan auch selbst erfahren hat, im Mittelpunkt seiner Kollektionen. So war etwa seine Kollektion Frühjahr/Sommer 2003 von den Kulturen der Wikinger, Byzantiner, Georgier und Armenier inspiriert, nachdem der Designer sich einem DNA-Test unterzogen hatte. Außer für das nach ihm benannte Label hat er im Laufe seiner Karriere für die Kaschmirmarke TSE sowie von 2001 bis 2004 als Creative Director für Asprey entworfen. Seine kreativen Prüfsteine sind Wissenschaft und neue Technologien. Er wurde zweimal mit dem Titel British Designer of the Year ausgezeichnet (1999 und 2000). 2004 eröffnete Chalayan seinen ersten Laden in Tokio. Und als Ergänzung der Damen- und Herrenkollektion lancierte er 2005 mit Chalayan noch eine jüngere Linie. Mit Chalayans Karriere geht es weiter bergauf. 2006 wurde er für seine Verdienste um die Modeindustrie in der Liste der Geehrten anlässlich des Geburtstags der Queen als Member of the Order of the British Empire ausgezeichnet. 2007 erhielt er den angesehenen Design Star Honoree der Fashion Group International. 2008 wurde Chalayan Creative Director des Sportartikel-Herstellers Puma, wo sein Faible für Technologie und zukunftsorientiertes Design der 80 Jahre alten Marke neues Leben einhauchte. Die Chalayan-Retrospektive im Londoner Design Museum (2009) feierte 15 Jahre bahnbrechendes experimentelles Design und beleuchtete die Inspirationen und Themen, die den Designer nach wie vor beschäftigen, insbesondere die Bereiche kulturelle Identität, Heimatverlust und Migration.

Hussein Chalayan repousse la frontière de la mode aux confins de la sculpture, du mobilier, du théâtre et même au-delà. Depuis sa collection de fin d'études à Central Saint Martins en 1993 il a confirmé sa réputation de créateur parmi les plus originaux actuellement en exercice dans le monde. Chalayan est connu pour ses défilés spectaculaires où tout peut arriver, des tables basses transformées en robes aux confessionnaux et trampolines utilisés en guise de podiums. Parallèlement, le créateur fait preuve d'une attention exceptionnelle aux détails techniques, à la structure et aux coutures. Ses collections parlent souvent du «déplacement culturel», une expérience vécue par Chalayan en personne; par exemple, pour sa collection printemps/été 2003 «Kinship Journey», il s'est inspiré des cultures viking, byzantine, géorgienne et arménienne après avoir obtenu les résultats de son test ADN. Outre sa griffe éponyme, Chalayan a travaillé pour la marque de cachemire TSE. En 2001, il a été nommé styliste d'Asprey, une maison qu'il quittera en 2004. Les pierres d'angle de sa démarche créative sont les sciences et les nouvelles technologies, et il a été couronné deux fois British Designer of the Year (1999 et 2000). En 2004, Chalayan a ouvert sa première boutique à Tokyo. Afin de compléter ses collections pour homme et pour femme, il a également lancé en 2005 une ligne plus jeune baptisée Chalayan. Depuis, la carrière de Chalayan reste sur une pente ascendante. En 2006, il a été nommé Membre de l'Ordre de l'Empire Britannique sur la «Birthday Honours List» de la Reine d'Angleterre pour services rendus à l'industrie de la mode, tandis qu'en 2007, Fashion Group International lui a décerné son prestigieux Design Star Honoree. En 2008, Chalayan est devenu directeur de la création de la griffe sportswear allemande Puma: grâce à sa passion de la technologie et sa créativité visionnaire, cette marque de 80 ans semble sans cesse se renouveler. La rétrospective Chalayan au Design Museum de Londres (2009) célèbre quinze années de création expérimentale révolutionnaire en revenant sur les sources d'inspiration et les thèmes qui continuent d'influencer le créateur, notamment les questions de l'identité, du «déplacement culturel» et de l'immigration.   SKYE SHERWIN

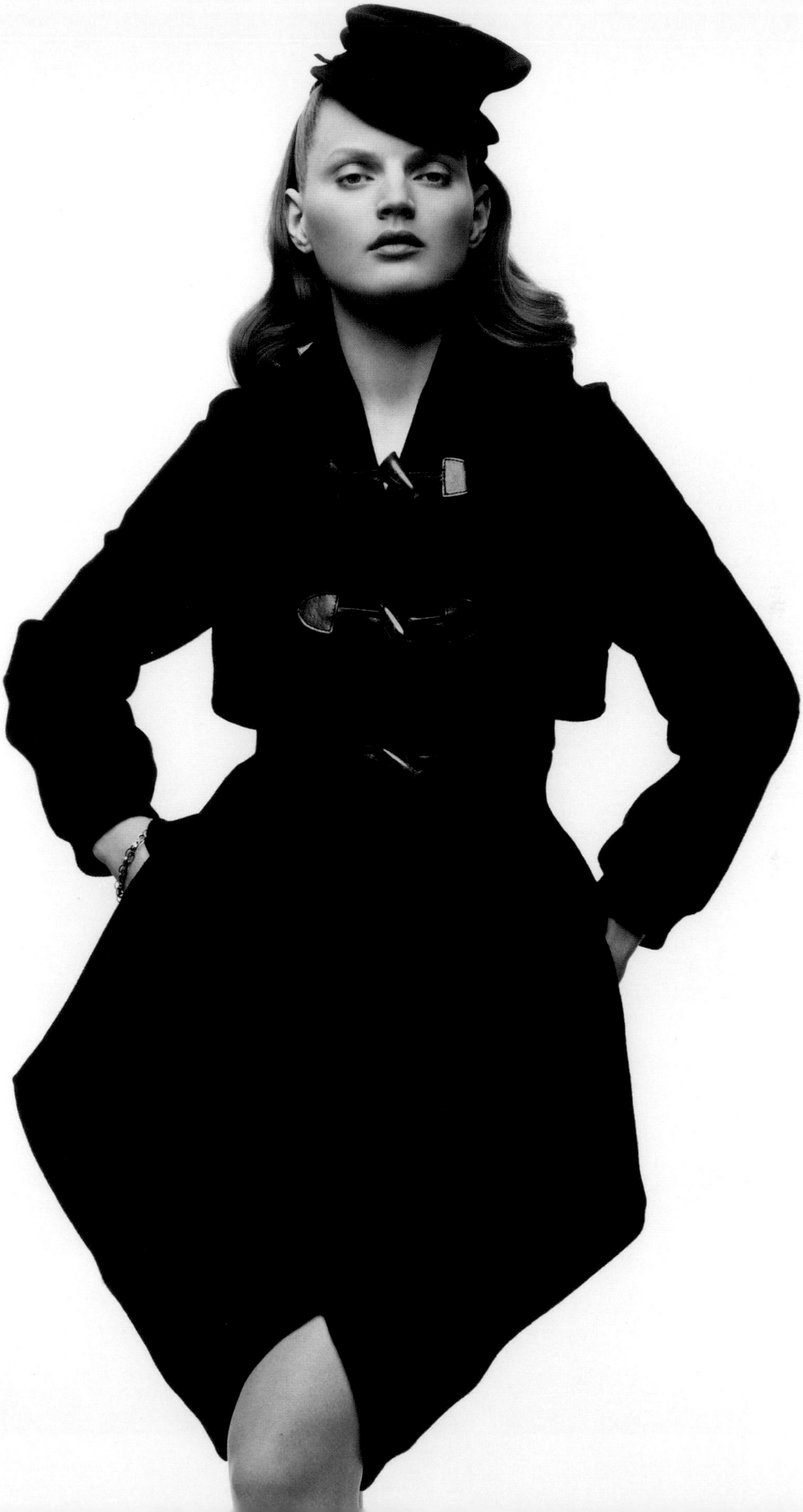

HUSSEIN CHALAYAN

What are your signature designs? It's hard to define the signature designs as each project for me has different monuments, but roughly speaking I would say they are: the buried dresses, the paper floral suits, airmail clothing, the shaved tulle dresses, all the mechanical dresses, all the low-armholed loop dresses, the historically layered collection etc. However, ultimately the sequential way in which we work creates the basis of the signature **What is your favourite piece from any of your collections?** My favourite pieces to date are the printed dresses based on the Cyprus border, spring/summer 2004 **How would you describe your work?** I feel that my work somehow lies in a gap between reality and fantasy **What's your ultimate goal?** My ultimate goal is to have a stable life, where I don't have to travel to fit a seam, and to have the opportunity to build up my vision without too much conflict. But ultimately to live in an environment where prejudice does not eat me up **What inspires you?** My inspiration comes from anthropology, genetic anthropology, migration, history, social prejudice, politics, displacement, science fiction and, I guess, my own cultural background **Can fashion still have a political ambition?** Fashion can be informed and inspired by political aspirations but to actually make it literally carry it is in my view often contrived **Who do you have in mind when you design?** Mostly Jane How (my long-term stylist and consultant), partly an architect woman and partly for a girl who is more boy-like but who can dress in a surprisingly feminine way for a special occasion **Is the idea of creative collaboration important to you?** Creative and practical collaboration is what makes things actually happen even if the project and the approach are the vision of one person. You can have the vision, but I think it's also important to recognise what other people can add to it **Who has been the greatest influence on your career?** My driving influence is not one person **How have your own experiences affected your work as a designer?** My experience has made me feel that being independent is what I value the most **Which is more important in your work: the process or the product?** The product, ultimately, is the most important thing but it can be said that the final product is for the buyer, and the process, which other people don't always need to know about, is the part that is for your personal satisfaction and, at times, growth **Is designing difficult for you? If so, what drives you to continue?** Designing is not difficult. Doing it under strict deadlines when there is no time makes it difficult. What drives me to continue is the feeling that I still have new things to learn **Have you ever been influenced or moved by the reaction to your designs?** If people are moved by what you do, who wouldn't be affected? However, to base your selfconfidence on fickle remarks and inconsistent journalists who don't know your history is disastrous **What's your definition of beauty?** My definition of beauty is a kind of 'truth' that may not always be aesthetically beautiful (Patti Smith... one minute the childlike smile on stage... one minute the hard-core spitting of gob on the floor whilst performing... what a beauty she is...) **What's your philosophy?** My philosophy (not as a part of any dogmatic belief) is based on the idea that whatever you do comes back to you **What is the most important lesson you've learned?** The realisation that you should live ultimately for yourself and less for others. And that people in the world are not really that different when it comes down to the basic facts.

"By questioning what you are doing, you evolve"
MARIA CORNEJO · ZERO

Chilean-born Maria Cornejo first arrived in the UK with her parents, having left their native country as political refugees. She later shot to prominence in the '80s, having graduated with flying colours with a fashion degree at Ravensbourne College. Her subsequent designs, produced in conjunction with John Richmond, under the label Richmond-Cornejo, were championed by the style press and garnered a strong cult following, helping to further establish her as a creative force – one able to see beyond mere seasonal modishness. From the outset of her career, Cornejo has been clear about her wish for longevity as a designer. By the late '80s, she had split from Richmond and was based in France, presenting her womenswear collections in Milan and Paris to much acclaim. She was also consulting and designing for British high street chain Jigsaw, in addition to overhauling the French ready-to-wear label Tehen, as their creative director. Now based in New York under the label Zero, with her own store situated in the city's fashionable NoLita district, she continues to refine her design aesthetic, one that is wholly wearable yet ever-so-slightly unconventional. Her geometric constructions and pared-down approach to cutting attract a certain type of intelligent, open-minded woman. High-profile advocates of Cornejo's clothing include actresses Tilda Swinton and Sigourney Weaver and the artist Cindy Sherman. In 2006, Cornejo won the prestigious fashion prize from the Smithsonian Cooper-Hewitt National Design Award. Now she has moved the atelier and new Zero store to 33 Bleecker Street, New York. Together with her husband, the photographer Mark Borthwick, she has retained a truly personal vision with her recent autumn/winter 2009 collection, returning to her Punk/Goth roots as a student in London. With global stockists currently ranging from stores such as Barneys in New York or Isetan in Japan, Cornejo clearly produces a style that can both cut though cultural difference and enhance the individuality of those who wear it.

Die in Chile geborene Maria Cornejo kam schon als Kind mit ihren Eltern nach Großbritannien, weil die Familie ihr Heimatland aus politischen Gründen verlassen musste. Anfang der 1980er-Jahre wurde sie auf einen Schlag prominent, nachdem sie ihr Modestudium am Ravensbourne College mit Bravour absolviert hatte. Ihre nächsten Entwürfe, die sie zusammen mit John Richmond unter dem Namen Richmond-Cornejo realisierte, brachten den beiden viel Lob von Modejournalisten und eine treue Fangemeinde ein. Cornejo half dieser Erfolg, sich als kreative Größe zu etablieren – und zwar als eine, die über die modischen Trends der aktuellen Saison hinaus Bestand hat. Denn in der Tat war der Designerin vom Beginn ihrer Karriere an Langlebigkeit ganz wichtig. Ende der 1980er-Jahre hatte Cornejo sich von Richmond getrennt und sich in Frankreich niedergelassen. Ihre Damenkollektionen präsentierte sie unter großem Beifall in Mailand und Paris. Außerdem war sie als Consultant und Designerin für die britische Nobel-Kaufhauskette Jigsaw tätig und hatte beim französischen Prêt-à-porter-Label Tehen die Funktion des Creative Director inne. Inzwischen arbeitet sie in New York für die Marke Zero und betreibt einen eigenen Laden im angesagten Viertel NoLita. Sie beschäftigt sich weiterhin mit der Verfeinerung ihrer Designästhetik, die absolut tragbare, aber sehr oft eine Spur unkonventionelle Stücke hervorbringt. Ihre geometrischen Konstruktionen und betont schlichten Schnitte sprechen einen bestimmten Typ intelligenter, aufgeschlossener Frauen an. Zu den angesehensten Fürsprecherinnen von Cornejos Mode zählen Schauspielerinnen wie Tilda Swinton, Sigourney Weaver und die Künstlerin Cindy Sherman. 2006 gewann Cornejo den prestigeträchtigen Smithsonian Cooper-Hewitt National Design Award. Inzwischen ist sie mit ihrem Atelier und dem neuen Zero-Laden in die New Yorker Bleecker Street Nr. 33 umgezogen. Gemeinsam mit ihrem Ehemann, dem Fotografen Mark Borthwick, hat sie sich in ihrer jüngsten Kollektion, Herbst/Winter 2009, eine wirklich persönliche Sicht der Dinge erhalten, indem sie zu ihren Punk/Goth-Wurzeln ihrer Studentenzeit in London zurückkehrte. Gegenwärtig findet man ihre Entwürfe in Nobelkaufhäusern rund um die Welt, etwa bei Barneys in New York oder bei Isetan in Japan. Ihre Mode besitzt zweifellos die Fähigkeit, kulturelle Grenzen zu überwinden und gleichzeitig die Individualität der Trägerin zu unterstreichen.

La Chilienne Maria Cornejo est arrivée en Angleterre avec ses parents, qui fuyaient la répression politique dans leur pays natal. Au début des années 80, elle se fait déjà remarquer en obtenant son diplôme de mode avec les félicitations du jury du Ravensbourne College. Elle s'associe ensuite avec John Richmond pour fonder la griffe Richmond-Cornejo. Encensées par la presse, les créations du duo remportent un énorme succès et deviennent rapidement culte, ce qui aide Maria à faire reconnaître son talent créatif: une force capable de voir au-delà des modes éphémères. Dès le début de sa carrière, Maria Cornejo déclarait déjà que son but était de durer dans le métier. A la fin des années 80, elle se sépare de John Richmond et s'installe en France, présentant avec grand succès ses collections pour femme à Milan et à Paris. Elle travaille également comme consultante et styliste pour la chaîne britannique des magasins Jigsaw, tout en assumant ses fonctions de directrice de la création du prêt-à-porter de Tehen. Aujourd'hui installée à New York sous la griffe Zero, avec sa propre boutique dans le quartier très tendance de NoLita (nord de Little Italy), elle continue à parfaire son esthétique de la mode à travers des créations très faciles à porter, mais toujours un peu surprenantes. Ses constructions géométriques et son approche épurée de la coupe attirent un certain type de femmes, intelligentes et ouvertes d'esprit. Les étendards du style Cornejo incluent donc des actrices telles que Tilda Swinton et Sigourney Weaver, ou encore la comédienne Cindy Sherman. En 2006, Maria Cornejo remporte le prestigieux Smithsonian Cooper-Hewitt National Design Award. Son atelier et sa nouvelle boutique Zero sont désormais installés au 33 Bleecker Street à New York. Dans la collection automne/hiver 2009, Maria Cornejo et son mari, le photographe Mark Borthwick, présentent une vision toujours aussi personnelle en revenant aux influences punk goth qui ont marqué la créatrice pendant ses années d'étudiante à Londres. Distribuée dans le monde entier, de Barneys (à New York) à Isetan (au Japon), Maria Cornejo produit une mode qui fait clairement fi des différences culturelles tout en soulignant l'individualité de celles qui la portent.

JAMES ANDERSON

What are your signature designs? Circle top, drape front top, curve waistcoat, bike pants **What is your favourite piece from any of your collections?** The bubble dress, which was in the collection for the first time autumn/winter 2001. It's a circular dress which is elasticated at the hem, creating a bubble shape **How would you describe your work?** Organic, sculptural and three-dimensional **What's your ultimate goal?** To be fulfilled and keep learning, to be successful and still have a life **What inspires you?** Architecture, people, all forms of organic life **Can fashion still have a political ambition?** Fashion can provoke thought and discussion, and through uniforms provoke fear and repression **Who do you have in mind when you design?** No particular person but shapes and forms **Is the idea of creative collaboration important to you?** Yes, collaborations are very important. They push you in different directions and, by questioning what you are doing, you evolve **Who has been the greatest influence on your career?** My greatest influence in spirit is my husband, Mark Borthwick. He has given me the confidence to find my identity as a designer **How have your own experiences affected your work as a designer?** I came from Chile with my parents as political refugees, so I am not sentimental about change **Which is more important in your work: the process or the product?** Both **Is designing difficult for you? If so, what drives you to continue?** Yes at times it is difficult, the challenges **Have you ever been influenced or moved by the reaction to your designs?** The different reactions always interest me as they can vary from a very intellectual point to a very amusing interpretation or a love of the way something fits **What's your definition of beauty?** Beauty in a person is a combination of the emotional and superficial **What's your philosophy?** Don't sweat the small stuff – look at the big picture **What is the most important lesson you've learned?** To trust my instincts.

"I really enjoy translating an idea into a real product – it's energising"
FRANCISCO COSTA · CALVIN KLEIN

It's hard to imagine a young Francisco Costa growing up in the small Brazilian town where he was born (even to a family already rooted in fashion) and having even an inkling of the career he has now – a career that, in some ways, is only just starting. In the early '90s, the diminutive and cherubic immigrant arrived in New York as bright-eyed in the big city as any who had come before. He set about learning English and enrolled at the Fashion Institute of Technology, where he won the Idea Como/Young Designers of America award. After graduation, he was recruited to design dresses and knits for Bill Blass. But fate soon swept Costa towards his first big break when Oscar de la Renta asked him to oversee the signature and Pink Label collections of his own high-society house, plus Pierre Balmain haute couture and ready-to-wear. In 1998, at Tom Ford's bidding, Costa decamped for the red-hot Gucci studio, where he served as senior designer of eveningwear, a position in which he was charged with creating the custom designs for both high-rolling clients and high-profile celebrities. This is where Costa cut his teeth, acquiring the skills required to direct a major label, as he would soon do, returning to New York in 2002 to work for Calvin Klein. Here he assumed the role of creative director of the women's collections, where he remains today. Costa's first marquee Calvin Klein collection was shown in the autumn of 2003, following the departure of the namesake designer (and, as the man who invented designer denim and who, in 1968, founded one of New York's mega-brands, Klein was hardly the easiest act to follow). Costa's debut drew rave reviews across the board for its seamless integration of the label's signature minimalism with a deft vision of how fashion looks now.

Man kann sich den jungen Francisco Costa kaum vorstellen, wie er in seiner kleinen brasilianischen Heimatstadt (wenn auch als Kind einer Familie, die bereits mit Mode zu tun hat) aufwächst und noch keinen Schimmer von seiner späteren Karriere hat. Wobei diese Karriere genau genommen erst der Anfang ist. Zu Beginn der 1990er-Jahre kam er als kleiner, unschuldiger Immigrant so blauäugig wie viele andere in die Großstadt New York. Er machte sich daran, Englisch zu lernen, und schrieb sich am Fashion Institute of Technology ein, wo er später den Preis Idea Como/Young Designers of America gewann. Nach dem Studium bot sich ihm die Möglichkeit, bei Bill Blass Kleider und Strickwaren zu entwerfen. Das Schicksal bescherte Costa jedoch schon den ersten Durchbruch, als Oscar de la Renta ihm die nach ihm benannte Kollektion Oscar de la Renta und Pink Label seines High-Society-Modehauses sowie die Haute Couture und die Prêt-à-porter-Linie von Pierre Balmain anvertraute. 1998 folgte Costa dem Ruf von Tom Ford und wechselte in das damals absolut angesagte Atelier von Gucci, wo er als Chefdesigner der Abendmode fungierte. In dieser Position war

er für die maßgefertigten Kreationen sowohl der betuchtesten Kunden als auch der Super-Promis verantwortlich. Costa verdiente sich seine Sporen und eignete sich die Fähigkeiten an, die man braucht, um ein großes Label zu führen, was er auch bald tun sollte, denn 2002 kehrte er nach New York zurück, um für Calvin Klein zu arbeiten. Hier übernahm er den Posten des Creative Director für alle Damenkollektionen, den er bis heute innehat. Costas erste unverkennbare Calvin-Klein-Kollektion wurde im Herbst 2003 gezeigt. Das war unmittelbar nach dem Ausscheiden des namengebenden Designers (der die Designerjeans erfunden und 1987 eines der New Yorker Mega-Labels gegründet hatte), in dessen Fußstapfen zu treten sicher keine leichte Aufgabe war. Costas Debüt erhielt durchweg Bombenkritiken für die nahtlose Integration des für die Marke so typischen Minimalismus in eine überzeugende Vision dessen, was Mode heute ausmacht.

Elevé dans sa petite ville natale du Brésil (au sein d'une famille déjà établie dans la mode), le jeune Francisco Costa ne pouvait sans doute pas imaginer sa carrière actuelle et qui, sous certains aspects, ne fait que commencer. Au début des années 90, ce minuscule immigrant au visage chérubin débarque à New York, les yeux pleins d'étoiles, à l'instar de tous ceux qui ont découvert la ville avant lui. Il apprend l'anglais et s'inscrit au Fashion Institute of Technology, où il remporte le prix Idea Como/Young Designers of America. Une fois diplômé, il dessine des robes et des pièces en maille pour Bill Blass. Mais le destin s'apprête à lui offrir sa première grande réussite : Oscar de la Renta lui demande de superviser sa collection signature et la griffe Pink Label de sa maison, si prisée par la haute société, ainsi que les lignes haute couture et prêt-à-porter de Pierre Balmain. En 1998, Tom Ford invite Costa à venir travailler dans l'atelier ultra-branché de Gucci en tant que styliste senior des tenues de soirée, où il est en charge des créations personnalisées sur mesure pour les clients les plus prestigieux et autres célébrités de premier plan. C'est là que Costa forge son style, acquérant les compétences requises pour diriger une grande marque, ce qu'il fera d'ailleurs rapidement en revenant à New York pour travailler chez Calvin Klein en 2002. Il y devient directeur de la création des collections pour femme, un poste qu'il occupe encore aujourd'hui. La première collection de Costa pour Calvin Klein est présentée à l'automne 2003, après le départ du fondateur de la maison (pas évident de reprendre le flambeau de l'homme qui a inventé le jean de créateur et fondé l'une des mégamarques new-yorkaises dès 1987). Les débuts de Costa suscitent les éloges de la critique, qui sait reconnaître son talent à fusionner le minimalisme signature de la griffe avec une vision habile de ce qu'est la mode aujourd'hui.

LEE CARTER

FRANCISCO COSTA

What is your favourite piece from any of your collections? Look #36 from the spring/summer 2005 show because it embodies two worlds. It's understated, but also eccentric. It's based on the simplicity of a T-shirt pattern, but it has volume and colour **How would you describe your work?** Eclectic, but consistent **What's your ultimate goal?** To be completely satisfied **What inspires you?** Nature, art, people, film, books, books, books **Can fashion still have a political ambition?** Yes, the more complicated and convoluted the world gets, the more influenced we are by our environment and international relations. We're much more likely to make a statement based upon where we live **Who do you have in mind when you design?** She is a confident individual with an ageless beauty. But, ultimately, I design for the consumer, and she is constantly evolving and so must each collection **Is the idea of creative collaboration important to you?** Yes, I believe very much in a free exchange of ideas and inspirations. We each absorb influences from all areas of our world and our environment and process them in different ways **Who has been the greatest influence on your career?** There is not one specific person. Again, I think as we go along working with different people, we absorb and learn from each of them and move on **How have your own experiences affected your work as a designer?** Definitely. Your own experiences are very telling. It is what you have learned and the way you choose to live **Which is more important in your work: the process or the product?** The product, although I love the process. The product is what gets represented – very few people want to know about process **Is designing difficult for you? If so, what drives you to continue?** Designing is the easiest thing for me. I really enjoy translating an idea into a real product – it's energising **Have you ever been influenced or moved by the reaction to your designs?** Yes, because a reaction – good or bad – creates momentum to further or improve an idea **What's your definition of beauty?** All elements in balance. Perfection of integration. Person: confidence. Object: proportion **What's your philosophy?** Be positive **What is the most important lesson you've learned?** Trust yourself.

"I am always happy if people give my designs the time of day"
GILES DEACON

From one-time fashion illustrator to the 2004 British Fashion Awards Best New Designer, Giles Deacon bridges the gap between cutting-edge East London and high-end couture. Following an art foundation course in Harrogate, England, he graduated in fashion design from London's Central Saint Martins in 1992 – a course selected, he has said, purely for novelty value. From here, Yorkshire-born Deacon worked with Jean-Charles de Castelbajac in Paris for two years before being appointed in 1998 to a dream job: he was selected by Tom Ford, then of the Gucci Group, as head designer for the luxury accessories brand Bottega Veneta. As it turned out, the experience was a salutary one that eventually persuaded Deacon to go it alone. In 2004, he launched his first full solo collection, which he titled 'Disco Jacobean Fairytale'. Sophisticated, feminine womenswear such as calf-length skirts, pussycat bow blouses, and '40s-style nipped-in jackets featured in his debut, which was shown during London Fashion Week, and modelled by world-famous supermodels. Deacon (born 1969) has been particularly quick to establish a glamorous signature look, one from which, he professes, there will be little deviation over the coming years. With his designs also showing an obvious leaning towards the handcrafted, Deacon is fast winning a reputation for working closely with many smaller British specialist companies – experts in their field of embroidery or beading, for instance. His prints are often inspired by Art Nouveau, which is perhaps a reflection of his ongoing interest in illustration. Deacon has also created a collection for the lingerie company Agent Provocateur. In 2006, Deacon collaborated with American Express on the Red project. In 2008, Deacon collaborated with New Look, Evoke Jewellery, designed a bar for the Elton John AIDS foundation and made a one-off denim dress in collaboration with Lee Cooper. Deacon introduced accessories in a two-season collaboration with Mulberry (Mulberry for Giles) and added an ongoing consultancy with high-street retailer New Look to design New Look Gold. Deacon continues to show in London, attracting the world's leading models to his catwalk.

Nachdem er es vom Modezeichner zum Best New Designer 2004 bei den British Fashion Awards gebracht hat, füllen Giles Deacons Entwürfe inzwischen genau die Lücke zwischen hippem East London und Haute Couture. Nach dem Grundstudium im englischen Harrogate machte er 1992 seinen Abschluss am Londoner Central Saint Martins. Laut eigener Aussage war für ihn allein der Reiz des Neuen ausschlaggebend für die Studienwahl. Später arbeitete der aus Yorkshire stammende Deacon zwei Jahre lang mit Jean-Charles de Castelbajac in Paris, bevor er 1998 das Angebot für einen Traumjob bekam: Tom Ford, damals noch bei Gucci, bestimmte ihn zum Chefdesigner der luxuriösen Accessoire-Marke Bottega Veneta. Diese Erfahrung war ein echter Segen, denn sie bewog Deacon, es schließlich allein zu versuchen. So lancierte er 2004 seine erste komplette Solokollektion unter dem Namen Disco Jacobean Fairytale. Raffiniert feminine Damenmode wie wadenlange Röcke, Blusen mit weichen Schleifen und Schlupfjacken im Stil der 1940er Jahre prägten sein Debüt, das auf der Londoner Modewoche von weltberühmten Supermodels präsentiert wurde und für phänomenale Kritiken sorgte. Der 1969 geborene Deacon schaffte es in unglaublich kurzer

Zeit, einen glamourösen eigenständigen Look zu entwickeln, von dem er nach eigener Aussage in den nächsten Jahren auch nicht stark abzuweichen gedenkt. Seine Entwürfe zeigen auch sein Faible für handwerklich Anspruchsvolles. So erwarb er sich rasch den Ruf, jemand mit engen Kontakten zu vielen kleinen britischen Spezialbetrieben zu sein – Experten in den Bereichen Stickerei oder Pailletten etwa. Seine Muster sind oft vom Jugendstil inspiriert, was mit seinem nach wie vor regen Interesse an Illustrationen zusammenhängen mag. 2006 kooperierte Deacon bei dem Projekt Red mit American Express. Im Jahr 2008 war er für New Look und Evoke Jewellery tätig, entwarf eine Bar für die Elton-John-AIDS-Stiftung und kreierte in Zusammenarbeit mit Lee Cooper ein einzigartiges Jeanskleid. Im Rahmen einer Kooperation über zwei Kollektionen (Mulberry for Giles) brachte Deacon Accessoires heraus. Darüber hinaus fungiert er als Berater der Nobel-Kette New Look, für die er New Look Gold designt. Deacon präsentiert weiterhin in London und schafft es, die weltweit gefragtesten Models für sich auf den Laufsteg zu bringen.

D'une expérience d'illustrateur de mode au prix de Best New Designer des British Fashion Awards 2004, les créations de Giles Deacon jettent un pont entre l'avant-garde d'East London et la haute couture de luxe. Après avoir suivi des cours à l'école d'art de Harrogate en Angleterre, il sort diplômé en mode de Central Saint Martins en 1992 : un cursus choisi, avoue-t-il, surtout pour l'attrait de la nouveauté. Ensuite, le jeune créateur du Yorkshire travaille pendant deux ans avec Jean-Charles de Castelbajac à Paris avant d'obtenir un job de rêve en 1998 : repéré par Tom Ford, qui travaille alors pour le Groupe Gucci, il est nommé styliste principal de la marque d'accessoires de luxe Bottega Veneta. Cette expérience s'avère salutaire pour Deacon, qui finit par trouver le courage de lancer sa propre griffe. En 2004, il présente une première collection complète baptisée « Disco Jacobean Fairytale » : les vêtements féminins et sophistiqués de ses débuts, tels que les jupes au mollet, les chemisiers à lavallière et les vestes cintrées très années 40, sont présentés lors de la London Fashion Week sur des top models mondialement célèbres et suscitent les louanges de la critique. Giles Deacon (né en 1969) a été particulièrement prompt à établir son glamour signature, dont il pense ne pas trop s'éloigner au cours de ces prochaines années. Avec des créations qui rendent un hommage évident au savoir-faire à l'ancienne, Deacon s'est aussi fait connaître pour ses étroites collaborations avec de petits artisans anglais, par exemple des experts spécialisés dans la broderie ou les perles. Ses imprimés puisent souvent leur inspiration dans l'Art Nouveau, peut-être en référence à son intérêt de longue date pour l'illustration. En 2006, Deacon collabore avec American Express sur le projet Red. En 2008, il travaille avec New Look, Evoke Jewellery, conçoit un bar pour la fondation Elton John de lutte contre le sida et crée une robe en jean unique en collaboration avec Lee Cooper. Dans le cadre d'une collaboration de deux saisons avec Mulberry, Deacon lance une ligne d'accessoires (Mulberry for Giles) et devient consultant permanent auprès du détaillant à succès New Look pour créer la ligne New Look Gold. Deacon continue de présenter ses collections à Londres avec des défilés qui attirent les plus grandes top-modèles du monde sur ses podiums. JOSH SIMS

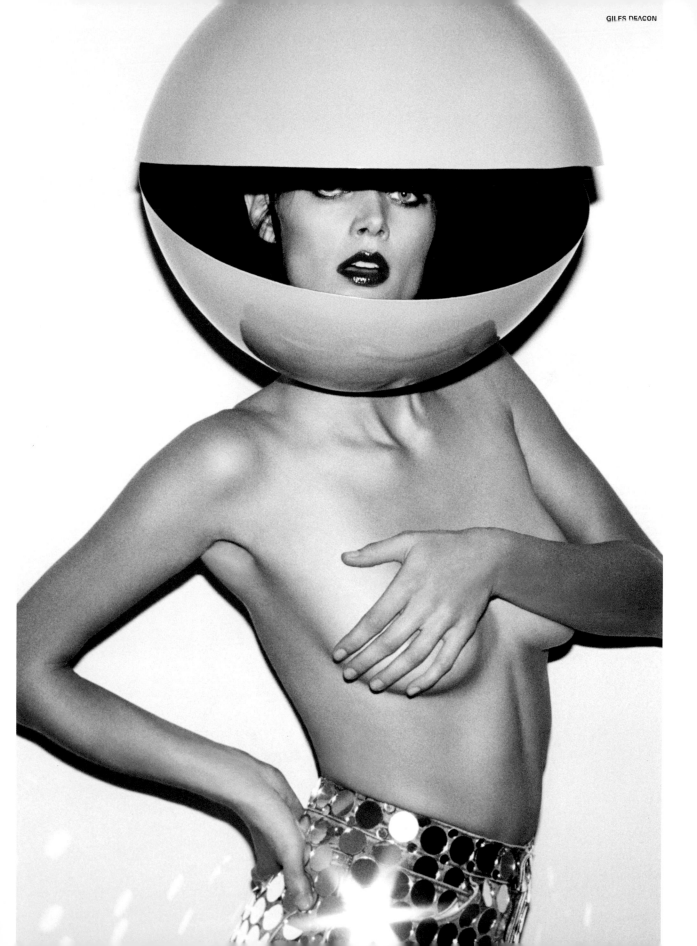

PHOTOGRAPHY WALTER PFEIFFER. STYLING ERIKA KURIHARA. JUNE 2009.

What are your signature designs? Specialist-designed fabrics, sharp suits and cult leader dresses **What is your favourite piece from any of your collections?** From the first collection, the glitter prints and rose jacquard suits, from spring/summer 2005 meteor print dresses and the 'dazzle' skirts/suits **How would you describe your work?** Hopefully an interesting, emotive thing **What's your ultimate goal?** Just to be happy working in an interesting environment keeps me going **What inspires you?** Nature, spontaneity and eccentricity **Can fashion still have a political ambition?** Only in an environmental way **Who do you have in mind when you design?** A mix of a whole host of various people's attributes **Is the idea of creative collaboration important to you?** I love it **Who has been the greatest influence on your career?** Keith Haring **How have your own experiences affected your work as a designer?** All the time and hopefully always will **Which is more important in your work: the process or the product?** Both are of equal importance, although the process is more fun **Is designing difficult for you? If so, what drives you to continue?** No, not difficult, though things do not always go to plan, which can also be interesting **Have you ever been influenced or moved by the reaction to your designs?** I am always happy if people give the designs the time of day to think about them **What's your definition of beauty?** Wit and a nice pair of legs **What's your philosophy?** The grass is always greener underneath you **What is the most important lesson you've learned?** Keep on working and have some fun.

"I want my clothes to be exclusive, but not too exclusive"
CHRISTOPHE DECARNIN • BALMAIN

Born in the coastal town of Le Touquet in northern France, Balmain's creative director Christophe Decarnin dreamed of working in fashion since he was a young boy. On graduating from the distinguished International Fashion University ESMOD in Paris, Decarnin consulted for various fashion houses, first as an illustrator and later as a designer, before working his way up to head designer of women's ready-to-wear at Paco Rabanne. Here he put his talents to work for ten years, before branching off to work as a consultant with several French contemporary brands in 2000. His hard work paid off and at the end of 2005, Decarnin was appointed Balmain's creative director, debuting his first collection for the heritage French fashion house in February 2006 to rapturous applause. He has since breathed new life into the label (founded in 1945 by Pierre Balmain and famed for its eveningwear), and today a heated buzz of excitement and anticipation greets every show. From the shortest, tightest Swarovski-spangled mini dress to sharp peak-shouldered military jackets (Decarnin's much copied signature shape for Balmain), again lathered in Swarovski crystals, stone-washed denim and studded high heels, Decarnin's clothes have become a byword for glamour, sophistication and after-dark cool. And, as a result, have earned their place as some of fashion's most highly coveted garments. The unremitting success meeting each of Balmain's womenswear collections provided Decarnin with the fuel he needed to relaunch Balmain Men in July 2008. The small but perfectly formed collection debuted in Paris to much critical acclaim. 2008 also saw Decarnin expand the brand to include fragrance, launching Balmain's first women's perfume, Ambre Gris, in partnership with Selective Beauty. Today Decarnin's designs for Balmain continue to be must-have items in the wardrobes of any discerning fashion lover.

Der in der nordfranzösischen Küstenstadt Le Touquet geborene Creative Director von Balmain, Christophe Decarnin, träumte schon als kleiner Junge davon, später einmal in der Modebranche zu arbeiten. Nach seinem Abschluss an der angesehenen internationalen Modeuniversität ESMOD in Paris arbeitete Decarnin für diverse Modehäuser, zunächst als Zeichner, später als Designer, bevor er sich zum Chefdesigner der Prêt-à-porter-Kollektion für Damen bei Paco Rabanne hochdiente. Dort ließ er seine Talente in den folgenden zehn Jahren wirken, bevor er ab 2000 als Berater für mehrere moderne französische Modemarken fungierte. Die harte Arbeit machte sich bezahlt, und Ende 2005 wurde Decarnin zum Creative Director bei Balmain ernannt. Seine Debüt-Kollektion für das altehrwürdige französische Modehaus im Februar 2006 wurde mit stürmischem Applaus aufgenommen. Seither hat er dem 1945 von Pierre Balmain gegründeten Label, das berühmt für seine Abendmode ist, neues Leben eingehaucht, so dass heute vor jeder Schau größte Spannung und Vorfreude herrschen. Vom kürzesten, engsten, mit Swarovski-Steinen übersäten Minikleid bis hin zu Armeejacken mit scharf geschnittenen Schultern (Decarnins oft kopiertes Markenzeichen bei Balmain) und ebenfalls unzähligen Swarovski-Kristallen, stone-washed Jeans und High-Heels mit Glitzerbesatz – Decarnins Kleidung ist zum Synonym für Glamour, Raffinesse und After-Dark-Coolness geworden. In der Folge haben einige seiner Kreationen sich einen Platz unter den begehrtesten Stücken der Modegeschichte verdient. Der ungebrochene Erfolg jeder einzelnen von Balmains Damenkollektionen verlieh Decarnin den Antrieb, den er für den Relaunch von Balmain Men im Juli 2008 brauchte. Die kleine, aber perfekt gestaltete Kollektion stieß bei ihrem Pariser Debüt auf große Zustimmung der Kritik. 2008 kümmerte sich Decarnin außerdem um die Expansion der Marke im Bereich Duft. Mit Ambre Gris kam im Zuge einer Partnerschaft mit Selective Beauty Balmains erstes Damenparfüm auf den Markt. Bis heute gehören Decarnins Entwürfe für Balmain zu den Must-Haves in den Kleiderschränken jeder anspruchsvollen Fashionista.

Né au Touquet dans le nord de la France, Christophe Decarnin, l'actuel directeur de la création Balmain, rêvait de travailler dans la mode depuis sa plus tendre enfance. Diplômé de la prestigieuse école ESMOD à Paris, il se lance d'abord en tant que consultant auprès de plusieurs maisons, d'abord comme illustrateur puis comme créateur. Il devient ensuite styliste principal du prêt-à-porter pour femme chez Paco Rabanne, où il affûte son talent pendant dix ans. En 2000, il revient au consulting pour différentes marques françaises contemporaines. Fin 2005, il voit ses efforts récompensés quand il est nommé directeur de création chez Balmain: en février 2006, sa première collection pour la vénérable maison française soulève un tonnerre d'applaudissements. Depuis, il ne cesse de renouveler la marque (fondée en 1945 par Pierre Balmain et connue pour ses tenues de soirée), chacun de ses défilés étant désormais attendu avec beaucoup d'effervescence. Ultra-minirobe franchement moulante, brodée de cristaux Swarovski, veste militaire aux épaules pointues, également parée de galons en strass Swarovski (un modèle Balmain caractéristique de Decarnin et largement copié), denim délavé et talons aiguille cloutés, les créations de Decarnin sont devenues synonymes de glamour, de sophistication et de soirées branchées, s'octroyant une place de choix parmi les vêtements les plus convoités de la mode. Grâce à l'implacable succès de chaque collection Balmain pour femme, Christophe Decarnin trouve en juillet 2008 l'énergie nécessaire pour relancer Balmain Homme. Lors de sa présentation à Paris, une critique unanime encense cette collection courte mais savamment composée. La même année, Decarnin lance aussi Ambre Gris, le premier parfum Balmain pour femme, en partenariat avec Selective Beauty. Aujourd'hui, les créations Decarnin pour Balmain sont de véritables must-have pour les amateurs de mode les plus exigeants.

HOLLY SHACKLETON

"Fashion has a reason 'to be' because in fashion you can find new kinds of expressions about human beings"
ANN DEMEULEMEESTER

Ann Demeulemeester once told an interviewer that women are not like Barbie dolls, and that she finds a subtle femininity in men most pleasing. Inevitably, then, her own designs for both sexes are far removed from the types of clothing in which bimbos and himbos might typically attire themselves. Hers is a far more personal, subtle and emotional aesthetic, one frequently, and lazily, labelled as androgynous, but which could more accurately be termed as romantically modernist. Born in Belgium, in 1959, Demeulemeester went on to study at Antwerp's Royal Academy, from which she graduated in 1981, as part of the now-legendary 'Antwerp Six' group of designers. In 1985, she launched her own label, along with her husband Patrick Robyn – a man she has cited as her biggest influence – and made her womenswear debut in Paris in 1992. By 1996, she would also be designing menswear collections. Given her long-entrenched fondness for the colour black (she has mainly clad herself in black since her Patti Smith-loving teens) along with the severity of her earlier work, with its wilfully unfinished look, she became known as a key figure of the deconstruction era of fashion during the late '80s and early '90s. Avoiding the fickle whims and fads of the fashion industry, Demeulemeester has subsequently carved out her own unique niche, not to mention a loyal fan-base, which continues to grow. Not surprisingly, the designer now also creates extremely successful shoe and accessory lines, and her collections are sold in more than 30 countries around the world. She continues to champion clothing that favours high-quality, natural materials – leather, wool and flannels – over less covetable synthetic fabrics, and her poetic mix of edgy rebellion with sensuality, plus slick tailoring with softer layers, creates an ever-intriguing design proposition. In 2007, Demeulemeester launched her first jewellery collection, opened an Ann Demeulemeester shop in Seoul and, in 2008, reissued key pieces from the Ann Demeulemeester archives.

Ann Demeulemeester erklärte einmal in einem Interview, dass Frauen keine Barbiepuppen seien und sie eine Spur Weiblichkeit an Männern schätze. Folglich sind auch ihre Entwürfe für beide Geschlechter weit von der Art Kleidung entfernt, die Lieschen Müller und ihr männliches Pendant üblicherweise tragen. Sie besitzen eine sehr viel individuellere, raffiniertere und emotionalere Ästhetik, die oft aus Bequemlichkeit mit dem Etikett „androgyn" versehen wird. Dabei wäre romantisch-modernistisch viel treffender. Die 1959 in Belgien geborene Demeulemeester studierte an der Königlichen Akademie in Antwerpen, wo sie 1981 als Mitglied des heute legendären Designerteams Antwerp Six ihren Abschluss machte. Ihr eigenes Label präsentierte sie 1985 gemeinsam mit ihrem Ehemann Patrick Robyn den sie ihren wichtigsten Einfluss von außen nennt. Ihr Damenmoden-Debüt in Paris gab sie 1992. Ab 1996 entwarf sie auch Herrenkollektionen. Ihre lang gehegte Liebe zur Farbe Schwarz (seit ihrer Begeisterung für Patti Smith im Teenageralter kleidet sie sich hauptsächlich schwarz) sowie die Strenge der frühen Arbeiten mit ihrem absichtlich unfertigen Aussehen machten sie zu einer Schlüsselfigur der dekonstruktivistischen späten 1980er und frühen 1990er

Jahre. Demeulemeester mied die kurzlebigen Launen und Marotten der Modeindustrie und schuf sich stattdessen bald eine einzigartige Nische im Markt. Von ihrer treuen, ständig wachsenden Fangemeinde ganz zu schweigen. Deshalb überrascht es auch nicht, dass die Designerin inzwischen außerdem äußerst erfolgreich Schuhe und Accessoires entwirft und ihre Kollektionen in mehr als dreißig Ländern weltweit verkauft. Dabei gibt sie weiterhin einer Mode hoher Qualität den Vorzug, meist aus natürlichen Materialien Leder, Wolle und Flanell, kaum einmal aus synthetischen Stoffen. Mit ihrem poetischen Mix aus dezidierter Rebellion und Sinnlichkeit sowie eleganter Schneiderkunst und weichem Lagenlook gelingt ihr ein immer wieder ansprechendes designerisches Statement. 2007 brachte Demeulemeester ihre erste Schmuckkollektion heraus und eröffnete einen Laden in Seoul. Im Jahr 2008 wurden Basis-Teile aus den Ann-Demeulemeester-Archiven neu aufgelegt.

Un jour, Ann Demeulemeester a déclaré dans une interview que les femmes n'étaient pas des poupées Barbie et qu'elle adorait les hommes un peu féminins. Ses créations pour les deux sexes n'ont donc strictement rien à voir avec l'attirail dont se parent généralement les bimbos, hommes ou femmes. Son esthétique, qui se veut avant tout personnelle, subtile et émotionnelle, est souvent étiquetée d'androgyne par les journalistes paresseux, alors qu'elle relève davantage d'un certain romantisme moderne. Née en 1959 en Belgique, Ann Demeulemeester étudie la mode à l'Académie Royale d'Anvers dont elle sort diplômée en 1981, membre d'une promotion de créateurs désormais légendaires : les Antwerp Six. Elle lance sa propre griffe en 1985 avec son mari Patrick Robyn, qu'elle considère comme sa principale influence, et présente son premier défilé pour femme en 1992 à Paris. En 1996, elle commence à dessiner des collections pour homme. Etant donné sa prédilection pour le noir (depuis sa passion adolescente pour Patti Smith, elle ne porte quasiment que du noir) et l'austérité de ses premières créations aux finitions délibérément brutes, elle émerge comme un personnage clé de l'ère déconstructionniste de la fin des années 80 et du début des années 90. Fuyant le grand cirque des médias et de l'industrie de la mode, Ann Demeulemeester s'est imposée sur un marché de niche et revendique un nombre de fans sans cesse croissant. Rien d'étonnant à ce que les lignes de chaussures et d'accessoires qu'elle s'est mise à dessiner remportent un tel succès, ni à ce que ses collections soient vendues dans plus de 30 pays à travers le monde. Elle continue à défendre une mode privilégiant les matières naturelles de qualité supérieure (cuir, laine et flanelles) aux tissus synthétiques moins précieux. Son mélange poétique de rébellion décalée et de sensualité, conjugué à des coupes parfaites et des superpositions de tissus plus douces, produit une mode créative et toujours intrigante. En 2007, la créatrice lance sa première collection de bijoux et ouvre une boutique éponyme à Séoul. En 2008, elle réédite des pièces majeures issues des archives Ann Demeulemeester.

JAMES ANDERSON

PHOTOGRAPHY TESH. FASHION DIRECTOR EDWARD ENNINFUL. MODEL NATASHA VOJNOVIC. NOVEMBER 2001.

What are your signature designs? My aim is that all my designs wear my signature **What is your favourite piece from any of your collections?** Too many to sum up... **How would you describe your work?** As a never-ending search **What's your ultimate goal?** To live every moment to the fullest **What inspires you?** Inspiration is very difficult to define, I think it is somehow given to you **Can fashion still have a** **political ambition?** Fashion has a reason "to be" because in fashion you can find new kinds of expressions about human beings **Who do you have in mind when you design?** Somebody I would love to meet **Is the idea of creative collaboration important to you?** Yes, I think it's part of my job **Who has been the greatest influence on your career?** My partner in life and work **How have your own experiences affected** **your work as a designer?** Everything that I have experienced in the 44 years that lie behind me has made me into the person I am now and that's my working tool **Which is more important in your work: the process or the product?** Both **Is designing difficult for you? If so, what drives you to continue?** Yes, it is. What drives me is my never-ending will to give it my best **Have you ever been influenced or moved by the** **reaction to your designs?** It's the communication, it is what keeps me going **What's your definition of beauty?** Beauty is constantly redefined. It is the joy that you feel when you discover it **What's your philosophy?** Get the maximum out of life **What is the most important lesson you've learned?** Stay true to yourself.

"We are both creative, both in a different way. We complete each other"
DOMENICO DOLCE & STEFANO GABBANA · DOLCE & GABBANA

Dolce & Gabbana are fashion's answer to Viagra: the full throbbing force of Italian style. The winning combination of Dolce's tailoring perfectionism and Gabbana's stylistic theatrics has made the label a powerhouse in today's celebrity-obsessed age and just as influential as the ambassadors of sport, music and film that they dress. Domenico Dolce was born in 1958 to a Sicilian family, his father a tailor from Palermo who taught him to make a jacket by the age of seven. Stefano Gabbana was born in 1962, the son of a Milanese print worker. But it was Sicily, Dolce's birthplace and Gabbana's favourite childhood holiday destination, that sealed a bond between them when they first met, and which has provided a reference for their aesthetic signatures ever since: the traditional Sicilian girl (opaque black stockings, black lace, peasant skirts, shawl fringing), the Latin sex temptress (corsetry, high heels, underwear as outerwear) and the Sicilian gangster (pinstripe suits, slick tailoring, fedoras). And it is the friction between these polar opposites – masculine/feminine, soft/hard and innocence/corruption – that makes Dolce & Gabbana so exciting. Established in 1985, the label continues to pay homage to such Italian film legends as Fellini, Visconti, Rossellini, Anna Magnani and Sophia Loren; in glossy art books, Dolce & Gabbana documents its own contribution to today's legends of film ('Hollywood'), music ('Music') and football ('Calcio'). They celebrated their 20th anniversary in 2005 and have now been designing for almost a quarter of a century. With an empire that includes the younger D&G line, childrenswear, swimwear, underwear, eyewear, fragrances, watches, accessories, the recently launched make-up line 'Dolce & Gabbana The Make-up' and a global distribution through their own boutiques, Dolce & Gabbana are, quite simply, fashion's Italian stallions.

Dolce & Gabbana sind quasi die Antwort der Mode auf Viagra: die ganze pulsierende Kraft italienischer Eleganz. Die gewinnbringende Kombination aus Dolces Schneiderkunst in Perfektion und Gabbanas stilvoller Theatralik verliehen dem Label in unserer promibesessenen Zeit denselben Einfluss wie den Vertretern aus Sport, Musik und Film, die sich in D&G kleiden. Domenico Dolce wurde 1958 auf Sizilien geboren. Schon im Alter von sieben Jahren lehrte ihn sein Vater, ein Schneider aus Palermo, ein Jackett zu nähen. Der 1962 geborene Stefano Gabbana ist der Sohn eines Mailänder Setzers. Es war jedoch Sizilien, wo Dolce geboren wurde und Gabbana als Kind die schönsten Ferien verbrachte, das die beiden von Anfang an verband. Die ästhetischen Markenzeichen der beiden haben seit jeher hier ihre Ursprünge: bei den traditionell streng erzogenen sizilianischen Mädchen (mit blickdichten schwarzen Strümpfen, schwarzer Spitze, Bauernröcken und Fransentüchern), beim Latino-Vamp (in Corsage, High Heels und gut sichtbar getragenen Dessous) und dem sizilianischen Gangster (in schick geschnittenem Nadelstreifenanzug und weichem Filzhut). Es sind die

Brüche zwischen diesen extremen Gegensätzen – maskulin/feminin, weich/hart, unschuldig/korrupt –, die Dolce & Gabbana so aufregend machen. Das 1985 gegründete Label zollt zum einen italienischen Filmlegenden wie Fellini, Visconti, Rossellini, Anna Magnani und Sophia Loren Tribut und dokumentiert zum anderen in Hochglanz-Kunstbänden seinen eigenen Beitrag zu Legenden des Films („Hollywood"), der Musik („Music") und des Fußballs („Calcio"). 2005 feierten die beiden ihr 20-jähriges Jubiläum und kreieren nun schon seit einem knappen Vierteljahrhundert Mode. Mit ihrem Firmenimperium, das inzwischen die jugendlichere D&G-Linie, Kinder- und Bademode, Dessous, Brillen, Düfte, Uhren, Accessoires sowie die kürzlich auf den Markt gebrachte Make-up-Linie „Dolce & Gabbana The Make-up" umfasst, und dem weltweiten Vertrieb durch eigene Boutiquen sind Dolce & Gabbana schlichtweg die typischen italienischen Machos der Modebranche.

Cœur palpitant du style italien, Dolce & Gabbana sont la réponse de la mode au Viagra. La combinaison gagnante formée par le perfectionnisme de Dolce et le cabotinage de Gabbana a imposé la griffe comme un incontournable de notre époque obsédée par la célébrité, comme une marque aussi influente que les ambassadeurs du sport, de la musique et du cinéma qu'elle habille. Domenico Dolce est né en 1958 dans une famille sicilienne ; son père, tailleur à Palerme, lui apprend à faire une veste alors qu'il n'a que sept ans. Stefano Gabbana est né en 1962, fils d'un ouvrier d'imprimerie milanais. Patrie de Dolce et destination de vacances favorite de Gabbana lorsqu'il était enfant, c'est la Sicile qui scelle leur relation dès la première rencontre, une référence qui transparaît continuellement dans leur esthétique : la fille sicilienne traditionnelle (bas noirs opaques, dentelle noire, jupes de paysanne, franges « châle »), la séductrice latine (corseterie, talons hauts, sous-vêtements portés en vêtements du dessus) et le gangster sicilien (costumes mille-raies, coupes élégantes, chapeaux mous). Ce sont ces oppositions de masculin et de féminin, de douceur et de dureté, d'innocence et de corruption qui rendent les créations de Dolce & Gabbana si fascinantes. Créée en 1985, la griffe continue de rendre hommage aux légendes du cinéma italien telles que Fellini, Visconti, Rossellini, Anna Magnani et Sophia Loren ; dans de superbes livres d'art, elle documente aussi sa propre contribution aux mondes du cinéma (« Hollywood »), de la musique (« Music ») et du football (« Calcio »). Aujourd'hui actifs depuis près d'un quart de siècle, les créateurs ont célébré les 20 ans de leur marque en 2005. Avec un empire incluant la ligne plus jeune D&G, une collection pour enfant, des maillots de bain, de la lingerie, des lunettes, des parfums (huit en tout), des montres, des accessoires, la toute nouvelle ligne de maquillage « Dolce & Gabbana The Make-up », mais aussi un réseau de distribution mondial composé de nombreuses boutiques indépendantes, Dolce & Gabbana restent, tout simplement, de vrais machos italiens.

JAMIE HUCKBODY

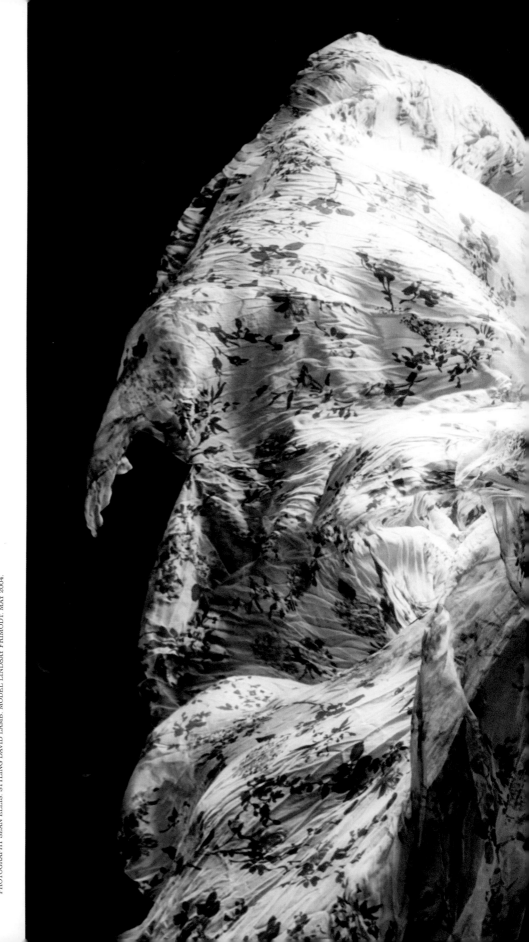

PHOTOGRAPHY SEAN ELLIS. STYLING DAVID LAMB. MODEL LINDSAY FRIMODT. MAY 2004.

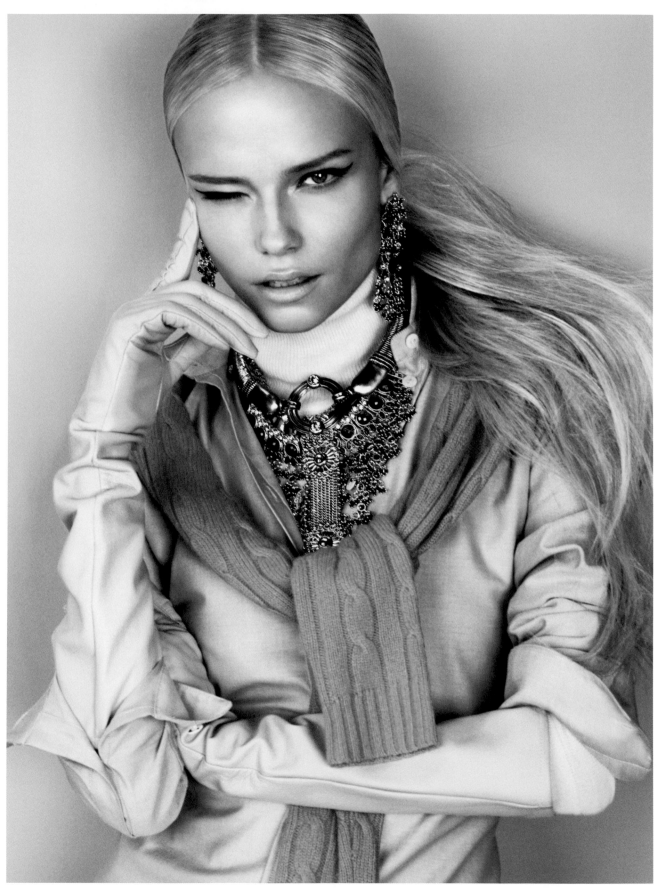

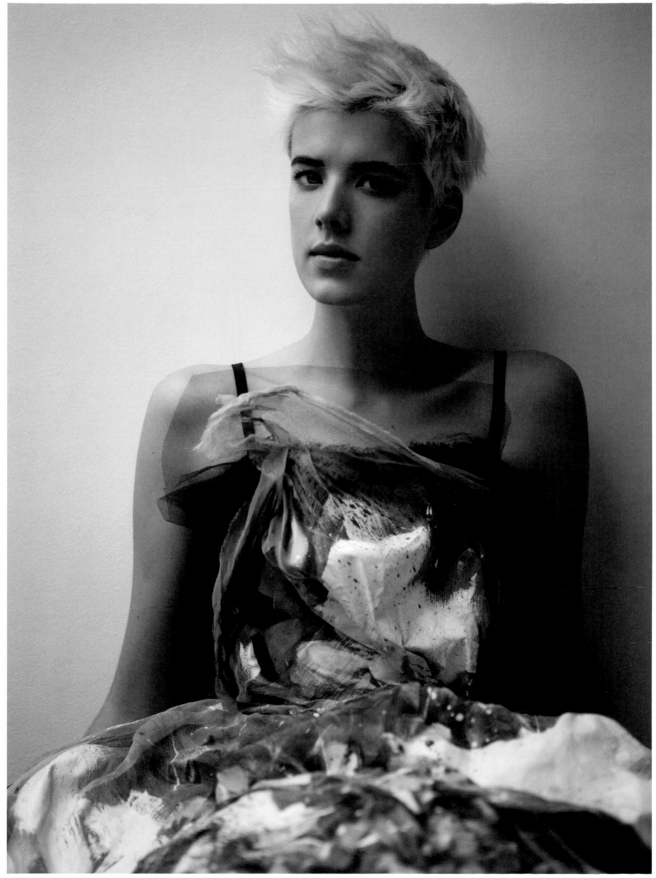

What are your signature designs? Guépière dresses, pinstripe suits, Sicilian caps, tank tops **What are your favourite pieces from any of your collections?** The above-mentioned because they are classic, signature pieces that we love and that we like to show again and again, reinterpreting them according to the spirit of each collection **How would you describe your work?** Our job is the most beautiful one in the world! It is very exciting, never boring and allows us to express our creativity and to experiment **What's your ultimate goal?** As far as our private life is concerned, our goal is happiness, always and everywhere! As far as our work, to create a style that will remain throughout the years and that will be remembered **What inspires you?** We are inspired by everyday life, by the world and by the people that surround us. Besides that, there are key elements that are our constant and continuous sources of inspiration (and that represent our identity and our roots); that is to say, the Mediterranean, Sicily, black and white, and the films of Italian neo-realism. But we are also inspired by opposites that attract each other, by contrasts, by music and cinema **Can fashion still have a political ambition?** Fashion is one of the expressions of the time we live in and of all changes that happen. It can have a specific position and make statements, but for us it is essentially a way of expressing creativity **What do you have in mind when you design?** When we sketch an outfit, we are at the end of an elaborate process because the sketch is the result of many conversations between the two of us, of many deep thoughts, of many notes that we have taken, of many different experiences that we have put together. When we design, we think about all these different things and about all that has led us to achieve that specific outfit **Is the idea of creative collaboration important to you?** For us it is the essence of our work. We are both creative, both in a different way because we complete each other. To have different opinions is important because it is a challenge **Who has been the greatest influence on your career?** For sure Madonna, who has been our muse and icon because of her strong personality **How have your own experiences affected your work as designers?** Our work is part of ourselves – our life. We reflect in the clothes we design all of our personal feelings **Which is more important in your work: the process or the product?** They are both important. However, the final product gives more satisfaction because when you see it, you forget all the efforts you've made to achieve it! **Is designing difficult for you?** We love our work – it is our passion, our life. To design clothes is a joy for us, it is a continuous challenge but, at the same time, it allows us to express ourselves. We are lucky to be in a privileged position; that is to say, our creations have a worldwide exposure and our message is accessible to a lot of people. This is a great support and it pushes us to go on, always and in the best possible way **Have you ever been influenced or moved by the reaction to your designs?** Of course we have, be these reactions positive or negative. If you listen to people's reactions, you are challenged and led to think **What's your definition of beauty?** Beauty is something you have inside. Beauty is life. Beauty is love **What's your philosophy?** To always be ourselves and consistent **What is the most important lesson you've learned?** That you always have to be yourself, without betraying your personality and without losing your identity.

"I guess it's the search for perfection from season to season that moves me forward"
ALBER ELBAZ • LANVIN

Alber Elbaz is a modern romantic who found his perfect match in Lanvin, the Parisian house where he has been artistic director since 2001. His signature designs for the label – pleated silk dresses, satin ribbon details and costume jewellery – are now among the most sought-after in fashion, making his switchback route to success all the more surprising. Elbaz was born in Casablanca, Morocco, and raised in the suburbs of Tel Aviv by his mother, a Spanish artist. He studied at the Shenkar College of Textile Technology and Fashion, Tel Aviv, but received some of his most valuable training in New York, where for seven years he was right-hand man to the late Geoffrey Beene, couturier to East Coast high society. In 1996, Elbaz was appointed head of ready-to-wear for Guy Laroche in Paris, where he remained for almost three years. During November 1998, he was appointed artistic director for Yves Saint Laurent Rive Gauche, effectively taking over design duties from Saint Laurent himself. During his tenure at YSL, Elbaz attracted a younger clientele – Chloë Sevigny wore one of his dresses to the Oscars. However, at the start of 2000, the Gucci Group took control of YSL Rive Gauche and Tom Ford stepped into Elbaz's position. Following a short but successful spell at Milanese brand Krizia and time out travelling the world, in October 2001, Elbaz returned to French fashion via Lanvin, the couture house founded by Jeanne Lanvin in the 1880s. Under his creative direction, Lanvin has reestablished itself, and now includes a jewellery, shoe and handbag collection. Elbaz's own accolades reflect the brand's success and include an array of internationally recognised awards, including the CFDA International Fashion Award (2005 and 2006), the prestigious Couture Council Award for Artistry of Fashion (2007) and an award at The Fashion Group International's 24th Annual. For Lanvin, he continues to recommend an urban elegance of emotion and optimism.

Alber Elbaz ist ein moderner Romantiker, der bei Lanvin seine ideale Heimat gefunden hat. Seit 2001 ist er künstlerischer Direktor des Pariser Modehauses. Seine Markenzeichen bei diesem Label – plissierte Seidenkleider, Verzierungen aus Satinband und Modeschmuck – gehören inzwischen zum Gefragtesten in der Modewelt und lassen seinen Zickzackkurs zum Erfolg umso erstaunlicher erscheinen. Geboren wurde Elbaz im marokkanischen Casablanca. Seine Mutter, eine spanische Künstlerin, zog ihn in der Vorstadt von Tel Aviv groß. Am Shenkar College of Textile Technology and Fashion in Tel Aviv absolvierte Elbaz sein Studium, seine wertvollsten Erfahrungen erwarb er jedoch in den sieben Jahren in New York. Dort war er die rechte Hand des heute verstorbenen Geoffrey Beene, des legendären Couturiers der Ostküsten-High-Society. 1996 wurde Elbaz für knapp drei Jahre Chef des Prêt-à-porter-Bereichs bei Guy Laroche in Paris. Im November 1998 übernahm er praktisch von Monsieur Saint Laurent höchstpersönlich die Designerpflichten, als er zum Artistic Director von Yves Saint Laurent Rive Gauche berufen wurde. In seiner Zeit bei YSL zog er eine deutlich jüngere Klientel an – so trug etwa Chloë Sevigny bei einer Oscar-Verleihung eines seiner Kleider. Anfang 2000 machte ihm jedoch das Big Business zu

schaffen, als der Gucci-Konzern die Kontrolle über YSL Rive Gauche erwarb und Tom Ford seine Position einnahm. Es folgten ein kurzes, aber erfolgreiches Intermezzo beim Mailänder Label Krizia und eine Auszeit, in der er durch die Welt reiste. Im Oktober 2001 kehrte Elbaz über das in den 1880er Jahren gegründete Modehaus Lanvin in die französische Couture zurück. Unter seiner Ägide hat sich Lanvin auf der internationalen Modebühne erneut als Marke etabliert, und inzwischen gehören auch eine Schmuck-, eine Schuh- sowie eine Handtaschenkollektion dazu. Elbaz' eigene Auszeichnungen spiegeln den Erfolg der Marke und umfassen international hochgeschätzte Preise wie den CFDA International Fashion Award (2005 und 2006), den angesehenen Couture Council Award for Artistry of Fashion (2007) und einen Preis bei The Fashion Group International's 24th Annual. Für Lanvin propagiert der Designer weiterhin urbane Eleganz, die auf Emotion und Optimismus baut.

Le romantique moderne Alber Elbaz a fini par trouver le job idéal chez Lanvin, maison parisienne dont il occupe la direction artistique depuis 2001. Ses créations signature pour la griffe (robes plissées en soie, détails en rubans de satin et bijoux fantaisie) comptent aujourd'hui parmi les pièces de mode les plus recherchées, ce qui rend son retour au succès d'autant plus surprenant. Né à Casablanca au Maroc, Alber Elbaz grandit auprès de sa mère, une artiste espagnole, dans la banlieue de Tel Aviv. Il étudie au Shenkar College of Textile Technology and Fashion de Tel Aviv, mais c'est New York qui lui offre sa formation la plus précieuse : pendant sept ans, Elbaz sera le bras droit de feu Geoffrey Beene, le couturier de l'élite de la côte est. En 1996, il est nommé directeur de la création du prêt-à-porter chez Guy Laroche à Paris, où il passe près de trois ans. En novembre 1998, il devient directeur artistique d'Yves Saint Laurent Rive Gauche, succédant avec efficacité à monsieur Saint Laurent en personne. Pendant cette période, Elbaz réussit à attirer une clientèle plus jeune : Chloë Sevigny portera l'une de ses robes pour la nuit des Oscars. Mais au début de l'an 2000, le groupe Gucci prend le contrôle d'YSL Rive Gauche et remplace Elbaz par Tom Ford. Après avoir travaillé avec succès pour la maison milanaise Krizia pendant quelques mois et pris un congé sabbatique pour voyager à travers le monde, Elbaz fait son retour dans la mode parisienne en octobre 2001 via Lanvin, maison de haute couture fondée par Jeanne Lanvin dans les années 1880. Sous sa direction, celle-ci retrouve la place qui lui revient sur la scène mondiale de la mode. Lanvin propose désormais une collection de bijoux, de chaussures et de sacs à main. A travers tout un éventail de prix mondialement reconnus, dont l'International Fashion Award du CFDA (2005 et 2006), le prestigieux Couture Council Award for Artistry of Fashion (2007) et une récompense à la 24ème édition annuelle des Fashion Group International Awards, les honneurs rendus à Alber Elbaz reflètent le succès de Lanvin. Aujourd'hui, il continue à prescrire une élégance urbaine empreinte d'émotion et d'optimisme.

SUSIE RUSHTON

What are your signature designs? A mix of two worlds, the old and the new. Old technique with new proportions **What is your favourite piece from any of your collections?** It's like asking a mother who is her favourite kid! I can't! I love them all **How would you describe your work?** Passioning, passioning, passioning! **What's your ultimate goal?** To make women beautiful **What inspires you?** Everything, everybody, anywhere and all the time **Can fashion still have a political ambition?** Politics was never my thing, therefore I moved to Paris rather than Washington **Who do you have in mind when you design?** Women I know, women I want to know, women I love **Is the idea of creative collaboration important to you?** Very much. The best of fashion was in the '20s and in the '60s, when everybody collaborated: artists, fashion designers, musicians… all working together, inspired each other and gave to each other. I believe that working with others can only give **Who has been the greatest influence on your career?** Geoffrey Beene **How have your own experiences affected your work as a designer?** My work is a voyage of my life. A voyage between Morocco, Tel Aviv, New York and Paris. Each city, each country, gave me different colours, different senses, different feelings **Which is more important in your work: the process or the product?** Both. The process leads to the product **Is designing difficult for you? If so, what drives you to continue?** In theory, designing should not be difficult. In reality, unfortunately, it is. So, it's not easy being me. My drive is to perfect the last collection, which I never find perfect. I guess it's the search for perfection from season to season that moves me forward. The moment I find perfection I guess I'll retire **Have you ever been influenced or moved by the reaction to your designs?** All the time **What's your definition of beauty?** Individuality **What's your philosophy?** Being me.

"When I design, sometimes I have sensations which I could call 'visionary'"
SILVIA VENTURINI FENDI • FENDI

Fendi is a house of extremes: big furs and little handbags, a family business with a worldwide reputation, a chic past and a street-cool future. Established in 1925, the Fendi empire was founded by Adele Fendi from a small leather-goods shop and workroom in Rome, where she and her husband, Eduardo, worked with private clients. The family business expanded with the opening of a larger shop in 1946, but it wasn't until the death of Eduardo, eight years later, that the modern Fendi image emerged, when the family's five daughters injected the little company with some youthful glamour. After the death of Adele in 1978, each sister adopted a corner of the empire to look after. Paola (born 1931) worked with the furs, Anna (born 1933) the leather goods, Franca (born 1935) the customer relations, Carla (born 1937) the business co-ordination, and Alda (born 1940) the sales. By the end of the '80s, the name of Fendi had become shorthand for jet-set elitist luxury, thanks to its signature furs and instantly recognisable double 'F' logo (designed by Karl Lagerfeld). The politically correct '90s saw the company refocus on Adele Fendi's traditional leather goods, and so the Baguette bag was reborn and Fendi's star was in the ascendant yet again. Amid the late-'90s' appetite for baroque excess, LVMH and Prada bought a 51 per cent stake in the label, with LVMH eventually becoming the sole partner in 2001. But Fendi is still very much a family business. The future lies with Silvia Venturini Fendi (born 1960, the daughter of Anna Fendi), who created the Fendissime line in 1987 and is now designer of accessories and menswear. Karl Lagerfeld, as chief designer, continues to work with the sisters – as he has done since 1965.

Fendi ist ein Modehaus der Extreme: mit opulenten Pelzen und winzigen Handtaschen, ein Familienbetrieb vom Weltruf, einer eleganten Vergangenheit und zeitgemäß cooler Zukunft. Das Fendi-Imperium wurde 1925 von Adele Fendi gegründet, in einem kleinen römischen Laden für Lederwaren mit angeschlossener Werkstatt. Dort arbeiteten sie und ihr Mann für einen kleinen Kreis von Privatkunden. 1946 expandierte das Familienunternehmen mit der Eröffnung eines größeren Geschäfts. Das moderne Image von Fendi begann sich jedoch erst acht Jahre später nach dem Tod von Eduardo Fendi herauszukristallisieren, als die fünf Töchter jugendlichen Charme in die Firma brachten. Nachdem 1978 auch Adele gestorben war, übernahm jede der Schwestern einen eigenen Bereich: die 1931 geborene Paola die Pelzabteilung, die 1933 geborene Anna die Lederwaren, die 1935 geborene Franca Werbung und PR, die 1937 geborene Carla die Finanzen und die 1940 geborene Alda den Verkauf. Ende der 1980er-

Jahre war der Name Fendi dank der typischen Pelze und dem unverwechselbaren Logo aus zwei Fs (eine Idee von Karl Lagerfeld) zum Synonym für elitären Luxus des Jet-Set avanciert. In den 1990er-Jahren mit ihrer Political Correctness besann man sich wieder verstärkt auf Adele Fendis traditionelle Lederwaren, entdeckte die Baguette-Tasche neu, und Fendis Stern stieg erneut. Angesichts der Lust an barocker Üppigkeit Ende der 1990er-Jahre kauften zunächst LVMH und Prada 51 Prozent des Unternehmens; seit 2001 ist LVMH einziger Partner. Trotzdem hat Fendi noch viel von einem Familienbetrieb. Die Zukunft liegt in den Händen von Silvia Venturini Fendi (der 1960 geborenen Tochter von Anna Fendi). Sie gründete 1987 die Linie Fendissime und ist heute die Designerin von Accessoires und Herrenmode. Chefdesigner Karl Lagerfeld arbeitet – wie seit 1965 – weiterhin mit den Schwestern zusammen.

Fendi est la marque des extrêmes : grosses fourrures et petits sacs à main, affaire familiale et réputation internationale, passé chic et avenir « street-cool ». L'empire Fendi a été fondé en 1925 par Adele Fendi à partir du petit atelier de maroquinerie de Rome où elle travaillait pour une clientèle privée avec son mari Eduardo. La petite affaire familiale se développe grâce à l'ouverture d'une plus grande boutique en 1946, mais ce n'est que huit ans plus tard, à la mort d'Eduardo, que naît l'image moderne de Fendi, lorsque leurs cinq filles commencent à insuffler tout leur glamour et leur jeunesse à l'entreprise. Quand Adele meurt en 1978, chaque sœur hérite d'un morceau de l'empire : Paola (née en 1931) s'occupe des fourrures, Anna (née en 1933) de la maroquinerie, Franca (née en 1935) des relations avec les clients, Carla (née en 1937) des finances et Alda (née en 1940) des ventes. A la fin des années 80, le nom Fendi est devenu synonyme de luxe élitiste et jet-set grâce à ses fourrures signature et à son logo en double F immédiatement identifiable (dessiné par Karl Lagerfeld). Pendant les années 90, ère du politiquement correct, l'entreprise ressort les sacs d'Adele Fendi : la Baguette est ressuscitée et l'étoile de Fendi remonte au firmament. L'appétit pour les excès baroques de la fin des années 90, ère voit LVMH et Prada racheter 51 % de la griffe, mais c'est LVMH qui finit par en devenir l'unique partenaire en 2001. Toutefois, Fendi reste encore une affaire très familiale : son avenir repose sur les épaules de Silvia Venturini Fendi (née en 1960, fille d'Anna Fendi), à l'origine de la ligne Fendissime en 1987 et qui occupe aujourd'hui la direction des départements Accessoires et Mode pour homme. Karl Lagerfeld, directeur de la création, continue à travailler pour les sœurs, comme il fait depuis 1965.

JAMIE HUCKBODY

What are your signature designs? Manual ability and technique **What's your favourite piece from any of your collections?** The Baguette **How would you describe your work?** Dreaming and realising **What's your ultimate goal?** The Ostrik bag **What inspires you?** Anything, but above all, the challenges **Can fashion still have a political ambition?** It should not – but it can because fashion has great power when it influences costume and society **What do you have in mind when you design?** It depends. Sometimes I have images in mind, sometimes I have only sensations which I would call 'visionary' **Is the idea of creative collaboration important to you?** Creativity grows when it is shared **Who has been the greatest influence on your career?** My mother **How have your own experiences affected your work as a designer?** Irony, which I have acquired through my life experiences, allows me to have a sort of detachment and to dampen the creative obsession **Which is more important in your work: the process or the product?** It is impossible to separate one from the other. However, the process is the longer and more fascinating phase, which culminates in the realisation of the product **Is designing difficult for you? If so, what drives you to continue?** It is not easy, but always challenging **Have you ever been influenced or moved by the reaction to your designs?** Yes, because creativity is neither blind nor deaf **What's your definition of beauty?** Energy **What's your philosophy?** To be afraid of convictions and to have the courage to change ideas **What is the most important lesson you have learned?** To be ready to reverse the norms that up to that moment seemed to be absolute.

"I try to transform a dream's magic into reality"
ALBERTA FERRETTI

As a woman famed for her fragile little dresses blown together from raw-edged chiffon, appliquéd ribbon and intricate rivulets of beading, Alberta Ferretti is an unlikely player in the boardroom wars of the world's luxury goods groups. Yet Aeffe SpA, the company she founded in 1980 with her brother Massimo as chairman, now owns the controlling stake in Moschino and brokered production and distribution deals with Jean Paul Gaultier (1994) and Narciso Rodriguez (1997). As well as Alberta Ferretti and her successful diffusion line, Philosophy di Alberta Ferretti, Aeffe owns swimwear/lingerie label Velmar and shoemaker Pollini. Born in 1950 in Cattolica, Italy, Ferretti is the daughter of a dressmaker and was raised assisting in her mother's atelier. Not for her are the sharp, tight and angular silhouettes of the male Parisian couturiers. Ferretti was inspired instead by a lyrical femininity and fluidity as celebrated in the Fellini movies being made around Cattolica in the 1950s. At the age of 18, Ferretti opened a boutique in her hometown and in 1974 unveiled her own label. 1980 saw Alberta and Massimo go into business together. Alberta Ferretti's debut on the catwalk in Milan came in 1981 with sheer, ethereal chiffons and pin-tucked satin dresses. In 1994, Aeffe annexed the medieval village of Montegridolfo as its Italian headquarters. More than a decade later, her delicate, romantic but modern take on fashion is as relevant as it was when she started; with the label growing in size to include Alberta Ferretti Girls, a childrenswear line, a hugely successful diffusion line Philosophy, a stylish eyewear range in conjunction with Elite Group SpA, and most recently an Alberta Ferretti fragrance with Elizabeth Arden.

Diese Frau, die für ihre zarten Kleidchen aus ungesäumtem Chiffon mit applizierten Bändern und raffinierten Perlenstickereien bekannt ist, kann man sich als Kämpferin auf dem Schlachtfeld der Luxuswarenkonzerne kaum vorstellen. Dabei besitzt Aeffe SpA, die 1980 mit Bruder Massimo als Geschäftsführer gegründete Firma, inzwischen die Mehrheit bei Moschino und blickt auf Produktions- und Vertriebskooperationen mit Jean Paul Gaultier (1994) und Narciso Rodriguez (1997) zurück. Neben dem Label Alberta Ferretti und der erfolgreichen Nebenlinie Philosophy di Alberta Ferretti gehört Aeffe auch noch das Bademoden- und Dessoushaus Velmar sowie die Schuhmarke Pollini. Ferretti kam 1950 im italienischen Cattolica als Tochter einer Schneiderin zur Welt und half schon in ihrer Kindheit im mütterlichen Atelier. Die scharfen, harten und geometrischen Silhouetten der Pariser Couturiers waren noch nie ihre Sache. Ferretti ließ sich stattdessen von einer lyrischen Weiblichkeit und den weichen Konturen inspirieren, wie sie in den Fellini-Filmen gefeiert wurden, die in den 1950er Jahren in der Gegend um Cattolica gedreht wurden. Mit 18 eröffnete Ferretti in ihrer Heimatstadt einen Laden, 1974 präsentierte sie ihr eigenes Label. 1980 schließlich taten sich die Geschwister Alberta und Massimo geschäftlich zusammen. Ihr Debüt auf dem Laufsteg gab Alberta 1981 in Mailand mit hauchdünnen ätherischen Chiffonkleidchen und mit Stecknadeln gerafften Satinroben. 1994 erkor Aeffe das mittelalterliche Städtchen Montegridolfo zu seinem Firmensitz in Italien. Fünfzehn Jahre danach besitzt Ferrettis zarte, romantische, aber dennoch moderne Mode nach wie vor dasselbe Gewicht wie zu Beginn ihrer Karriere. Das beständig wachsende Label umfasst inzwischen auch die Kindermarke Alberta Ferretti Girls, eine ungeheuer erfolgreiche Nebenlinie namens Philosophy, elegante Brillen in Kooperation mit Elite Group SpA sowie das erst kürzlich bei Elizabeth Arden auf den Markt gekommene Parfüm Alberta Ferretti.

Réputée pour ses délicates petites robes en mousseline de soie aux finitions brutes, applications de rubans et rivières de perles très élaborées, Alberta Ferretti fait figure de personnage improbable au sein des guerres que se livrent les conseils d'administration des grands groupes de luxe mondiaux. Pourtant, Aeffe SpA, l'entreprise qu'elle fonde en 1980 avec son frère Massimo au poste de président, possède aujourd'hui une part majoritaire dans la société Moschino et a conclu des accords de production et de distribution avec Jean Paul Gaultier (1994) et Narciso Rodriguez (1997). Aux côtés de la griffe Alberta Ferretti et de sa ligne à succès Philosophy di Alberta Ferretti, Aeffe possède la marque de maillots de bain et de lingerie Velmar, ainsi que le fabricant de chaussures Pollini. Fille de couturière, Alberta Ferretti est née en 1950 à Cattolica en Italie et grandit dans l'atelier de sa mère dont elle est aussi l'assistante. Les silhouettes acérées, angulaires et restreintes des couturiers parisiens ne la séduisent pas. Elle s'inspire au contraire de la féminité lyrique et de la fluidité célébrées dans les films que Fellini tourne dans la région de Cattolica dans les années 1950. A 18 ans, Alberta Ferretti ouvre une boutique dans sa ville natale avant de lancer sa propre griffe en 1974. En 1980, Alberta et Massimo s'associent en affaires. Pour son premier défilé à Milan en 1981, Alberta Ferretti présente des robes transparentes et aériennes en mousseline de soie et en satin nervuré. En 1994, Aeffe installe son siège italien dans le village médiéval de Montegridolfo. Quinze ans plus tard, sa mode délicate et romantique mais néanmoins moderne n'a rien perdu de sa pertinence. Sa griffe s'est développée pour inclure Alberta Ferretti Girls, une collection pour enfant, la ligne à succès Philosophy plus accessible, une gamme de lunettes très stylées conçue en collaboration avec Elite Group SpA, et tout récemment, le parfum Alberta Ferretti avec Elizabeth Arden.

JAMES SHERWOOD

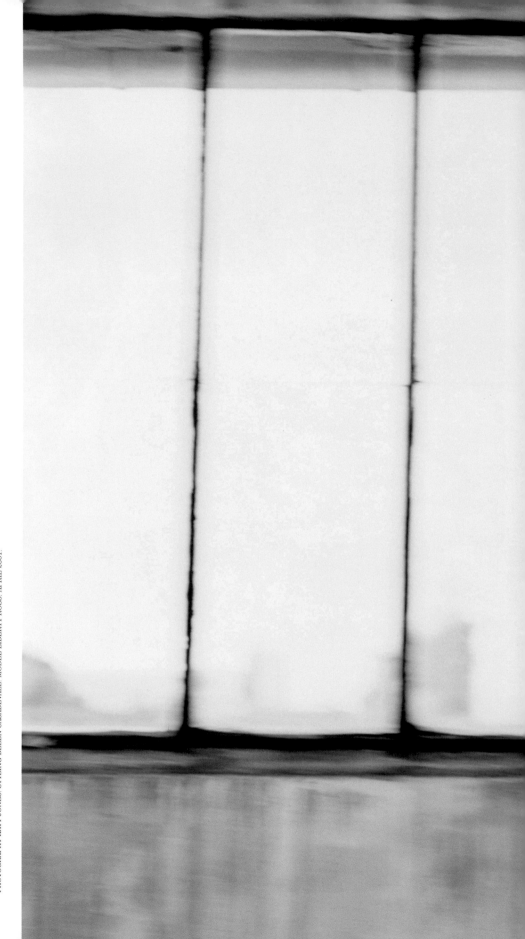

ALBERTA FERRETTI

What are your signature designs? Lightness **What is your favourite piece from any of your collections?** The one that best represents my style **How would you describe your work?** Challenging, stimulating, satisfying **What's your ultimate goal?** To create a dress like the Intarsia dresses of my Alberta Ferretti autumn/winter 2004 collection. Like the one that Scarlett Johansson wore for the Oscars in 2004 **What inspires you?** Emotions **Can fashion still have a political ambition?** Particular styles in dressing can underline belonging to a group with a specific and identifiable ideology. Only in that sense can we say that fashion has political ambitions **Who do you have in mind when you design?** Not a specific person, but I try to transform a dream's magic into reality **Is the idea of creative collaboration important to you?** Yes, as working with others is essential to moving forward **Who has been the greatest influence on your career?** Myself: from the endless challenges I face to the effort I make to improve myself and reach new goals **How have your own experiences affected your work as a designer?** I decided to become a designer watching my mother working in her atelier and there I started loving fabrics and dresses, draped carefully following the harmony and proportions of the feminine silhouette **Which is more important in your work: the process or the product?** There is no outcome without process, elaborating without producing is sterile. The result really only comes from the union of these two phases **Is designing difficult for you? If so, what drives you to continue?** No, designing is my passion. It's almost a necessity, keeping the creativity alive **Have you ever been influenced or moved by the** reaction to your designs? I consider the opinions of others, but it is fundamental to maintain my concept of elegance, femininity and sensuality **What's your definition of beauty?** In my opinion, beauty is the harmony created by the dress and the woman who wears it **What's your philosophy?** In addition to my younger line, I try to emphasise the personality and elegance of women **What is the most important lesson you've learned?** Everyday life is full of lessons. All of them are important. There is always something to learn.

"I'm more of a patternmaker than a designer"
LIMI FEU

Limi Feu, born Limi Yamamoto to the acclaimed Japanese fashion designer Yohji Yamamoto, grew up with fashion in her DNA. Born in Fukuoka in southern Japan, Limi moved to Tokyo in 1994 to enrol at the acclaimed Bunka Fashion College. Two years later, she began her official training as a patternmaker for Yohji's diffusion line, Y's. Here she perfected her skills, before branching out on her own as a designer in 1999 with Y's bis LIMI, presenting her first collection for autumn/winter 2000-2001 at the Garden Hall in Ebisu, Tokyo. With Yohji as her mentor, the collection was naturally a success and, in 2002, Limi changed the label's name from Y's bis LIMI to Limi Feu, 'feu' meaning 'fire' in French. The change in name not only mirrored her passion but marked a new direction for the young Japanese designer, with Limi establishing Limi Yamamoto Inc soon after, in 2006. After several successful shows in Tokyo, Limi moved the collection to Paris to show her debut collection for spring/summer 2008 at the Garage Turenne. Highly anticipated by the international press, the collection did not disappoint, firmly establishing Limi's position at the forefront of a new wave of Japanese designers. From Yohji she inherited her conceptual use of layering, asymmetry and a predominantly monochromatic palette. But that is where the similarities end. Limi's love of oversized proportions, and masculine/feminine interplay, place her firmly in a league of her own – a position that was cemented in 2008, when she received the prestigious Designer of the Year award from The 51st Fashion Editor's Club of Japan. Based in Nishi-Azabu in Tokyo, Limi Feu has since expanded her business to include three flagship stores around the city.

Limi Feu, geborene Yamamoto, ist die Tochter des gefeierten japanischen Designers Yohji Yamamoto und wuchs bereits mit Mode in ihrer DNA auf. Von ihrem Geburtsort Fukuoka im Süden Japans zog sie 1994 nach Tokio, um sich am berühmten Bunka Fashion College einzuschreiben. Zwei Jahre später begann sie ihre offizielle Ausbildung in der Schnittabteilung von Yamamotos Nebenlinie Y's. Dort perfektionierte sie ihre Fähigkeiten, bevor sie sich 1999 mit Y's bis LIMI als eigenständige Designerin versuchte und ihre erste Kollektion, Herbst/Winter 2000/2001, in der Ebisu Garden Hall in Tokio präsentierte. Mit ihrem Vater als Mentor war die Kollektion selbstverständlich ein Erfolg, und 2002 änderte Limi den Namen des Labels von Y's bis LIMI in Limi Feu, nach dem französischen Wort für „Feuer". Diese Änderung sollte nicht nur ihre Leidenschaft zum Ausdruck bringen, sondern auch die Neuausrichtung der jungen japanischen Designerin kennzeichnen, die im Jahr 2006 die Limi Yamamoto Inc. gründete. Nach einigen erfolgreichen Schauen in Tokio zog Limi

mit ihrer Kollektion nach Paris, wo sie mit ihrer Kollektion Frühjahr/Sommer 2008 ihr Debüt in der Garage Turenne gab. Von der internationalen Presse mit reichlich Vorschusslorbeeren bedacht, enttäuschte sie nicht, sondern festigte ihre Position an der Spitze einer neuen Generation japanischer Designer. Von ihrem Vater Yohji Yamamoto hat sie die konzeptionelle Vorliebe für Lagen, Asymmetrie und eine vornehmlich monochrome Farbpalette geerbt. Doch damit endet die Ähnlichkeit auch schon. Limis Faible für überdimensionale Proportionen und das Wechselspiel zwischen maskulin und feminin hat ihr eine solide Eigenständigkeit eingebracht. Gefestigt wurde diese Position nicht zuletzt 2008, als sie vom 51st Fashion Editor's Club of Japan mit dem angesehenen Preis Designer of the Year ausgezeichnet wurde. Der Firmensitz liegt im Tokioter Viertel Nishi-Azabu, allerdings hat Limi Feu ihre Geschäfte inzwischen auf drei Flagship Stores an verschiedenen Stellen der Stadt ausgedehnt.

Fille du brillant créateur japonais Yohji Yamamoto, Limi Feu est née avec le gène de la mode dans son ADN. Originaire de Fukuoka au sud du Japon, elle s'installe à Tokyo en 1994 pour suivre des études au prestigieux Bunka Fashion College. Deux ans plus tard, elle entame sa formation pratique et se perfectionne dans l'art du traçage de patrons pour Y's, la ligne de diffusion de Yohji Yamamoto. En 1999, elle se lance en tant que styliste avec la griffe Y's bis LIMI et présente sa première collection automne/hiver 2000-2001 au Garden Hall d'Ebisu à Tokyo. Avec un mentor tel que Yohji, Limi remporte évidemment un grand succès et rebaptise sa griffe Limi Feu en 2002. Référence littérale au terme français, ce changement de nom reflète sa passion tout en ouvrant un nouveau chapitre dans la carrière de la jeune créatrice japonaise, qui fonde Limi Yamamoto Inc. en 2006. Après plusieurs défilés acclamés à Tokyo, Limi fait son « baptême du feu » à Paris en présentant sa collection printemps/été 2008 au Garage Turenne. Loin de décevoir la presse internationale, cette collection très attendue installe fermement Limi à l'avant-garde de la nouvelle vague de créateurs nippons. De son père, elle a hérité un usage conceptuel des superpositions, l'asymétrie et une palette principalement monochrome, mais ce sont bien là leurs seules similitudes. Le penchant de Limi pour les proportions exagérées et les interactions masculin/féminin la classe dans une catégorie à part entière, une originalité distinguée en 2008 par le prestigieux prix de Designer of the Year remis lors de la 51e édition du Fashion Editor's Club of Japan. Depuis son Q.G. de Nishi-Azabu à Tokyo, Limi Feu a développé son activité en ouvrant trois boutiques à travers la ville.

HOLLY SHACKLETON

What are your signature designs? White shirts and trousers **What is your favourite piece from any of your collections?** I like Look 24 from my autumn/winter 2008/2009 collection **How would you describe your work?** I'm more of a patternmaker than a designer, and I am also a producer who directs both sides **What's your ultimate goal?** It's to maintain the environment, which allows me to create the clothes I like to design, as long as I can **What inspires you?** The personalities of the people I directly meet, and their enthusiasm toward their work **Can fashion still have a political ambition?** It should always have **Who do you have in mind when you design?** Myself **Is the idea of creative collaboration important to you?** Yes, it's important **Who has been the greatest influence on your career?** It's Mr Yohji Yamamoto **How have your own experiences affected your work as designer?** Not really. I'm a high-school dropout... **Which is more important in your work: the process or the product?** The product result **Is designing difficult for you? If so, what drives you to continue?** Because I love clothes **Have you ever been influenced or moved by the reaction to your designs?** No, but I like to hear the reaction **What's your definition of beauty?** Capability to be strong or brave enough to deal with all the things that could happen to us, yet to be warm-hearted, as if you feel hugged, at the same time **What's your philosophy?** The continuation is the power.

"I like to think that I brought a certain hedonism back to fashion"
TOM FORD

Tom Ford has redefined the role of fashion designer. Born in Austin, Texas, in 1961, spending his teenage years in Santa Fe, New Mexico, before enrolling in an art history course at New York University. In Manhattan, Ford's extracurricular activities included acting in TV advertisements and hanging out at both Studio 54 and Warhol's Factory. He eventually transferred to and was studying architecture at Parsons School of Design in New York and Paris, studying architecture, but by the end of the course, Ford had realised that he wanted to work in fashion. In 1986, back in New York, he joined the design studio of Cathy Hardwick, moving to Perry Ellis two years later as design director. In 1990, Ford became womenswear designer at Gucci. In 1994, he was made creative director at Gucci and the following March showed a landmark collection. His velvet hipster trousers and jewel-coloured satin shirts – unbuttoned to the navel and impossibly lean – were part of a slick, alluring package of unapologetic flash and sex appeal. Almost overnight, Gucci became a byword for desirability, offering the most aspirational and hedonistic kind of fashion. When the Gucci Group purchased Yves Saint Laurent in January 2000, Ford began designing menswear and womenswear for Yves Saint Laurent Rive Gauche. In 2002, he was awarded Accessory Designer of the Year for his work, and soon earned the titles of both creative director of the Gucci Group, and vice-chairman of the management board of Gucci Group. In 2004, Ford left the company and exactly one year later announced the creation of the Tom Ford brand, which today includes luxury men's ready-to-wear and made-to-measure clothing, footwear and accessories, in addition to an award-winning eyewear label in conjunction with the Marcolin Group, and a glossy men's fragrance and beauty range with Estée Lauder. Ford opened his flagship store in New York in 2007. His success as a designer and a personality increases with every passing year. He has received dozens of industry awards, including four from the prestigious CFDA and five from the VH-1/ Vogue Fashion Awards. Meticulous in his own personal appearance, Ford has also been awarded for his personal style, winning ‚Elle' magazine's Style Icon Award and GQ's International Man of the Year Award.

Tom Ford hat die Rolle des Modeschöpfers neu definiert. Er wurde 1961 in Austin, Texas, geboren und studierte Architektur an der Parsons School of Design in New York und in Paris, doch gegen Ende der Ausbildung erkannte Ford, dass er eigentlich in der Modebranche arbeiten wollte. 1986 schloss er sich, nach New York zurückgekehrt, dem Designatelier von Cathy Hardwick an. Zwei Jahre später ging er als Design Director zu Perry Ellis. 1990 wurde er Designer für Damenmode bei Gucci. Dort wurde Ford 1994 zum Creative Director befördert und zeigte im darauf folgenden März eine Kollektion, die den Wendepunkt darstellen sollte. Seine Hüfthosen aus Samt und Satinblusen in Edelsteintönen – bis zum Nabel aufgeknöpft und unglaublich schmal geschnitten – waren Teil eines raffinierten, verführerischen, keineswegs zurückhaltenden sexy Looks. Fast über Nacht wurde Gucci zum Synonym für Begehrlichkeit, zu einem Label, das die ambitionierteste und hedonistischste Mode von allen bot. Als der Gucci-Konzern im Januar 2000

Yves Saint Laurent kaufte, begann Ford, Herren- und Damenmode für Yves Saint Laurent Rive Gauche zu entwerfen. Im Jahr 2002 wurde er für seine Arbeit als Accessory Designer of the Year ausgezeichnet und avancierte bald zum Creative Director sowie zum stellvertretenden Vorstandsvorsitzenden des Gucci-Konzerns. 2004 verließ Ford das Unternehmen und gab genau ein Jahr später die Gründung der Marke Tom Ford bekannt, die heute luxuriöse Prêt-à-porter sowie Maß-Mode für Herren umfasst, dazu Schuhwerk, Accessoires, inklusive eines presigekrönten Brillenlabels in Zusammenarbeit mit der Marcolin Group sowie ein glanzvolles Duft- und Beauty-Sortiment für Herren unter dem Dach von Estée Lauder. Den eigenen Flagship-Store in New York eröffnete Ford 2007. Sein Erfolg als Designer und als Persönlichkeit wächst mit jedem Jahr. Ford hat dutzende Branchenpreise gewonnen, darunter vier der angesehenen CFDA und fünf VH-1/Vogue Fashion Awards. Sorgsam auf seine persönliche Erscheinung bedacht, wurde Ford auch für seinen eigenen Stil schon ausgezeichnet, mit dem Style Icon Award der Zeitschrift Elle und mit GQ's International Man of the Year Award.

Tom Ford a redéfini le rôle du créateur de mode. Né en 1961 à Austin au Texas, Tom Ford étudie l'architecture à la Parsons School of Design de New York, puis à Paris. Ce n'est qu'une fois ses études terminées que Ford prend enfin conscience de sa vocation. En 1986, de retour à New York, il rejoint le studio de création de Cathy Hardwick, avant de partir travailler deux ans plus tard chez Perry Ellis comme directeur de la création. En 1990, Ford devient styliste pour femme chez Gucci. En 1994, Ford est nommé directeur de la création de Gucci et présente au mois de mars une collection qui fait date : ses pantalons taille basse en velours et ses chemises en satin aux couleurs de pierres précieuses, déboutonnées jusqu'au nombril et très près du corps, font partie d'une collection séduisante et maline au sex-appeal sans complexe. Quasiment du jour au lendemain, Gucci devient une marque indispensable en proposant la mode la plus désirable et la plus hédoniste du moment. Quand le Groupe Gucci rachète Yves Saint Laurent en janvier 2000, Ford commence à concevoir les collections pour homme et pour femme Yves Saint Laurent Rive Gauche. En 2002, son travail sur les accessoires lui vaut le titre d'Accessory Designer of the Year. Il devient rapidement directeur de la création et vice-président du conseil d'administration du Groupe Gucci. Il quitte l'entreprise en 2004 et exactement un an plus tard, annonce la création de la marque Tom Ford, qui propose actuellement du prêt-à-porter de luxe et sur mesure pour homme, des chaussures et des accessoires – notamment une collection de lunettes primée, conçue en collaboration avec le Groupe Marcolin – ainsi qu'un parfum et une gamme de produits cosmétiques pour homme avec Estée Lauder. En 2007, Tom Ford ouvre sa boutique phare à New York. Son succès en tant que star et créateur de mode ne fait qu'augmenter chaque année. Il a reçu des dizaines de prix, dont quatre du prestigieux CFDA et cinq des VH-1/Vogue Fashion Awards. Très soigneux de sa propre apparence, Ford a aussi été distingué pour son style personnel par un Style Icon Award du magazine Elle et le titre d'International Man of the Year de GQ.

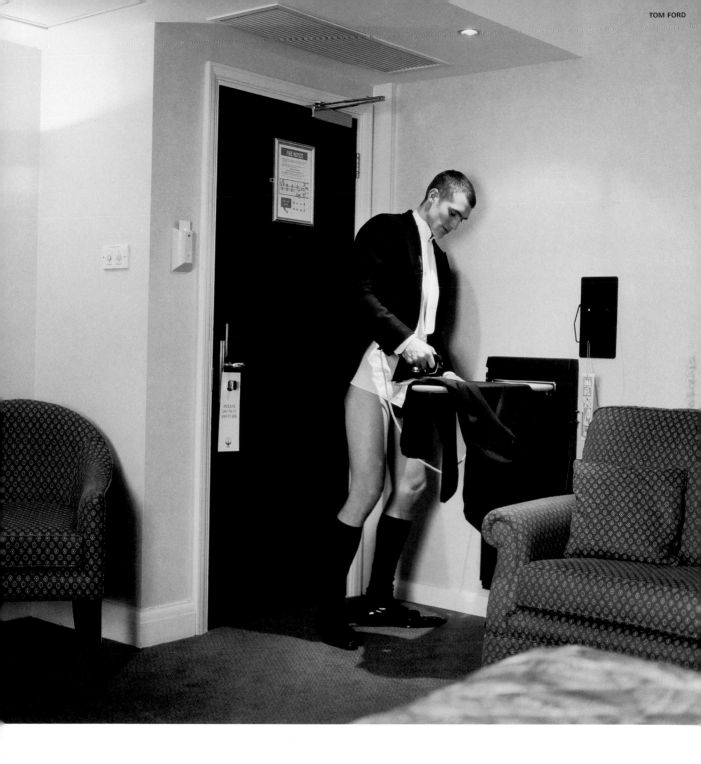

What are your signature designs? I like to think that in the mid '90s I brought a certain hedonism back to fashion. Sensuality is always present in my work **How would you describe your work?** Hard. I love what I do but it can be incredibly draining to constantly generate things that feel fresh and new **Who do you have in mind when you design?** A woman who's confident, intelligent and uses fashion to express different aspects of her personality. And who knows how to walk in heels **Can fashion still have a political ambition?** I don't think that clothes can start a revolution, but I do believe that fashion is often a manifestation of a sociological or political climate **What has been the greatest influence on your career?** My constant drive **How have your own experiences affected your work as a designer?** If you are a writer you write about what you know, if you are a designer you design for the world that you know. My experiences are my work **Is designing difficult for you? If so, what drives you to continue?** No. I become bored very easily and I love change **What inspires you?** Chicks with Dicks.

"Creations from a fresh and innovative vision, which are free from the existing theories of making clothes"
DAI FUJIWARA • ISSEY MIYAKE

Dai Fujiwara joined the Issey Miyake Design Studio in 1994, after graduating from Tokyo's Tama Art University in textile design. As part of Miyake's collection staff, he collaborated with Miyake on the A-POC (A Piece of Cloth) project, which wowed editors, journalists and buyers alike when 23 models appeared on the Paris catwalk in 1998 connected by one tube of fabric. For his work on A-POC, Fujiwara was awarded the Good Design Grand Prize in 2000 and was nominated for the Mainichi Design Award in 2003. Three years later, his continued dedication to fabric research and development culminated in the appointment of creative director of the Issey Miyake collections, with Fujiwara unleashing his debut collection 'Rondo' for autumn/winter 2007. Just like Miyake, Fujiwara enjoys collaborating with artists and product designers across the globe. Spring/summer 2008 saw him join forces with James Dyson – inventor of the dual cyclone vacuum cleaner – on an atmospheric wind stage set. For his autumn/winter 2008 collection, 'Apocalyptic Lovers', the maverick designer took part in Finland's 5th International Alvar Aalto Design Seminar 'It's a Beautiful Day', working closely with some of the world's most renowned design companies to visualise and kit out the wedding of an ordinary Finnish couple. Always one to think outside the box, Fujiwara goes to great lengths to research the theme of his collection, flying a part of his design team to the Amazon rainforest to research 'real colour' for his spring/summer 2009 collection 'Colour Hunting'. Autumn/winter 2009 saw the Japanese designer recruit Karate Kata masters as models to accurately demonstrate the high-performance quality of his clothing. The Issey Miyake men's collections continue to be shown in the Paris showroom in Place des Vosges twice yearly. August 2009 marked the much-awaited launch of Issey Miyake's new fragrance, A Scent. Housed in a slick glass bottle designed by Paris-based designer Arik Levy, the fragrance follows 17 years after the huge success of L'Eau D'Issey.

Dai Fujiwara fing 1994 im Issey Miyake Design Studio an, nachdem er seinen Abschluss in Textildesign an der Tokioter Tama Art University gemacht hatte. Als Mitglied von Miyakes Kollektionsteam war er an dessen Projekt A-POC (A Piece of Cloth) beteiligt, das Journalisten und Einkäufer gleichermaßen begeisterte, als 1998 auf einem Pariser Catwalk 23 Models auftraten, die alle durch einen Stoffschlauch miteinander verbunden waren. Für seine Arbeit an A-POC wurde Fujiwara 2000 mit dem Good Design Grand Prize ausgezeichnet und 2003 für den Mainichi Design Award nominiert. Drei Jahre später fand seine anhaltende Hingabe zur Materialforschung und -entwicklung ihren Höhepunkt in der Ernennung zum Creative Director der Kollektionen von Issey Miyake. Seine Debütkollektion in dieser Position war „Rondo" für Herbst/Winter 2007. Ganz wie Miyake hat auch Fujiwara seine Freude an der Zusammenarbeit mit Künstlern und Produktdesignern aus aller Welt. Für Frühjahr/Sommer 2008 tat er sich etwa mit James Dyson – dem Erfinder des Dual-Zyklon-Staubsaugers – zusammen, um eine atmosphärereiche Bühne mit viel Wind zu kreieren. Für „Apocalyptic Lovers", seine Kollektion für Herbst/Winter 2008, nahm der rebellische Designer an Finnlands 5. Internationalem Alvar Aalto Design Seminar „It's a Beautiful Day" teil und arbeitete eng mit einigen der bekanntesten

Designfirmen der Welt zusammen, um die Hochzeit eines ganz normalen finnischen Paares zu visualisieren und auszustatten. Als passionierter Querdenker scheut Fujiwara keine Mühen, um das Thema einer Kollektion zu erforschen. So ließ er etwa einen Teil seines Designteams in den Regenwald am Amazonas fliegen, um dort „echte Farben" für seine Kollektion „Colour Hunting" für Frühjahr/Sommer 2009 zu studieren. Für Herbst/Winter 2009 rekrutierte der japanische Designer dagegen Karate-Kämpferinnen als Models, um die Strapazierfähigkeit seiner Kleidung anschaulich zu demonstrieren. Die Herrenkollektionen von Issey Miyake werden weiterhin zweimal jährlich im Pariser Showroom an der Place des Vosges gezeigt. Im August 2009 kam mit A Scent der langersehnte neue Duft von Issey Miyake auf den Markt. Er steckt in einer raffinierten Glasflasche, die der in Paris lebende Designer Arik Levy entworfen hat, und soll an den Riesenerfolg von L'Eau d'Issey vor 17 Jahren anknüpfen.

Dai Fujiwara rejoint le studio de création Issey Miyake en 1994, après avoir obtenu son diplôme en design textile de la Tama Art University de Tokyo. Membre de l'équipe en charge des collections, il collabore avec Miyake sur le projet A-POC (A Piece of Cloth) qui laisse les rédacteurs, les journalistes et les acheteurs sans voix devant les 23 mannequins défilant toutes reliées par un tube de tissu en 1998 à Paris. Son travail sur A-POC vaut à Fujiwara le Good Design Grand Prize en 2000 et une nomination au Mainichi Design Award en 2003. Trois ans plus tard, son constant dévouement à la recherche et au développement de tissus est récompensé par son accession au poste de directeur de la création des collections Issey Miyake : Fujiwara présente sa première collection baptisée « Rondo » pour l'automne/hiver 2007. Tout comme Miyake, Fujiwara aime collaborer avec des artistes et des designers du monde entier. Pour la saison printemps/été 2008, il travaille avec James Dyson – l'inventeur de l'aspirateur cyclonique sans sac – sur la création d'un podium balayé par le vent. Pour « Apocalyptic Lovers », sa collection automne/hiver 2008, le créateur dissident participe à « It's a Beautiful Day », le 5e Séminaire international Alvar Aalto en Finlande, où il collabore étroitement avec certaines des entreprises de design les plus célèbres au monde pour imaginer et créer les objets du mariage d'un couple finnois ordinaire. Privilégiant systématiquement le décalage, Fujiwara est prêt à tout pour trouver le thème de ses collections : pour « Colour Hunting », la collection printemps/été 2009, il emmène son équipe dans la forêt amazonienne en quête de « vraies couleurs ». Pour la collection automne/hiver 2009, le créateur japonais recrute des maîtres de karaté comme mannequins pour démontrer avec précision la qualité et les hautes performances de ses vêtements. Les collections pour homme Issey Miyake sont toujours présentées deux fois par an dans le showroom parisien de la griffe place des Vosges. Le mois d'août 2009 voit le lancement d'A Scent, le nouveau parfum très attendu d'Issey Miyake : présenté dans un flacon en verre épuré conçu par le designer parisien Arik Levy, il fait suite à L'Eau D'Issey, immense succès de parfumerie depuis 17 ans.

JAMES SHERWOOD

What are your signature designs? It's 'King & Queen', which we presented in 1997 when I was working with Mr Miyake. It's my representative clothes that were accepted into the permanent collection of the Architecture and Design Department at The Museum of Modern Art, New York, in 2006 **What is your favourite piece from any of your collections?** I've been creative director at Issey Miyake since 2006. Above all, my favourite piece is the autumn/winter 2009 'Frame Stretch' jacket, which was made out of a textile that was developed in collaboration with karate masters. In this special textile, three different stretches are applied **How would you describe your work?** Right now, I'm creative director at Issey Miyake, but I am first and foremost a designer **What's your ultimate goal?** Perhaps it's to wake up nicely in the morning. It's not ultimate, but it's something I want to start doing soon. I think as times have changed, textiles have greatly influenced the history of the computer. I would like to research a textile compendium, from ancient times to the present day **What inspires you?** Nature, cultures and information technology **Can fashion still have a political ambition?** Clothes used to be the centre of fashion. Now it extends to the fields of home electronics and architecture. Its influence on society is increasing every day. Therefore, fashion should be able to continue to create a new method of expressing a political ambition **Who do you have in mind when you design?** I always have three people in mind: the customer who pays for our clothes, the customer who comes to our shop to return our clothes and the customer who will come to our shop in the future **Is the idea of creative collaboration important to you?** Modern society is inundated with goods. The ideas underlining them are hard to see. Collaboration is a convenient method of sharing ideas about these goods. It also helps people to understand the ideas. Collaboration is an effective way to mix things **Who has been the greatest influence on your career?** Issey Miyake, Antoni Plàcid Guillem Gaudí i Cornet, William Paul Thurston **How have your own experiences affected your work as a designer?** My way of understanding **Is designing difficult for you? If so, what drives you to continue?** Designing is the most enjoyable part of my life **Have you ever been influenced or moved by the reaction to your designs?** Modes of thought change from one generation to the next, like geological layers **What's your definition of beauty?** Liberal excitement **What's your philosophy?** The Why? **What is the most important lesson you've learned?** To place importance on light and space.

"I am here to make people dream, to seduce them into buying beautiful clothes and to strive to make amazing clothing to the best of my ability. That is my duty"
JOHN GALLIANO + CHRISTIAN DIOR

John Galliano is one of Britain's fashion heroes. Born in 1960 to a working-class Gibraltan family, Galliano lived on the island until leaving at the age of six for south London. But it was the young Juan Carlos Antonio's early life, with its religious ceremonies and sun-drenched culture, which has proved a constant inspiration for Galliano; stylistic eclecticism wedded to the Latin tradition of 'dressing-up' has become his signature. Having attended Wilson's Grammar School for boys, Galliano won a place at Central Saint Martins, graduating in 1984. And it was that graduation collection – inspired by the French Revolution and titled 'Les Incroyables' – that was bought by Joan Burstein of Browns, catapulting the young designer into the spotlight. In 1990 – after suffering a period notorious for problems with backers and collections deemed 'uncommercial' because they dared to dream beyond the conventional – Galliano started to show in Paris, moving to the city in 1992. A champion of the romantic bias-cut dress and the dramatic tailoring of '50s couture at a time when minimalism and grunge dominated fashion, it was announced in 1995 that Galliano would succeed Hubert de Givenchy at the dusty maison de couture. Two seasons later, and with an unprecedented four British Designer of the Year awards under his belt, Galliano became creative director at Christian Dior, presenting his first collection for the spring/summer 1997 haute couture show. Since then, Galliano has financially and creatively revitalised the house, while continuing to design his own collections for men and women in Paris, a city where he is accorded the status of fashion royalty, who celebrated a decade at Christian Dior in 2007. Now designing 17 collections a year for Dior and for his own label, 2009 will mark 25 years of the John Galliano line, further cementing his status as fashion royalty.

John Galliano ist eine Ikone der britischen Mode. Er wurde 1960 als Arbeiterkind auf Gibraltar geboren und verbrachte die ersten sechs Lebensjahre auf der Insel. Dann zog er mit seiner Familie in den Süden Londons. Es waren jedoch die frühen Jahre des Juan Carlos Antonio mit ihren religiösen Zeremonien und der sonnendurchfluteten Umgebung, die Galliano bis heute inspirieren. Eklektizismus in Verbindung mit der südländisch-katholischen Tradition des „Sich-schön-Anziehens" wurde zu seinem Markenzeichen. Nach dem Besuch der Wilson's Grammar School for Boys ergatterte Galliano einen Studienplatz am Central Saint Martins, das er 1984 abschloss. Seine von der Französischen Revolution inspirierte Schlusskollektion mit dem Namen „Les Incroyables", die Joan Burstein für Browns aufkaufte, katapultierte den Jungdesigner ins Rampenlicht. Nach einer schwierigen Phase – geprägt von Problemen mit Geldgebern und Kollektionen, die als nicht kommerziell genug abgeschmettert wurden, weil er darin Unkonventionelles wagte – begann Galliano 1990, seine

Kreationen in Paris zu präsentieren. Zwei Jahre später verlegte er auch seinen Wohnsitz hierher. Als Verfechter des romantischen Diagonalschnitts und der dramatischen Effekte der Couture der 1950er-Jahre in einer Zeit, als Minimalismus und Grunge die Mode dominierten, wurde Galliano 1995 als Nachfolger von Hubert de Givenchy in dessen leicht verstaubtes Couture-Haus gerufen. Zwei Saisons später und mit noch nie da gewesenen vier Titeln als British Designer of the Year in der Tasche wurde Galliano schließlich Creative Director bei Christian Dior, wo er als erste Kollektion die Haute Couture für Frühjahr/ Sommer 1997 präsentierte. Seit damals ist es dem Designer gelungen, das Haus sowohl in finanzieller wie in kreativer Hinsicht zu revitalisieren. 2007 feierte er sein zehnjähriges Jubiläum bei Christian Dior. Inzwischen entwirft er alljährlich 17 Kollektionen für Dior und für sein eigenes Label. Mit seiner 2009 bereits 25 Jahre bestehenden Marke John Galliano wird der Designer seinem Ruf als Modezar absolut gerecht.

John Galliano est un héros de la mode britannique. Né en 1960 à Gibraltar dans une famille d'ouvriers, il quitte son île natale pour le sud de Londres à l'âge de six ans. La tendre enfance du jeune Juan Carlos Antonio, avec ses cérémonies religieuses et sa culture du soleil, représente une source d'inspiration constante pour Galliano ; l'éclectisme stylistique et la tradition du « chic latin » sont devenus sa signature. En sortant du lycée pour garçons Wilson's Grammar School, Galliano réussit à entrer à Central Saint Martins, dont il sort diplômé en 1984. Inspirée par la Révolution française et baptisée « Les Incroyables », sa collection de fin d'études est achetée par Joan Burstein de chez Browns, ce qui le catapulte directement sur le devant de la scène. En 1990, après de célèbres déboires avec ses financiers et des collections vouées à l'échec commercial parce qu'elles osaient défier les conventions, Galliano commence à présenter ses défilés à Paris, où il s'installe en 1992. Fervent défenseur des coupes asymétriques romantiques et de la haute couture théâtrale des années 50 au sein d'une mode alors dominée par le minimalisme et le grunge, sa nomination à la succession d'Hubert de Givenchy dans l'antique maison éponyme est annoncée en 1995. Deux saisons plus tard et couronné de quatre British Designer of the Year Awards, un exploit sans précédent, Galliano devient directeur de la création chez Christian Dior et présente sa première collection aux défilés haute couture printemps/été 1997. Depuis, Galliano a redonné vie à la maison Dior, tant sur le plan financier que créatif, et a fêté ses dix ans chez Christian Dior en 2007. Il conçoit désormais 17 collections par an pour Dior et pour sa propre griffe. En 2009, la collection John Galliano célèbrera son 25e anniversaire, un événement qui ne fera qui confirmer sa place au sein de la famille royale de la mode.

JAMIE HUCKBODY

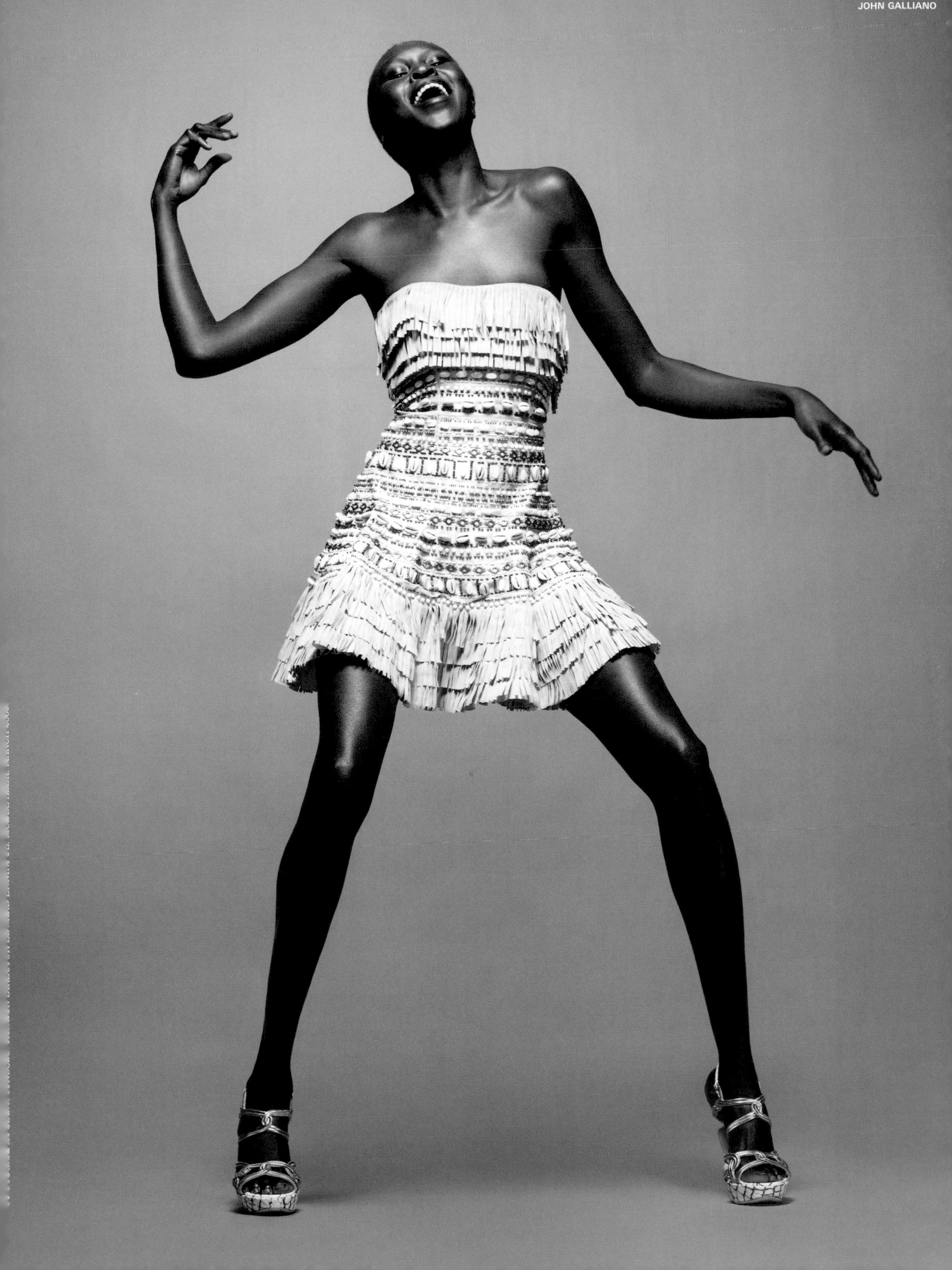

What are your signature designs? The bias cut for women and now for men as well **What is your favourite piece from any of your collections?** It is too difficult to give an answer. It would be like choosing which of your children you like best **How would you describe your work?** My work is about femininity and romance, about pushing the boundaries of creation. It is a constant search for new creative solutions **What's your ultimate goal?** To live life to the fullest, to hold on to every minute as if it were my last **What inspires you?** Everything that surrounds me can be an inspiration. I am inspired by music, film, art, street culture, my girlfriends… **Can fashion still have a political ambition?** I am a fashion designer, not a politician. I am here to make people dream, to seduce them into buying beautiful clothes and to strive to make amazing clothing to the best of my ability. That is my

duty **Who do you have in mind when you design?** In the course of my career, I have discovered that having a specific muse (either a historical figure or a living person) can be inhibiting rather than inspiring. Now I would say that I think of a more abstract notion of a modern-day woman, someone who is assertive and controls her own destiny **Is the idea of creative collaboration important to you?** I share my passion and my love of clothing with my creative team, the Studio, the Ateliers at both Dior and Galliano, with the fantastic French artisans and embroiderers like Lesage… **Who has been the greatest influence on your career?** My mother and my grandmother and their love for life and their sense of occasion for dress have been the first and lasting influence on me. When I lived in Gibraltar, to go to school in Spain, I had to go through Tangiers. The souks,

the markets, the fabrics, the carpets, the smells, the herbs, the Mediterranean colour is where my love of textiles comes from. Later, when I started my studies at Saint Martins, I was greatly influenced by the fantastic teachers I had and by the theatre **How have your own experiences affected your work as a designer?** My experiences are a vital part of my work… **Which is more important in your work: the process or the product?** One is nothing without the other **Is designing difficult for you? If so, what drives you to continue?** I have always seen work as a positive challenge. I love what I am doing, I love the very act of creating. Even in my darkest moments, I would continue working – I had no choice. Then and now, it was all I could and can do **Have you ever been influenced or moved by the reaction to your designs?** A few weeks

before the showing of the autumn/winter 2002 collection, I received a letter with some drawings from a ten-year-old boy. It turns out that he had seen the Dior show on the telly. He did not want to go to sleep and stayed up until two in the morning drawing the clothes. His mother was first exasperated but then moved by his enthusiasm and she sent us the drawings. The drawings were so lovely; I was very touched. I invited the boy to the Dior show and met him afterwards. Something like this makes it all worth while **What's your definition of beauty?** A woman in charge of her own destiny **What is the most important lesson you've learned?** Mr Arnault once told me, "John, you have to learn to live with your critics." That was a very good lesson.

"I love fashion and I love making fashion"
JEAN PAUL GAULTIER + HERMÈS

The former 'enfant terrible' of French fashion is one of the most significant designers working today, his appeal bridging the elite and mass markets. On one hand, Jean Paul Gaultier is hailed as the saviour of haute couture (Gaultier Paris was launched 1997) and since 2004, has designed refined womenswear for Hermès, alongside his own well-established ready-to-wear label. On the other, he is one of the world's most famous living Frenchmen, partly due to a presenting job on the TV show Eurotrash in the early '90s (not to mention his personal fondness for striped Breton shirts and other Gallic clichés). Born in 1952, he was beguiled by fashion from a young age and would sketch showgirls from the Folies Bergère to impress his classmates. In the early '70s, he trained under Pierre Cardin and Jean Patou, eventually launching his own ready-to-wear collection in 1976. He soon became known for iconoclastic designs such as the male skirt, corsetry worn as outerwear and tattoo-printed body stockings. The classics of Parisian fashion are also central to his repertoire, particularly the trench coat and 'le smoking'. In 1998, he launched a diffusion line, Junior Gaultier (since replaced by JPG), followed by excursions into perfumes (1993) and film costume (notably for Luc Besson's 'The Fifth Element' and Peter Greenaway's 'The Cook, The Thief, His Wife and Her Lover'). But it was his wardrobe for Madonna's Blonde Ambition tour of 1990 that made him world-famous, in particular for a certain salmon-pink corset with conical bra cups. A celebrity and a genius possessed of both a piquant sense of humour and a deadly serious talent, in 2004 Gaultier staged a unique exhibition at the Fondation Cartier in Paris, entitled 'Pain Couture', that showcased clothing constructed entirely from bread. Gaultier celebrated his 30th anniversary as a fashion designer in 2006 with a fashion show in Paris recapping his greatest hits followed by magic show and party. Grace Coddington, Suzy Menkes, Hillary Alexander, Audrey Marnay, Lily Cole and Lucinda Chambers participated in magic tricks entertaining an audience of celebrities and journalists.

Das frühere Enfant terrible der französischen Mode ist einer der bedeutendsten Designer der Gegenwart, dem es gelingt, Eliteklientel und breite Masse gleichermaßen anzusprechen. Einerseits wurde Jean Paul Gaultier als Retter der Haute Couture gepriesen (Gaultier Paris existiert seit 1997) und entwirft seit 2004 neben seinem eigenen bestens eingeführten Prêt-à-porter-Label elegante Damenmode für Hermès. Andererseits ist er einer der berühmtesten Franzosen weltweit, nicht zuletzt dank seiner Moderation der Fernsehshow Eurotrash Anfang der 1990er-Jahre (von seiner Vorliebe für gestreifte bretonische Fischerhemden und andere gallische Klischees ganz zu schweigen). 1952 geboren, war er schon früh von Mode fasziniert und beeindruckte seine Klassenkameraden mit Zeichnungen der Tänzerinnen der Folies Bergère. In den frühen 1970er-Jahren lernte er bei Pierre Cardin und Jean Patou, bis er schließlich 1976 seine eigene Prêt-à-porter-Kollektion herausbrachte. Er erlangte bald Berühmtheit für ikonoklastische Entwürfe wie Männerröcke, Korsetts als Oberbekleidung und Bodystockings mit Tatoo-Muster. Aber auch die Klassiker der Pariser Mode sind aus seinem Repertoire nicht wegzudenken, insbesondere der Trenchcoat und der Smoking. 1998 gründete er die Nebenlinie Junior Gaultier (inzwischen ersetzt durch JPG), unternahm Ausflüge zu den Parfümeuren (1993) und in die Kostümbildnerei beim Film (für Luc Bessons „Das Fünfte Element" und für Peter Greenaways „Der Koch, der Dieb, seine Frau und ihr Liebhaber"). Weltberühmt machten ihn jedoch erst die Kostüme für Madonnas „Blonde Ambition"-Tour 1990, insbesondere das lachsrosa Korsett mit den konischen Körbchen. Inzwischen ist er selbst Promi und Genie, besessen von einem pikanten Sinn für Humor und todernstem Talent. 2004 präsentierte er in der Pariser Fondation Cartier eine einzigartige Ausstellung unter dem Titel „Pain Couture" mit Kleidungsstücken, die ausschließlich aus Brot gefertigt waren. Sein 30-jähriges Jubiläum als Modedesigner feierte Gaultier 2006 mit einer Modenschau in Paris, auf der man seine größten Erfolge rekapitulierte und anschließend eine Zauberschau und Party erlebte. Grace Coddington, Suzy Menkes, Hillary Alexander, Audrey Marnay, Lily Cole und Lucinda Chambers beteiligten sich an Zaubertricks, die ein Publikum von Prominenten und Journalisten unterhielten.

L'ancien «enfant terrible» de la mode française reste l'un des plus importants couturiers actuellement en exercice, capable de bâtir un pont entre le marché du luxe et celui de la grande consommation. D'une part, Jean Paul Gaultier est acclamé comme le sauveur de la haute couture (la collection Gaultier Paris a été lancée en 1997) et depuis 2004, il dessine également une ligne pour femme très raffinée chez Hermès, en plus de sa propre griffe de prêt-à-porter déjà bien établie. D'autre part, c'est aussi l'un des Français vivants les plus connus au monde, en grande partie grâce à son job de présentateur dans l'émission de télé Eurotrash au début des années 90 (sans parler de sa passion pour les pulls rayés bretons et autres clichés gaulois). Né en 1952, il s'intéresse très tôt à la mode et dessine des danseuses des Folies Bergère pour impressionner ses petits camarades de classe. Au début des années 70, il entame sa formation auprès de Pierre Cardin et de Jean Patou, avant de lancer sa propre collection de prêt-à-porter en 1976. Il se fait rapidement remarquer par ses créations iconoclastes comme la jupe pour homme, le corset porté en vêtement de dessus et les collants de corps imprimés de tatouages. Les classiques de la mode parisienne occupent aussi un rôle central dans son répertoire, en particulier le trench-coat et le smoking. En 1998, il crée Junior Gaultier, une ligne de diffusion (remplacée depuis par JPG) suivie par le lancement de plusieurs parfums (1993), puis par la création de costumes pour le cinéma (pour «Le Cinquième Elément» de Luc Besson et «Le Cuisinier, le Voleur, sa Femme et son Amant» de Peter Greenaway, entre autres). Mais ce sont les costumes dessinés en 1990 pour la tournée Blonde Ambition de Madonna qui lui valent sa notoriété mondiale, notamment un certain corset rose saumon à bonnets coniques. Star et génie doté d'un sens de l'humour piquant et d'un talent incontestable, Gaultier a organisé en 2004 une exposition exclusive à la Fondation Cartier de Paris : baptisée «Pain Couture», elle présentait des vêtements entièrement faits de pain. En 2006, il a célébré ses 30 ans de carrière lors d'un défilé parisien qui présentait ses plus grandes créations, suivi d'un kitschissime spectacle de magie et d'une grande fête. Grace Coddington, Suzy Menkes, Hillary Alexander, Audrey Marnay, Lily Cole et Lucinda Chambers ont toutes participé aux tours de magie pour divertir un public composé de célébrités et de journalistes. SUSIE RUSHTON

PHOTOGRAPHY SØLVE SUNDSBØ. FASHION DIRECTOR EDWARD ENNINFUL. MODEL NAOMI CAMPBELL. MARCH 2009.

PHOTOGRAPHY DONALD CHRISTIE. STYLING KARL PLEWKA. SEPTEMBER 2001.

What are your signature designs? The corset is probably the thing I am known for **What are your favourite pieces from any of your collections?** Probably the ones that other people have liked most, because I do the collections for people to like. And through that, to like me. So I love the clothes which they love, because it makes me loved **What inspires you?** I think that to look is my biggest pleasure. Once I was in Ibiza, in a very, very bad club, and there was a live parrot in a cage. And I just looked at him for three hours. I wanted to absorb all the colours. And that inspired a dress in my first couture show. I had no photo, nothing but my memory. I truly love that **Who do you have in mind when you design?** Not one person, because I want to be open to difference. That would be too restrictive. I like very different types of people, different types of beauty, different types of living **Is the idea of creative collaboration important to you?** I enjoy collaboration… Exactly what kind of collaboration do you mean? **What has been the greatest influence on your career?** Seeing the scandal Yves Saint Laurent caused in the '70s was important, because he captured everything that I love – glamour and sexual aggressiveness and even political shock. It was all the things that ever made me dream about being a part of the world of fashion. What he did definitely influenced me later and also made me realise the point in fashion: that if you are too much in advance, it appears as a provocation **How have your own experiences affected your work as a designer?** I was quite rejected at school because, let's say, I was more effeminate. So I was always on my own, sketching. One time, when I was about seven, I saw the Folies Bergère on TV – the feathers, the fishnets – and I drew it at school the next day. The teacher, wanting to punish me, pinned it to my back and made me walk from class to class. But everyone was smiling. So I thought, well, people like you when you do your sketches. It comforted me and gave me a lot of confidence. After that I drew a lot of fishnets and feathers **Is designing difficult for you? If so, what drives you to continue?** I love fashion and I love making fashion. But to deal with problems of organisation is not exactly my cup of coffee **What's your definition of beauty?** I don't have one. You can find beauty everywhere **What's your philosophy?** In fashion, you are supposed to hate what you have loved before. I cannot do that. And I do not appreciate that part of the industry. It's a kind of snobbery. You feel like you have to hate something to show that you are a part of the new trend **What is the most important lesson you've learned?** To be yourself. I am still very shy; I suppose you'd say I have a complex that people only like me because of what I do.

"The history of the house is incredible, which means I can work with a lot of freedom"
NICOLAS GHESQUIÈRE · BALENCIAGA

When the great Cristobal Balenciaga closed the doors of his couture house in 1968, he lamented, "There is no one left worth dressing." For decades, the house lay dormant, until 26-year-old Frenchman Nicolas Ghesquière was appointed creative director of Balenciaga in 1997 after the departure of Josephus Thimister. Since 1995, Ghesquière had quietly freelanced for Balenciaga's licences. Three years later, Ghesquière won the Vogue/VH1 Avant Garde Designer of the Year Award. Suzy Menkes of 'The International Herald Tribune' called him "the most intriguing and original designer of his generation". Though relatively unknown when he was appointed to Balenciaga, Ghesquière's is a life in fashion. He won work placements at agnès b. and Corinne Cobson while still at school in Loudon, central France. At 19, he became an assistant designer to Gaultier and then Mugler, before a brief tenure as head designer at Trussardi. But his great achievement has been his revival of Balenciaga. His green silk crop combat pants for spring/summer 2002, were the most copied garment of the season and Neoprene mini skirts and dresses for spring/summer 2003 kept Balenciaga on the edge, creatively and commercially. In 2002, a menswear line was launched, a year after the house of Balenciaga was bought by the Gucci Group. For autumn/winter 2005, he showed A-line leather dresses trimmed with pale ostrich feathers and sleek tailoring fitted with chrome fastenings. He was elected as one of The 100 Most Influential People in the World by 'Time' magazine in 2006, and awarded the prestigious Insigne de Chevalier des Arts et des Lettres for his continued creativity in 2008. Under Ghesquière's influence, Balenciaga today includes seven extremely lusted-after diffusion lines: Balenciaga Edition, a collection of items inspired by Cristobal Balenciaga's haute couture archives Balenciaga Leather, Balenciaga Pants, Balenciaga Knits, Balenciaga Denim, Balenciaga Black Dress and Balenciaga Silk. Former Gucci CEO Domenico De Sole has said: 'Balenciaga has one fantastic asset. He's called Nicolas Ghesquière'.

Als der große Cristobal Balenciaga 1968 die Tore seines Couture-Hauses schloss, klagte er: „Es gibt niemanden mehr, der es wert wäre, eingekleidet zu werden." Danach lag das Modehaus jahrzehntelang in einer Art Dornröschenschlaf, bis der Franzose Nicolas Ghesquière 1997 nach dem Weggang von Josephus Thimister Chefdesigner von Balenciaga wurde. Bereits ab 1995 hatte Ghesquière im Stillen als freier Mitarbeiter für Balenciagas Lizenzmarken entworfen. Drei Jahre später gewann er den Avant Garde Designer of the Year Award von Vogue und VH1. Suzy Menkes von der International Herald Tribune nannte ihn „den faszinierendsten und originellsten Designer seiner Generation". Auch wenn er bei seiner Verpflichtung für Balenciaga noch relativ unbekannt war, drehte sich doch auch bis dahin schon sein ganzes Leben um Mode. Bereits während seiner Schulzeit im französischen Loudon ergatterte er Praktikumsplätze bei agnès b. und Corinne Cobson. Mit 19 assistierte er Gaultier, anschließend Thierry Mugler, dann folgte ein kurzes Intermezzo als Chefdesigner bei Trussardi. Seine größte Leistung bis dato ist jedoch die Wiederbelebung von Balenciaga. Die abgeschnittenen Army-Hosen aus grüner Seide für Frühjahr/Sommer 2002 gehörten zu den meistkopierten Kleidungsstücken der Saison. Die Miniröcke und -kleider aus Neopren für Frühjahr/Sommer 2003 sorgten dafür, dass Balen-

ciaga führend blieb – kreativ wie kommerziell. 2002 wurde erstmals eine Herrenkollektion präsentiert, ein Jahr später kaufte der Gucci-Konzern Balenciaga. Im Herbst/Winter 2005 zeigte Ghesquière Lederkleider in A-Form mit hellem Straußenfederbesatz, schmaler Silhouette und Verschlüssen aus Chrom. So wählte das Time Magazine ihn 2006 unter die 100 einflussreichsten Menschen der Welt. 2008 wurde er für seine unerschöpfliche Kreativität mit dem angesehenen Insigne de Chevalier des Arts et des Lettres ausgezeichnet. Ghesquières Einfluss verdankt Balenciaga heute sieben ausgesprochen gefragte Nebenlinien: Balenciaga Edition, eine von Cristobal Balenciagas Haute-Couture-Klassikern inspirierte Kollektion, Balenciaga Leather, Balenciaga Pants, Balenciaga Knits, Balenciaga Denim, Balenciaga Black Dress und Balenciaga Silk. Der ehemalige CEO von Gucci, Domenico De Sole, sagte einmal: „Balenciaga besitzt einen fantastischen Aktivposten. Er heißt Nicolas Ghesquière."

Quand le grand Cristobal Balenciaga ferme sa maison en 1968, il déplore que « plus personne ne mérite d'être habillé ». Pendant plusieurs décennies, la griffe semble plongée dans un sommeil de Belle au bois dormant jusqu'à ce que Nicolas Ghesquière, un jeune Français de 26 ans, soit nommé directeur de la création de Balenciaga en 1997, après le départ de Josephus Thimister. Depuis 1995, Ghesquière travaillait tranquillement comme styliste free-lance pour les collections sous licence de Balenciaga. Trois ans plus tard, il remporte le prix d'Avant Garde Designer of the Year décerné par Vogue et la chaîne VH1. Suzy Menkes de l'International Herald Tribune le considère alors comme « le créateur le plus fascinant et le plus original de sa génération ». Presque inconnu lorsqu'il a pris ses fonctions chez Balenciaga, Ghesquière revendiquait déjà un beau parcours dans la mode. Il avait suivi des stages chez agnès b. et Corinne Cobson alors qu'il était encore lycéen à Loudon dans le centre de la France. A 19 ans, il devient assistant-styliste chez Gaultier puis chez Mugler, avant de travailler pendant une brève période comme styliste principal chez Trussardi. Mais la renaissance de Balenciaga reste sa plus grande réalisation. Le treillis-pantacourt en soie verte de sa collection printemps/été 2002 devient le vêtement le plus copié de la saison ; quant aux minijupes et robes en néoprène du printemps/été 2003, elles placent Balenciaga au pinacle de la mode, tant sur le plan créatif que commercial. En 2002, Balenciaga lance une ligne pour homme, un an après le rachat de la maison par le groupe Gucci. Pour l'automne/hiver 2005, il présente des robes trapèze en cuir, ornées de plumes d'autruche aux couleurs pâles, ainsi que des tailleurs épurés dotés d'attaches en chrome. Elu parmi les « 100 personnes les plus influentes du monde » par le magazine Time en 2006, il a été distingué du prestigieux titre de Chevalier des Arts et des Lettres en 2008 en récompense de son inépuisable créativité. Grâce à sa contribution, Balenciaga commercialise désormais sept lignes de diffusion extrêmement convoitées : Balenciaga Edition, une collection de pièces inspirées par les archives haute couture de Cristobal Balenciaga, ainsi que Balenciaga Leather, Balenciaga Pants, Balenciaga Knits, Balenciaga Denim, Balenciaga Black Dress et Balenciaga Silk. Domenico De Sole, ancien PDG de Gucci, a un jour déclaré : « Balenciaga possède un atout fantastique. Il s'appelle Nicolas Ghesquière ». JAMES SHERWOOD

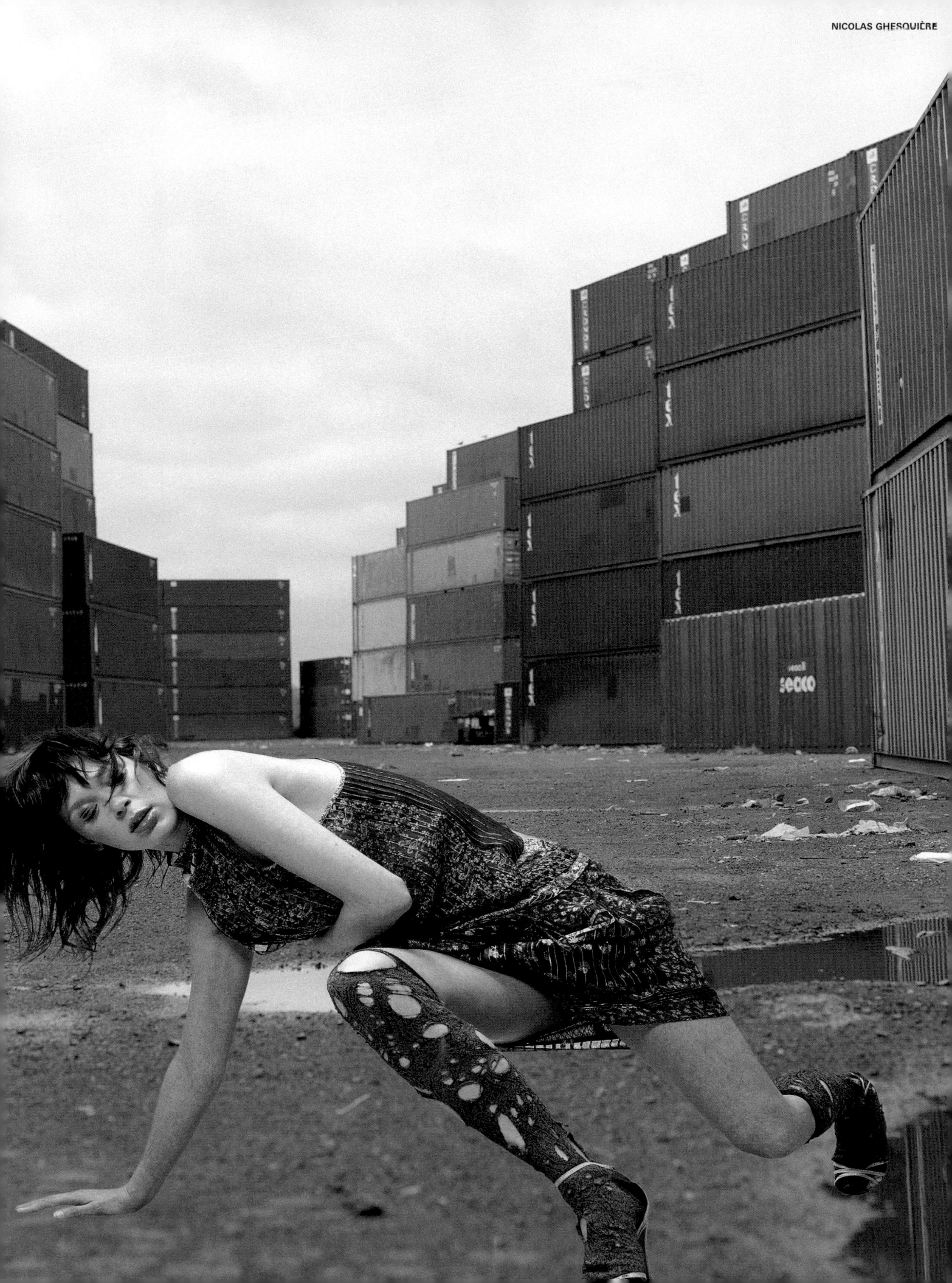

What are your signature designs? I can't define what I do and I don't really want to. If people interpret this or that in a certain way, it's fine. It's done for that reason – to be open **How would you describe your work?** What I do is always because of last season, not a reaction against it. I always want to find a surprising way to go, but beneath that, I want to try and say the same things **What's your ultimate goal?** I've never really wanted to be famous. That, for me, is not the intention **What inspires you?** I'm an '80s child, so it's completely natural for me to be inspired by that decade. I've always used those references. I think, in a way, you always have to use the same thing in fashion, but you must find a new way to tell it **Who do you have in mind when you design?** Any girl who puts on Balenciaga is a muse. I don't like to think of one in particular when I'm designing **How have your own experiences affected your work as a designer?** The history of the house is incredible, which means I can work with a lot of freedom. Cristobal Balenciaga discovered so many things, was so inventive, it's astonishing. I can work on something and then look back through the archives and find it already. I am very respectful of Balenciaga, but this is another time and it is my vision of what Balenciaga is now **What's your philosophy?** For me it's about evolution, not revolution **What is the most important lesson you've learned?** If you want to be happy, then keep yourself a little hidden.

"I think of a mood, a way of living, of certain needs"
FRIDA GIANNINI · GUCCI

In March 2005, Frida Giannini was charged with pushing Gucci, one of the most recognisable status labels of the late 20th century, into a new era. She is responsible for its high-profile accessories and womenswear collections, which has become synonymous with figure-hugging pencil skirts, glamorous sportswear and vixenish eveningwear, a look established by Gucci's former designer, Tom Ford, during the '90s. Established in 1921 by Guccio Gucci as a saddlery shop in Florence, the company had been a traditional family-run Italian business until Guccio's grandson Maurizio sold his final share of the brand in 1993. It was Guccio who first intertwined his initials to create the iconic logo. Yet until Tom Ford came along in the mid-'90s, the brand's image was lacklustre. In 2004, Ford exited Gucci, and new management filled his position not with a single designer but with a team of three, all of whom were promoted internally: John Ray for menswear, Alessandra Facchinetti for womenswear and Frida Giannini for accessories. In March 2005, Facchinetti also left Gucci, and Giannini was then also made responsible for women's clothing collections. Born in Rome in 1972, Giannini studied at the city's Fashion Academy; in 1997, she landed a job as ready-to-wear designer at Fendi, before first joining Gucci in 2002. Her 'Flora' collection of flowery-printed accessories was the commercial hit of 2004. By 2005, she was named creative director of Gucci Women's ready-to-wear. In 2006, she took over menswear. Frida has since put her distinctive stamp on the label, celebrating the house's inimitable past and expertise in luxury craftsmanship, while adding youth, colour and a playful extravagance. Giannini has also been integral in bringing celebrities to the brand – Drew Barrymore and Claire Danes for the jewellery campaigns, James Franco for fragrance, while working closely with Madonna and Rihanna on charitable initiatives.

Im März 2005 erhielt Frida Giannini den Auftrag, eines der bekanntesten Statuslabels des ausgehenden 20. Jahrhunderts in eine neue Ära zu führen. Sie ist zuständig für Guccis viel beachtete Accessoires sowie für die Damen-kollektionen, die für ihre figurbetonten Bleistiftröcke, glamouröse Sportswear und aggressive Abendmode bekannt ist. Diesen Look hatte der frühere Gucci-Designer Tom Ford etabliert. 1921 hatte Guccio Gucci die Firma in Florenz als Sattlerei gegründet. Und sie blieb auch ein traditioneller italienischer Familien-betrieb, bis Guccios Enkel Maurizio seine letzten Anteile an der Marke 1993 ver-kaufte. Doch war es bereits Guccio gewesen, der seine Initialen zum berühmten Logo zusammenfügte. Bis Tom Ford Mitte der Neunziger auf den Plan trat, war das Markenimage jedoch ziemlich glanzlos. 2004 verließ Ford Gucci. Das neue Management entschied sich bei der Nachfolge nicht für einen einzigen Designer, sondern für ein Dreierteam, dessen Mitglieder alle aus dem eigenen Haus stammten: John Ray für die Herrenmode, Alessandra Facchinetti für die Damen-mode und Frida Giannini für die Accessoires. Als Facchinetti im März 2005 das Unternehmen verließ, übernahm Giannini die Damenmode noch mit. Giannini

wurde 1971 in Rom geboren und studierte an der dortigen Modeakademie. 1997 erhielt sie bei Fendi den Job der Designerin für Prêt-à-porter. 2002 fing sie dann bei Gucci an. Dort landete sie mit ihrer blumenbedruckten Kollektion Flora den kommerziellen Hit des Jahres 2004. 2005 wurde sie Creative Director von Guccis Prêt-à-porter für Damen. 2006 übernahm sie auch die Menswear. Seither hat Frida Giannini das Label auf unübersehbare Weise geprägt, indem sie die unnachahmliche Vergangenheit und Erfahrung in luxuriöser Handwerkskunst feiert und zugleich Jugendlichkeit, Farbe und eine ausgelassene Extravaganz ins Spiel bringt. Giannini war auch dafür verantwortlich, Prominente an die Marke zu binden – Drew Barrymore und Claire Danes für die Schmuck-Kampagnen oder James Franco für den Duft. Gleichzeitig arbeitet sie eng mit Madonna und Rihanna an Wohltätigkeitsprojekten zusammen.

En mars 2005, Frida Giannini se voit confier la mission de faire entrer Gucci, l'une des griffes les plus incontournables de la fin du XXᵉ siècle, dans une nouvelle ère. Elle y est responsable des collections pour femme et des lignes d'accessoires de luxe, qui est surtout connue pour ses jupes droites moulantes, son sportswear glamour et ses tenues de soirée archi-sexy, un look établi par Tom Ford, anciennement styliste de Gucci. La petite boutique de sellier fondée en 1921 à Florence par Guccio Gucci reste une affaire familiale traditionnelle à l'italienne jusqu'à ce que Maurizio, petit-fils de Guccio, revende sa dernière part de l'entreprise en 1993. C'est Guccio le premier qui a entrecroisé ses initiales pour produire le logo signature. Mais jusqu'à l'arrivée de Tom Ford au milieu des années 90, l'image de la marque manquait sérieusement de lustre. En 2004, Tom Ford quitte Gucci. La nouvelle équipe de direction le remplace non pas par un nouveau créateur, mais par une écurie de trois stylistes, tous promus en interne : John Ray à la mode masculine, Alessandra Facchinetti à la collection pour femme et Frida Giannini aux accessoires. En mars 2005, Alessandra Facchinetti quitte également Gucci et c'est désormais Frida Giannini, qui dirige les collections pour femme. Née en 1972 à Rome, Frida Giannini étudie à l'Académie de mode de la ville ; en 1997, elle décroche un poste de styliste en prêt-à-porter chez Fendi, puis rejoint Gucci en 2002. Sa collection « Flora » aux imprimés floraux s'impose comme le grand succès de l'année 2004, et en 2005, elle est nommée directrice de la création du prêt-à-porter Gucci pour femme, puis pour homme en 2006. Depuis, Frida Giannini imprime son style bien particulier à la griffe en célébrant le passé inimitable de la maison et son expertise du luxe artisanal tout en lui insufflant plus de jeunesse, de couleur et une extravagance ludique. Frida Giannini a aussi joué un rôle crucial pour attirer les célébrités vers la marque : Drew Barrymore et Claire Danes ont prêté leurs visages aux campagnes publicitaires pour les bijoux, et James Franco aux parfums. De plus, elle travaille étroitement avec Madonna et Rihanna sur des projets caritatifs.

SUSIE RUSHTON

PHOTOGRAPHY IAN McFELL STYLING MAY PEARMAN MODEL JOSH BIDELL FEBRUARY 2009

PHOTOGRAPHY TODD COLE. STYLING BENJAMIN STURGILL. MODEL NOREEN. JULY 2007.

How would you describe your work? Great research. Necessary adaptation. Fabulous team work. Very hard work. Reflection. Attention to what is happening in the world. Great results **Can fashion still have a political ambition?** Fashion and politics do not go hand in hand, but generally speaking, I believe that fashion can reflect the sociological mood of the moment **What is your ultimate goal?** I have many. One of the most important is to live in harmony with myself and with others **What inspires you?** Jackie Kennedy Onassis, who, to me, is the ultimate in elegance **What do you have in mind when you design?** I think of a mood, a way of living, of certain needs of women and men. The possibility to link the history of the Gucci brand, of Gucci's iconic pieces, with contemporary design and styles **Who has been the greatest influence on your career?** My passion. My family. My drive. Music. The world of vintage **Have you ever been influenced or moved by reactions to your design?** All reactions from the 'public', whether positive or negative, can only be productive and open 'new roads' for the next direction **How have your own experiences affected your work as a designer?** Through my experience, I have learnt to become a leader, and have learnt how important communicating, expressing and listening is within your own team. I am not afraid to say the final 'yes' or to say the final 'no' **Which is more important in your work: the process or the product?** Definitely both. And the harmony that exists between the two. Always with the utmost respect for the brand **What is your definition of beauty?** Beauty is very subjective and personal, and I believe that when something gives pleasure to your eyes and to your soul… well, that's beautiful.

"Every experience permanently alters the way you perceive beauty"
KATHARINE HAMNETT

For many fans, Katharine Hamnett defines '80s style. Her trademark use of functional fabrics such as parachute silk and cotton jersey has continued to inspire many in the industry since. She spearheaded a number of style directions, including the military look, utility fashion and casual day-to-evening sportswear, all of which still resonate today. And 21 years after her logo T-shirts first became front-page news (in 1984, she famously met Mrs Thatcher and wore one that read: '58% Don't Want Pershing'), Hamnett can still make the fashion world sit up and pay attention to her ideas. Born in 1948, she graduated from Central Saint Martins in 1969 and freelanced for ten years before setting up her own label, Katharine Hamnett London. This was followed in 1981 by menswear and a denim diffusion range in 1982. She became the BFC's Designer of the Year in 1984 and her ad campaigns helped to launch the careers of photographers including Juergen Teller, Terry Richardson and Ellen von Unwerth. Projects such as her flagship stores in London's Brompton Cross and Sloane Street, designed by Norman Foster, Nigel Coates and David Chipperfield, were famous for their forward-thinking retail design. A political conscience has always been key to the Katharine Hamnett ethos. She created antiwar T-shirts ('Life is Sacred') in 2003 that were widely worn by peace protesters marching in London; Naomi Campbell modelled a 'Use a Condom' design for Hamnett's spring/ summer 2004 catwalk show in order to highlight the designer's concern over the AIDS epidemic in Africa. She decided to relaunch as Katharine E Hamnett for autumn/winter 2005 and often continues to voice her concerns about unethical and non-environmental manufacturing processes. In 2007, she was appointed professor at the University of the Arts London and launched a line of ethically and environmentally mined gold and diamond jewellery with Cred Jewellery.

Für viele Fans verkörpert Katharine Hamnett den Stil der 1980er-Jahre. Ihr Markenzeichen ist die Verwendung funktionaler Materialien wie Fallschirm-seide und Baumwolljersey, womit sie seither viele in der Modeindustrie inspi-riert hat. Sie war Vorkämpferin für viele Stilrichtungen wie etwa den Military Look, Utility Fashion und lässige Sportswear für tagsüber und abends. All diese Trends wirken bis heute fort. Und selbst 21 Jahre, nachdem sie mit ihren „Slogan"-T-Shirts erstmals Schlagzeilen machte (unvergessen, wie sie 1984 bei einem Treffen mit Margaret Thatcher ein T-Shirt mit dem Aufdruck „58% Don't Want Pershing" trug), gelingt es Hamnett immer noch, in der Modewelt für Aufmerksamkeit zu sorgen. Die 1948 geborene Designerin machte 1969 ihren Abschluss am Central Saint Martins. Danach war sie zehn Jahre lang freischaffend tätig, bevor sie ihr eigenes Label – Katharine Hamnett London – gründete. 1981 kam Herrenmode dazu, 1982 eine Nebenlinie für Jeans. Den Titel BFC's Designer of The Year erhielt Hamnett 1984. Nebenbei beflügelten ihre Werbekampagnen auch die Karrieren von Fotografen wie Jürgen Teller, Terry Richardson und Ellen von Unwerth. Projekte wie ihre Londoner Flagship Stores in Brompton Cross und der Sloane Street nach Entwürfen von Norman Foster, Nigel Coates und David Chipperfield erregten durch ihr innovatives

Ladenkonzept Aufsehen. Katharine Hamnetts Ethos war schon immer von politischem Bewusstsein geprägt. So kreierte sie T-Shirts gegen den Krieg („Life is Sacred"), die 2003 unter den Londoner Friedensdemonstranten sehr verbrei-tet waren. In Hamnetts Catwalk Show für Frühjahr/Sommer 2004 präsentierte Naomi Campbell den Schriftzug „Use a Condom", um die Betroffenheit der Designerin angesichts der Ausmaße der Aids-Epidemie in Afrika zum Ausdruck zu bringen. Für die Kollektion Herbst/Winter 2005 entschloss sie sich zu einem Relaunch ihres Labels unter dem Namen Katharine E Hamnett und kritisiert nach wie vor unmoralische und umweltschädliche Produktionsbedingungen. 2007 wurde sie als Professorin an die University of the Arts in London berufen und brachte außerdem zusammen mit Cred Jewellery eine Linie für Gold- und Diamantschmuck auf den Markt, deren Ausgangsprodukte nach ethischen und ökologischen Gesichtspunkten einwandfrei sind.

Aux yeux de ses nombreux fans, Katharine Hamnett est «la» créatrice des années 80. Son utilisation caractéristique de tissus utilitaires tels que les soies de parachute et le jersey de coton continue depuis à inspirer bon nombre de stylistes. Elle a lancé de nombreuses tendances, notamment le look militaire, la mode utilitaire et un sportswear décontracté à porter le jour comme le soir, autant d'innovations qui résonnent encore de nos jours. 21 ans après que ses T-shirts à slogan aient fait la une des journaux (en 1984, elle a rencontré Margaret Thatcher vêtue d'un T-shirt proclamant : «58% Don't Want Pershing»), Katharine Hamnett peut encore étonner l'univers de la mode et attirer l'attention sur ses idées. Née en 1948, elle sort diplômée de Central Saint Martins en 1969 et travaille en free-lance pendant 10 ans avant de fonder sa propre griffe, Katharine Hamnett London, qui sera suivie d'une ligne pour homme en 1981 et d'une autre collection en denim en 1982. Elle est nommée British Designer of the Year en 1984, et ses campagnes publicitaires donnent un coup de pouce aux carrières des photographes Juergen Teller, Terry Richardson et Ellen von Unwerth. Des projets tels que ses boutiques de Brompton Cross et Sloane Street à Londres, conçues par Norman Foster, Nigel Coates et David Chipperfield, deviennent célèbres pour leur conception visionnaire en matière d'espace de vente. Une certaine conscience politique occupe toujours une place centrale dans l'éthique de Katharine Hamnett. En 2003, elle a créé des T-shirts anti-guerre («La vie est sacrée») largement portés par les défenseurs de la paix qui manifestaient à Londres; lors de son défilé printemps/été 2004, Naomi Campbell arborait un T-shirt proclamant «Use a Condom» afin d'exprimer les inquiétudes de la créatrice quant à l'épidémie du sida en Afrique. Pour la saison automne/hiver 2005, elle décide de relancer sa griffe sous le nom de «Katharine E Hamnett» et continue à clamer son inquiétude face aux procédés de fabrication non équitables et nuisibles à l'environnement. En 2007, elle est devenue professeur à l'University of the Arts de Londres et a lancé avec Cred Jewellery une collection de bijoux fabriqués à partir d'or et de diamants extraits dans le respect des règles éthiques et environnementales.

TERRY NEWMAN

What are your signature designs? Nice clothes you don't throw away **What is your favourite piece from any of your collections?** I am not interested in what I have done before **How would you describe your work?** Creating a fresh persona **What's your ultimate goal?** Reforesting the desert **What inspires you?** Banishing ugliness, not having anything to wear. Being horrified by the clothes your date is wearing **Can fashion still have a political ambition?** Yes, industry runs the planet and the fashion industry is the fourth largest. How we design and consume fashion to an extent decides our future **Who do you have in mind when you design?** Myself, my friends, beautiful strangers **Is the idea of creative collaboration important to you?** No, I'm a loner with occasional exceptions, design by committee is death **Who has been the greatest influence on your career?** My parents, movies and everybody I've ever met or read **How have your own experiences affected your work as a designer?** Every experience permanently alters the way you perceive beauty **Which is more important in your work: the process or the product?** The idea **Is designing difficult for you? If so, what drives you to continue?** It's easy when you're happy. Bills and the fact that every thousand pair of organic cotton trousers we sell means another African farmer can convert from pesticide intensive farming to growing cotton organically which has the potential to deliver a 50 per cent increase in income as well as huge health benefits **Have you ever been influenced or moved by the reaction to your designs?** I am really touched by people who keep on contacting us and say that I made the best pair of trousers they ever had or Andy Birkin at the Stop the War Coalition telling me that the marches they organised all over the world against the invasion of Iraq, came from the T-shirts we did straight after September 11th after Bush declared "The War on Terror": Stop and Think, No War, Life is Sacred **What's your definition of beauty?** The outward appearance of an inner quality **What's your philosophy?** If you take on something, you have to do it with a passion, to the best of your ability or not at all **What is the most important lesson you've learned?** Fame is a mistake, thank God I always wore dark glasses in the '80s so nobody recognises me.

"I work on the cut"
ANNE VALÉRIE HASH

Anne Valérie Hash is a thoroughly modern couturière. Known for her virtuoso cutting skills, Hash transforms pieces of classic men's tailoring into elegant and unusual womenswear. For example, a man's white shirt is upended to become a sculpted blouse, or pleated pinstriped trousers are deconstructed to become a strapless dress. Hash, who was born in Paris in 1971, was one of the first of a younger generation of designers to be invited to show during haute couture week, despite being unable to fulfil all the traditional requirements for qualification as an haute couture house. She made her debut in July 2001. Before this, Hash had studied at both the Ecole des Arts Appliqués Duperré (1992) and the prestigious Ecole de la Chambre Syndicale de la Couture Parisienne (1995). She also completed internships at Nina Ricci, Chloé, Christian Lacroix and Chanel – the latter a particular high point for Hash, who has been constantly rereading the biography of Coco Chanel since the age of 18. From her first collection, Hash has demonstrated how the refined handcraft techniques of haute couture can be applied to an aesthetic that has more in common with Martin Margiela than Valentino. In recent seasons, Hash has softened her androgynous look to allow for the inclusion of more obviously romantic pieces such as layered tulle dresses – an aesthetic also seen in her handbags line (launched in 2007) and Anne Valérie Hash Mademoiselle collection for girls aged 4 to 14 (2008). However, the skeleton of her garments – their bindings, linings and seams – remain deliberately exposed, the result of her investigations into tailoring. Hash has further expanded into shoes (2006) and a capsule collection called 'Dress Me' (2007). In January 2009, Hash was honoured with the L'Ordre des Arts et des Lettres from France's Ministry of Culture.

Anne Valérie Hash ist eine durch und durch moderne Couturière. Berühmt für ihre virtuosen Schnitte, transformiert sie Kleidungsstücke aus der klassischen Herrenschneiderei zu eleganter und außergewöhnlicher Damenmode. Da wird beispielsweise ein weißes Herrenhemd zur skulpturalen Bluse umgestülpt oder eine Nadelstreifenhose mit Bügelfalte zum schulterfreien Kleid umgeschneidert. Die 1971 in Paris geborene Hash war eine der Ersten einer jüngeren Designergeneration, die man einlud, bei der Haute-Couture-Woche zu präsentieren, auch wenn sie nicht alle traditionellen Anforderungen erfüllte, um als echtes Haute-Couture-Haus zu gelten. Ihr Debüt gab sie im Juli 2001. Zuvor hatte Hash sowohl an der Ecole des Arts Appliqués Duperré (1992) als auch an der angesehenen Ecole de la Chambre Syndicale de la Couture Parisienne (1995) studiert. Sie absolvierte auch Praktika bei Nina Ricci, Chloé, Christian Lacroix und Chanel. Wobei Chanel einen besonderen Höhepunkt für Hash darstellte, weil sie sich schon seit ihrem 18. Lebensjahr intensiv mit Coco Chanels Biografie auseinandergesetzt hatte. Bereits mit ihrer ersten Kollektion bewies die Designerin,

dass die raffinierten handwerklichen Techniken der Haute Couture sich auf eine Ästhetik anwenden lassen, die mehr mit Martin Margiela als mit Valentino verbindet. In den letzten Saisons hat Hash ihren androgynen Look etwas abgemildert und sich auch eindeutig romantische Kreationen wie mehrlagige Tüllkleider gestattet. Diese Ästhetik findet man übrigens auch in ihren Handtaschenkollektionen (seit 2007) sowie bei Anne Valérie Hash Mademoiselle für Mädchen von 4 bis 14 Jahren (2008). Das Gerüst ihrer Kleidung – Einfassungen, Futter und Säume – bleibt jedoch bewusst sichtbar, sozusagen als Ergebnis ihrer Recherchen in der hohen Schneiderkunst. Hash hat ihre Produktpalette seit 2006 um Schuhe erweitert und entwirft zudem eine Extra-Kollektion namens Dress Me (2007). Im Januar 2009 ehrte das französische Kultusministerium sie mit dem Ordre des Arts et des Lettres.

Anne Valérie Hash est une couturière résolument moderne. Réputée pour ses coupes virtuoses, elle transforme les pièces du costume classique pour homme en vêtements pour femme élégants et insolites. Par exemple, elle renverse une chemise blanche masculine pour la transformer en un sculptural chemisier, ou déconstruit un pantalon mille-raies à pinces pour en faire une robe bustier. Née en 1971 à Paris, Anne Valérie Hash figure parmi la nouvelle génération de créateurs invités à défiler pendant la semaine de la haute couture, bien qu'elle ne soit pas en mesure de satisfaire à tous les critères traditionnels requis pour être officiellement qualifiée de styliste de haute couture. Elle fait ses débuts en juillet 2001, après avoir étudié à l'Ecole des Arts Appliqués Duperré (1992) et dans la prestigieuse Ecole de la Chambre Syndicale de la Couture Parisienne (1995). Elle effectue également des stages chez Nina Ricci, Chloé, Christian Lacroix et surtout Chanel, grande source d'inspiration pour elle, qui depuis l'âge de 18 ans ne cesse de relire la biographie de Coco Chanel. Depuis sa première collection, Anne Valérie Hash démontre comment les techniques artisanales raffinées de la haute couture peuvent être appliquées à une esthétique plus proche de Martin Margiela que de Valentino. Ces dernières saisons, elle a atténué son look androgyne pour permettre l'introduction de pièces franchement plus romantiques, telles que ses robes composées de plusieurs couches de tulle, une approche esthétique que l'on retrouve dans sa ligne de sacs à main (lancée en 2007) et la collection Anne Valérie Hash Mademoiselle destinées aux filles de 4 à 14 ans (2008). Toutefois, l'ossature de ses vêtements (leurs points de liage, leurs doublures et leurs coutures) reste délibérément exposée, conséquence de ses recherches sur la coupe. Anne Valérie Hash a poursuivi sa diversification à travers une ligne de chaussures (2006) et une mini-collection baptisée Dress Me (2007). En janvier 2009, le ministère français de la Culture l'a décorée de l'Ordre des Arts et des Lettres.

SUSIE RUSHTON

What are your signature designs? A pant-dress mixture of femininity and masculinity **What is your favourite piece from any of your collections?** Lace dress, it is my contradiction **How would you describe your work?** I work on the cut **What's your ultimate goal?** Jocker **What inspires you?** My muse Lou Lisa Lesage was ten years old when we started my work and she is now almost 13. She inspires me. We work as we play **Can fashion still have a political ambition?** Yes, to start with pants for women were a revolution. To stop wearing the corset was also a new way to see women. The best example is the tiny shoes that the Chinese women had to wear during the last century in order to get married — we used to teach them that small feet were more precious! **Who do you have in mind when you design?** It depends on the season **Is the idea of creative collaboration important to you?** Yes, I love to collaborate with different illuminated spirits **Who has been the greatest influence on your career?** Fontana, the artist **How have your own experiences affected your work as a designer?** It is not so clear yet **Which is more important in your work: the process or the product?** The product is the result of the process, the product is what you see at the end **Is designing difficult for you? If so, what drives you to continue?** My team **Have you ever been influenced or moved by the reaction to your designs?** Each season I move to another reflection **What's your definition of beauty?** The heart hides the absolute beauty **What's your philosophy?** CUT **What is the most important lesson you've learned?** To stay simple — I could die any minute — so stay calm and enjoy being alive. To do what I love.

"We don't design things we would not need if we were the client"
DESIRÉE HEISS & INES KAAG · BLESS

Whether Bless counts as a fashion label at all is a moot point. Preferring to describe their venture as "a project that presents ideal and artistic values to the public via products", Desirée Heiss (born 1971) and Ines Kaag (born 1970) formed Bless in 1995, positioning themselves as a collaborative experiment in fashion. The business is split between two European capitals: Heiss, who graduated from the University of Applied Arts in Vienna in 1994, is based in Paris, while Kaag, who graduated from the University of Arts and Design in Hanover in 1995, is based in Berlin. The two met by chance when their work was shown adjacently at a Paris design competition. The Bless modus operandi is to re-invent existing objects to produce new garments and accessories that are released in quarterly limited editions and are available through subscription. Their work has included fur wigs for Martin Margiela's autumn/winter 1997 collection, customisable trainers for Jean Colonna and the creation of 'Human-Interior-Wear' for Levi's. While these all function as wearable garments, many of their products cross entirely into the realm of art. 'Embroidered Flowers', for instance, is a series of photographic prints, while their 'Hairbrush Beauty-Product' (a brush with human hair for bristles) is closer to the work of Joseph Beuys or Marcel Duchamp than that of any fashion designer. Consequently, when the 'Bless Shop' goes on tour, it visits Europe's alternative galleries, rather than department stores. Heiss and Kaag's success is in providing a unique comment on fashion that can also (usually) be worn. For their autumn/winter 2009 presentation in a disused restaurant, models banged out a beat on ten classic drum kits while circulating among the spectators.

Ob man Bless überhaupt zu den Modelabels zählen kann, ist umstritten. Desirée Heiss (Jahrgang 1971) und Ines Kaag (Jahrgang 1970) bezeichnen ihr Unternehmen lieber als „ein Projekt, das der Öffentlichkeit mittels Produkten ideelle und künstlerische Werte präsentiert". Sie gründeten Bless 1995 und positionierten sich selbst als kollaboratives Modeexperiment. Das Unternehmen ist auf zwei europäische Hauptstädte aufgeteilt: Heiss, die 1994 ihren Abschluss an der Wiener Universität für angewandte Kunst machte, ist in Paris stationiert, während Kaag, die an der Fachhochschule für Kunst und Design in Hannover studiert hat, von Berlin aus arbeitet. Kennen gelernt haben sich die beiden per Zufall, als ihre Arbeiten bei einem Pariser Designwettbewerb nebeneinander ausgestellt waren. Das Konzept von Bless besteht darin, bereits existierende Objekte neu zu erfinden. Diese Kleidungsstücke oder Accessoires werden vierteljährlich in limitierten Auflagen an Abonnenten verkauft. Zu ihren bisherigen Arbeiten gehören Pelzperücken für Martin Margielas Kollektion Herbst/Winter 1997, „verstellbare" Turnschuhe für Jean Colonna und eine Kreation namens

„Human Interior Wear" für Levi's. Die genannten Produkte lassen sich alle tragen, während viele andere reine Kunstobjekte sind. So etwa die Fotoserie „Embroidered Flowers". Mit ihrem „Hairbrush Beauty-Product" (einer Art Bürste mit „Borsten" aus Menschenhaar) nähern sich Heiss und Kaag mehr als jeder andere Modedesigner den Arbeiten von Joseph Beuys oder Marcel Duchamp an. Da ist es nur folgerichtig, dass man den „Bless Shop" auf Tour eher in Europas alternativen Galerien als in Kaufhäusern antrifft. Der Erfolg des Labels liegt wohl darin begründet, dass es einzigartige Kommentare zur Mode abgibt, die man (meistens) sogar anziehen kann. Bei der Präsentation für Herbst/Winter 2009 in einem nicht mehr genutzten Restaurant traktierten die Models zehn klassische Schlagzeuge, während sie sich zwischen den Zuschauern bewegten.

Peut-on vraiment considérer Bless comme une marque de mode ? Desirée Heiss (née en 1971) et Ines Kaag (née en 1970) décrivent plutôt leur association comme « un projet présentant au public des valeurs idéales et artistiques par le biais de produits ». Elles créent Bless en 1995 dans l'optique d'une collaboration expérimentale autour de la mode. Leur activité se divise entre deux capitales européennes : Desirée Heiss, diplômée de l'Université des Arts appliqués de Vienne en 1994, travaille à Paris, tandis qu'Ines Kaag, diplômée de l'Université des Arts et du Design de Hanovre en 1995, est installée à Berlin. Elles se sont rencontrées par hasard à Paris lors d'un concours de design où leurs travaux respectifs étaient présentés côte à côte. Le modus operandi de Bless consiste à réinventer des objets existants pour produire de nouveaux vêtements et accessoires, commercialisés chaque trimestre en édition limitée et uniquement sur abonnement. Entre autres, elles ont créé des perruques en fourrure pour la collection automne/hiver 1997 de Martin Margiela, des tennis personnalisables pour Jean Colonna et travaillé sur un concept de « Human-Interior-Wear » pour Levi's. Bien que toutes ces pièces soient portables, la plupart de leurs produits s'apparentent entièrement au domaine de l'art. Par exemple, « Embroidered Flowers » est une série d'impressions photographiques, tandis que leur « Hairbrush Beauty-Product » (une brosse en cheveux humains) relève davantage du travail de Joseph Beuys ou de Marcel Duchamp que de la pure création de mode. Quand le « Bless Shop » part en tournée, il préfère donc faire étape dans les galeries d'art alternatives d'Europe plutôt que dans les grands magasins. Le succès de Desirée Heiss et d'Ines Kaag repose avant tout sur leur approche unique d'une mode que on peut aussi porter, la plupart du temps. Organisée dans un restaurant désaffecté, leur présentation automne/hiver 2009 a vu les mannequins circuler parmi le public et battre chacune un temps sur dix caisses claires.

MARK HOOPER

"The collection has so many different components. But that's how we design and how people dress - with intellect, with spirit and an eye for the mix"
LAZARO HERNANDEZ & JACK MCCOLLOUGH · PROENZA SCHOULER

Lazaro Hernandez and Jack McCollough are the American duo behind Proenza Schouler. The label has secured accounts with the world's most exclusive stores, won a Council of Fashion Designers of America (CFDA) award for new talent and, for many, has put the New York collections back on the must-see fashion map. Its fans include American Vogue's editor Anna Wintour and her super-chic French counterpart Carine Roitfeld. All this has been achieved within the space of a few seasons. Both born in 1978, Hernandez, who was born in Miami of Spanish Cuban heritage, and McCollough, who was born in Tokyo and raised in New Jersey, first met at Parson's College in New York City. After Hernandez completed an internship at Michael Kors (on Anna Wintour's recommendation) and McCollough at Marc Jacobs, they made the unusual decision of working together on their senior collection. Winning the Designer of the Year award at Parson's student show and with their whole graduation collection snapped up by Barneys, Hernandez and McCollough quickly had to find a name. They came up with the nom de plume Proenza Schouler, combining each of their mothers' maiden names. Since then, Proenza Schouler have become part of a new breed of American designers who are choosing polish and sincere sophistication over grunge and thrift store irony, quickly perfecting a style that is particular to New York: a blend of tailored uptown glamour with sporty downtown nonchalance. Inspired by '50s couture – Christian Dior, Cristobal Balenciaga and Coco Chanel – and pictures by Avedon and Penn, Proenza Schouler's signatures include their play with proportion, bolero jackets, bustiers and heavily worked detailing – a fusion of old-world luxury and new-world lifestyle. In 2004, the duo scooped the first-ever Vogue/CFDA Fashion Fund award, winning a $200,000 cash prize and business mentoring. In 2007, the duo received the esteemed award of CFDA Womenswear Designer of the Year award. Only a few months later, Proenza Schouler partnered with Valentino Fashion Group SpA.

Lazaro Hernandez und Jack McCollough sind das amerikanische Duo hinter Proenza Schouler. Das Label hat sich seinen Platz in den exklusivsten Läden der Welt gesichert, einen Preis des Council of Fashion Designers of America (CFDA) für neue Talente gewonnen und in den Augen vieler den New Yorker Kollektionen zu neuem Ansehen in der Modebranche verholfen. Zu den Fans gehören die Herausgeberin der amerikanischen Vogue, Anna Wintour, und deren französischer super-schicker Widerpart Carine Roitfeld. All das erreichte man innerhalb weniger Saisons. Hernandez, 1978 als Kind spanisch-kubanischer Eltern in Miami geboren, und der im selben Jahr in Tokio geborene, in New Jersey aufgewachsene McCollough lernten sich am Parson's College in New York kennen. Nachdem Hernandez (auf Empfehlung von Anna Wintour) ein Praktikum bei Michael Kors und McCollough eines bei Marc Jacobs absolviert hatte, fällten die beiden die ungewöhnliche Entscheidung, sich für ihre Abschlusskollektion zusammenzutun. Nachdem sie damit den Preis Designer of the Year bei der Studentenschau am Parson's gewonnen hatten und Barneys sich ihre komplette Kollektion gesichert hatte, mussten sich Hernandez und McCollough rasch einen Namen einfallen lassen. Sie kamen auf den Kunstnamen Proenza Schou-

ler, für den sie die Mädchennamen ihrer Mütter kombinierten. Seit damals ist Proenza Schouler Teil einer neuen Generation amerikanischer Designer, die strahlender echter Eleganz den Vorzug vor Grunge und Second-Hand-Ironie geben. Daraus entwickelte sich rasch ein Stil, der eng mit New York verbunden ist: ein Mix aus maßgeschneidertem Uptown-Glamour und sportlicher Downtown-Lässigkeit. Inspiriert von den Couturiers der 1950er-Jahre – Christian Dior, Cristobal Balenciaga und Coco Chanel – sowie den Bildern von Avedon und Penn, gehört das Spiel mit Proportionen, Bolerojäckchen, Bustiers und arbeitsaufwändige Details zu den Markenzeichen von Proenza Schouler. Kurz gesagt: eine Melange aus dem Luxus der Alten und dem Lifestyle der Neuen Welt. Im Jahr 2004 sicherte sich das Designerduo den erstmals ausgelobten Vogue/CFDA Fashion Fund, der 200.000 Dollar in bar und Business Mentoring umfass-te. Im Jahr 2007 verlieh die CFDA dem Designerduo den angesehenen Preis Womenswear Designer of the Year. Nur ein paar Monate später ging Proenza Schouler eine Partnerschaft mit der Valentino Fashion Group SpA ein.

Proenza Schouler est l'œuvre du duo américain formé par Lazaro Hernandez et Jack McCollough. Cette griffe vendue dans les boutiques les plus sélectives du monde leur a valu le prix du CFDA (Council of Fashion Designers of America) décerné aux nouveaux talents et beaucoup estiment qu'elle a contribué à remettre les collections new-yorkaises sur le devant de la scène. Proenza Schouler compte des fans tels que la rédactrice du Vogue américain Anna Wintour et son homologue française ultra-chic Carine Roitfeld, un exploit accompli en l'espace de quelques saisons seulement. Tous deux sont nés en 1978; Hernandez grandit à Miami dans une famille d'origine hispano-cubaine tandis que McCollough, né à Tokyo, grandit dans le New Jersey. Ils se rencontrent au Parson's College de New York et effectuent des stages pendant leurs études, Hernandez chez Michael Kors (sur les recommandations d'Anna Wintour) et McCollough chez Marc Jacobs. Contrairement aux habitudes, ils décident de travailler ensemble sur leur collection de fin d'études, avec un défilé couronné par le prix de Parson's Designer of the Year et une collection complète achetée par Barneys. Hernandez et McCollough doivent alors rapidement se trouver un nom de plume : ils optent pour Proenza Schouler, une combinaison des noms de jeune fille de leurs mères. Depuis, Proenza Schouler fait partie de la nouvelle génération de griffes américaines qui préfèrent la sophistication classe et sincère à l'ironie du grunge et du vintage, perfectionnant rapidement un style typiquement new-yorkais : coupes sophistiquées et glamour alliées à une nonchalance sport. Inspirées par la haute couture des années 50 (Christian Dior, Cristobal Balenciaga et Coco Chanel) comme par les photos d'Avedon et de Penn, les signatures de Proenza Schouler se distinguent par un jeu sur les proportions qui se décline dans des boléros, des bustiers et des détails très travaillés: une fusion entre luxe à l'ancienne et lifestyle du nouveau monde. En 2007, le duo a gagné le prix très convoité de Womenswear Designer of the Year remis par le CFDA. A peine quelques mois plus tard, Proenza Schouler s'associait avec Valentino Fashion Group SpA.

JAMIE HUCKBODY

PHOTOGRAPHY TERRY RICHARDSON. STYLING MEL OTTENBERG. MODELS LAZARO HERNANDEZ, KATE BOSWORTH AND JACK MCCOLLOUGH. SEPTEMBER 2007.

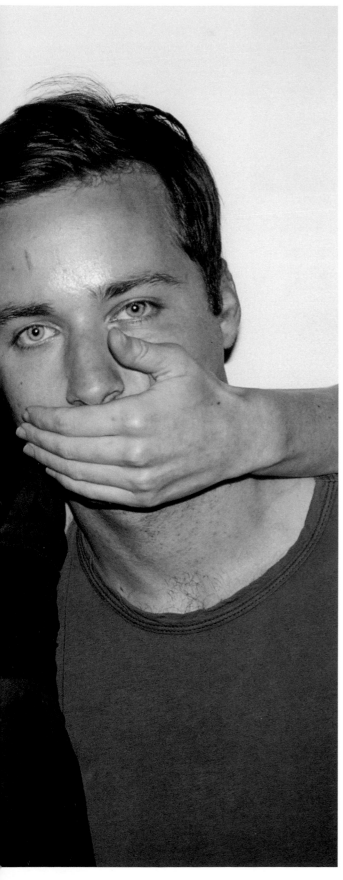

What are your signature designs? Many would say the bustier and the Trapunto stitching that we have visited in several of our collections, and we always show jackets, which we like because of their versatility. But we like to think of our clothes in terms of a signature theme instead, which is that they are both luxurious and comfortable. We hope they are pieces that have an easy dialogue with all parts of a woman's wardrobe and her life **What is your favourite piece from any of your collections?** It would be impossible to isolate a favourite because we have attachments to things for different reasons – you can love one thing because it was the first, or most successful, or the easiest – or the most challenging **What's your ultimate goal?** Right now it's not to have an "ultimate" goal – for things to constantly evolve without a particular destination in mind **What inspires you?** The visual arts, especially photography and painting. The work of master couturiers. Travel. But there is never one specific reference – inspiration comes from everything, even if you don't recognise it at the time **Who do you have in mind when you design?** It's not one person. There is not one woman who is quintessentially Proenza Schouler. One of the most interesting things we have learned from doing this is that we have teenagers who wear our clothes and grandmothers who do too – which we love. The collection has so many different components, and all of the components can have many different lives, depending on the point of view. But that's what we want because that's how we design and how people dress – with intellect, with spirit and an eye for the mix **Is the idea of creative collaboration important to you?** Is this a trick question? Naturally creative collaboration is our process and we share work and credit equally. But people do often wonder about the division of work and labour, which is not really how we work. We work separately for a period, then come together – and the results are often remarkably similar. We agree far more often than we argue, and we always refine silhouettes and ideas as a team **Which is more important in your work: the process or the product?** One can't be more important than the other because of how closely they are linked: the process drives the product, and the product enables the process to begin all over again **Is designing difficult for you? If so, what drives you to continue?** Like any job, there are periods, or projects, that are more challenging than others – but that doesn't force you to quit; you just get through it. This is what we do and enjoy and are trained for. So that, if nothing else, is what keeps us going **Have you ever been influenced or moved by the reaction to your designs?** One of the greatest compliments you can receive as a designer is to see a complete stranger wearing things you designed. Critical praise, awards and accolades, commercial success – those are a certain kind of award, but there is something so personal and immediate about seeing someone you have never seen before walking down the street wearing just one piece that you created with other things that she loves and expresses who she is. To know that someone has a reaction to this thing – encountered and pursued it and wanted to own it. It really affects you **What's your definition of beauty?** Beauty is not only hard to define but it's impossible to prescribe. One of the most arresting things about beauty is often that it's a surprise – it's something that takes you off guard. If you tried to define it, you might restrict it, or run the risk of diluting it **What is the most important lesson you've learned?** That the most important lesson is probably yet to be learned.

"People always want something unexpected and exciting.
That's what drives me"
TOMMY HILFIGER

Born one of nine children in 1951 in Elmira, New York, Tommy Hilfiger's eponymous brand is often viewed as epitomising the American Dream. His career famously began in 1969 with $150 and 20 pairs of jeans. When customers to his People's Palace store in upstate New York failed to find what they were after, he took to designing clothes himself, with no previous training. In 1984, having moved to New York City, Hilfiger launched his first collection under his own name. With his distinctive red, white and blue logo and collegiate/Ivy League influences, Hilfiger presented a preppy vision of Americana, which, coupled with his looser sportswear aesthetic, found a surprising new audience in the burgeoning hip-hop scene of the early '90s. Hilfiger, a dedicated music fan himself, welcomed this re-interpretation of his work, but rumours that he was less than enamoured of his new audience led him to make an admirable response, lending his support to the Anti-Defamation League and the Washington DC Martin Luther King Jr National Memorial Project Foundation. By 1992, his company had gone public and Hilfiger was named the CFDA's Menswear Designer of the Year in 1995. A new 'semi-luxe' line of tailored separates, entitled simply 'H', was launched in 2004 as a higher-priced, more upmarket addition to the global brand, which now incorporates everything from denim and eyewear to fragrances, homeware, sporting apparel and children's lines. In keeping with his music and fashion influences, Hilfiger chose to market his new 'grown-up' range by asking David Bowie and Iman to appear in ad campaigns for H. In December 2004, Hilfiger looked set on further expansion when he announced an agreement made with Karl Lagerfeld to globally distribute the latter's own-label collections. Hilfiger, in 2005, hosted and sponsored a CBS TV reality show called 'The Cut' in which contestants competed for a design job with Hilfiger. In 2006, Hilfiger sold his company for $1.6 billion to a private investment company, Apax Partners.

Die Marke des 1951 als eines von neun Kindern in Elmira, New York, geborenen Tommy Hilfiger gilt vielen als der Inbegriff des amerikanischen Traums. Seine Karriere begann, wie inzwischen allgemein bekannt ist, 1969 mit 150 Dollar und 20 Paar Jeans. Wenn die Kundschaft in seinem Laden People's Palace nicht fand, wonach sie suchte, stellte er die Stücke – ohne jegliche Vorkenntnisse – eben selbst her. Nach seinem Umzug nach New York City präsentierte Hilfiger 1984 seine erste Kollektion unter eigenem Namen. Mit seinem auffälligen Logo in Rot, Weiß und Blau sowie den Einflüssen des Ivy-League-Stils präsentierte Hilfiger eine Vision von Amerikana im Preppy-Look, die gepaart mit lässiger Sportswear-Ästhetik überraschenderweise eine neue Klientel in der gerade erblühenden Hip-Hop-Szene der frühen Neunziger fand. Als leidenschaftlicher Musikfan begrüßte Hilfiger diese Neuinterpretation seiner Arbeit. Dennoch brachten ihn Gerüchte, er sei von seiner neuen Anhängerschaft wenig angetan, zu dezidierten Reaktionen, etwa der Unterstützung der Anti-Defamation League und der Washington DC Martin Luther King Jr. National Memorial Project

Foundation. 1992 ging das Unternehmen an die Börse, 1995 wurde Hilfiger von der CFDA zum Menswear Designer of the Year gekürt. Unter dem schlichten Kürzel H kam 2004 eine neue, halb-luxuriöse Linie von aufwändiger geschneiderten Einzelstücken auf den Markt, quasi die höherpreisige, elitäre Ergänzung der internationalen Marke, die inzwischen von Jeans und Brillen über Düfte, Heimtextilien, Sportartikel bis hin zu Kinderkleidung praktisch alles umfasst. Passend zu seinen musikalischen und modischen Einflüssen entschloss sich Hilfiger, für seine neue „erwachsene" Linie bei David Bowie und Iman anzufragen, die anschließend in der Werbekampagne für H posierten. 2005 moderierte und sponserte Hilfiger eine Reality-Show namens ‚The Cut' beim TV-Sender CBS. Dort kämpften die Kandidaten um einen Job als Designer für Hilfiger. Im Jahr 2006 verkaufte Hilfiger sein Unternehmen für 1,6 Milliarden Dollar an die private Investmentfirma Apax Partners.

Né en 1951 dans une famille de neuf enfants à Elmira dans les environs de New York, Tommy Hilfiger et sa marque éponyme sont souvent considérés comme l'incarnation du rêve américain. La légende dit qu'il a entamé sa carrière en 1969 avec 150 dollars en poche et 20 paires de jeans. Comme les clients de sa boutique People's Palace au nord de l'Etat de New York n'arrivent pas à trouver ce qu'ils cherchent, il décide de dessiner lui-même des vêtements, sans formation préalable. En 1984, une fois installé à New York, Hilfiger lance une première collection baptisée de son propre nom. Avec son célèbre logo rouge, blanc et bleu et influencé par le style des universités de l'Ivy League, Hilfiger présente une vision BCBG du style américain qui, associée à une esthétique sportwear plus décontractée, séduit une clientèle inattendue au sein de la jeune scène hip-hop du début des années 90. Lui-même passionné de musique, Hilfiger accepte cette interprétation de son travail, mais les rumeurs qui courent sur le fait qu'il ne soit pas particulièrement fan de son nouveau public le conduisent à réagir admirablement en offrant son soutien à la ligue anti-raciste américaine (Anti-Defamation League) et à la Fondation du projet de mémorial national de Martin Luther King Junior. En 1992, son entreprise est introduite en bourse et le CFDA le couronne Menswear Designer of the Year en 1995. Une nouvelle ligne « semi-luxe » de séparés baptisée tout simplement « H » est lancée en 2004 en guise de complément plus haut de gamme et plus onéreux pour cette marque mondiale qui intègre aujourd'hui toutes sortes de lignes, du denim aux lunettes en passant par les parfums, le mobilier, les articles de sport et la mode pour enfant. Fidèle à ses influences vestimentaires et musicales, Hilfiger décide de commercialiser sa nouvelle gamme « adulte » en demandant à David Bowie et Iman d'apparaître dans les campagnes publicitaires de H. En 2005, il anime et sponsorise « The Cut », une émission de télé-réalité diffusée sur CBS où les candidats se disputent une place de styliste chez Hilfiger. En 2006, il vend son entreprise au fonds d'investissement Apax Partners pour un montant de 1,6 milliard de dollars.

MARK HOOPER

MENSWEAR 1998/99 HARPER MCELAN MSI ELAN MIKE EVA SIMON BORDON KIRCHENA 2000

PHOTOGRAPH BY ANGELA STILLING FRANCESCA BURNS. MODEL ALI STEPHENS. JULY 2008

PHOTOGRAPH BY BRUCE WEBER, STELLA MARA ANIMAL, JANUARY/FEBRUARY 2000.

PHOTOGRAPHY MATT JONES. STYLING CATHY DIXON. JANUARY/FEBRUARY 2000.

What are your signature designs? I am known best for 'classics with a twist'. For me it's about updating the classics **What is your favourite piece from any of your collections?** A classic oxford shirt with a contrast collar. It is timeless and classic, and always in fashion **How would you describe your work?** In one word, classic **What's your ultimate goal?** I don't think in terms of one ultimate goal. For me, it's about seizing each opportunity as it reveals itself **What inspires you?** For me, pop culture has been my greatest inspiration. Pop culture to me is about being relevant and being very 'now' I thrive on change, evolution and invention, and that's what pop culture is all about **Can fashion still have a political ambition?** Yes, but for me it's more about self-expression than about politics. People are moved and influenced by different things and for some people, it's politics **Who do you have in mind when you design?** I see everything through a pop-culture lens. Andy Warhol, Jackson Pollock, The Stones, The Who. These guys really paved the way for pop culture and changed the way people think about the world **Is the idea of creative collaboration important to you?** Absolutely. In fact, I acquired the Karl Lagerfeld trademark. Karl is a creative genius and I think we will learn a lot from each other **Who has been the greatest influence on your career?** My kids are an amazing influence. Their youth and vitality give me energy **How have your own experiences affected your work as a designer?** Every experience I have had has affected me in some way. Life is really made up of thousands of different experiences. That is how we learn and grow as individuals **Which is more important in your work: the process or the product?** Both. You can't do one successfully without the other. **Is designing difficult for you? If so, what drives you to continue?** Design is my first love, my passion in life, and when you're passionate about something, it never feels like hard work. It's a very organic and natural process for me. I love the challenge of reinterpreting things in new and different ways **Have you ever been influenced or moved by the reaction to your designs?** The most rewarding thing about being a designer is you can see how your designs impact people. There's nothing I enjoy more than seeing someone on the street wearing my designs with their own personal flair **What's your definition of beauty?** There is nothing more beautiful than self-confidence. With a great attitude and an open mind, you can do anything in life **What's your philosophy?** Be true to yourself **What is the most important lesson you've learned?** The most important thing in life is to never let anyone tell you that your dreams are impossible.

"The illusion that next time it might be perfect keeps us going"
VIKTOR HORSTING & ROLF SNOEREN · VIKTOR & ROLF

Inseparable since they met whilst studying at Arnhem's Fashion Academy, Dutch duo Viktor Horsting and Rolf Snoeren (both born 1969) decided to join forces after graduating in 1992. Their first feat was winning three awards at the 1993 Hyères Festival with a collection that already betrayed their preferences for sculptural, experimental clothes. Soon afterwards, they joined the ranks of Le Cri Néerlandais, a loose collective of like-minded young designers from the Netherlands who organised two shows in Paris. However, once Le Cri disbanded, Viktor & Rolf continued to produce collections, including one in 1996 called 'Viktor & Rolf On Strike' that decried the lack of interest in their work from press and buyers. Refusing to give up, the duo created a toy-like miniature fashion show and a fake perfume bottle with an accompanying ad campaign. These artefacts, presented in the Amsterdam art gallery Torch in 1996, established them as upstart designers with an unconventional agenda. But what really launched their careers was their introduction to Paris couture in 1998, where Viktor & Rolf stunned ever-growing audiences with their highly innovative creations based on exaggerated volumes and shapes. To everyone's surprise and delight, the duo have managed to translate their earlier spectacular couture designs into wearable yet groundbreaking prêt-à-porter pieces, showing their first ready-to-wear collection for autumn/winter 2000. Clinging to a love of ribbons and perfectly-cut smoking suits, Viktor & Rolf shows have become a must-see on the Paris prêt-à-porter schedule, and in 2004 they launched their first fragrance, Flowerbomb. The next few years saw the pair reach new heights: the opening of the Viktor & Rolf Boutique on Milan's Via Sant'Andrea (2005), a collaboration with H&M (2006) and their first-ever UK exhibition, at The Barbican (2008). They continue to live and work in Amsterdam.

Seit sie sich als Studenten an der Modeakademie von Arnheim kennen lernten, sind die beiden Holländer Viktor Horsting und Rolf Snoeren (beide Jahrgang 1969) unzertrennlich. Nach ihrem Studienabschluss 1992 beschlossen sie folglich, ihre Kräfte zu bündeln. Ihre erste Meisterleistung waren drei Preise beim Hyères-Festival 1993, und zwar mit einer Kollektion, die ihre Vorliebe für skulpturale, experimentelle Kleidung zum Ausdruck brachte. Bald danach reihten sie sich bei Le Cri Néerlandais ein, einem losen Kollektiv von gleichgesinnten Jungdesignern aus Holland, die zwei Schauen in Paris organisierten. Nachdem Le Cri sich aufgelöst hatte, machten Viktor & Rolf mit der Produktion von Kollektionen weiter, darunter eine von 1996 mit dem Titel ‚Viktor & Rolf On Strike', die das geringe Interesse von Journalisten und Käufern beklagte. Das Designerduo gab jedoch nicht auf und schuf eine spielzeugartige Modenschau in miniature und einen falschen Parfümflakon mit dazugehöriger Werbekampagne. Diese Artefakte wurden 1996 in der Amsterdamer Kunstgalerie Torch präsentiert und etablierten die beiden als Newcomer mit unkonventionellem Programm. Was ihrer Karriere jedoch den entscheidenden Schub gab, war ihre Einführung in die Pariser Couture 1998, wo Viktor & Rolf ein ständig wachsendes Publikum mit höchst innovativen Kreationen erstaunte, die auf extremem Volumen und überzeichneten Formen basierten. Zur allseitigen freudigen Überraschung gelang es dem Duo, seine frühere spektakuläre Couture in tragbare, aber dennoch völlig neuartige Prêt-à-porter zu transponieren, wovon man sich bei ihrer ersten Kollektion für Herbst/Winter 2000 überzeugen konnte. Mit ihrer Vorliebe für Bänder und perfekt geschnittene Smokings sind die Schauen von Viktor & Rolf Pflichtprogramm im Pariser Prêt-à-porter-Kalender. 2004 wurde mit Flowerbomb der erste Duft des Designerteams vorgestellt. In den darauffolgenden Jahren erzielte das Kreativ-Duo weitere Erfolge: die Eröffnung der Viktor & Rolf Boutique an der Mailänder Via Sant'Andrea (2005), die Zusammenarbeit mit H&M (2006) sowie ihre allererste Ausstellung in Großbritannien, im Londoner Barbican (2008). Die beiden Designer leben und arbeiten nach wie vor in Amsterdam.

Inséparables depuis leur rencontre sur les bancs de l'académie de mode d'Arnhem, les Hollandais Viktor Horsting et Rolf Snoeren (tous deux nés en 1969) décident de travailler ensemble après l'obtention de leurs diplômes en 1992. Ils réalisent un premier exploit en remportant trois prix au Festival de Hyères en 1993 grâce à une collection qui trahit déjà leur prédilection pour une mode sculpturale et expérimentale. Peu de temps après, ils rejoignent les rangs du Cri Néerlandais, collectif libre de jeunes designers hollandais partageant le même état d'esprit et qui a présenté deux défilés à Paris. Après la dissolution du Cri, Viktor & Rolf continuent pourtant à travailler ensemble. En 1996, ils baptisent l'une de leurs collections «Viktor & Rolf On Strike» pour dénoncer le manque d'intérêt de la presse et des acheteurs à leur égard. Refusant d'abandonner, ils créent un mini-défilé jouet, un faux flacon de parfum et une campagne publicitaire pour l'accompagner: ces artefacts, présentés dans la galerie d'art Torch à Amsterdam en 1996, les imposent comme de nouveaux rebelles à suivre de très près. Mais c'est lorsqu'ils débarquent dans la haute couture parisienne que leur carrière décolle enfin: depuis 1998, Viktor & Rolf éblouissent un public sans cesse croissant grâce à des créations très innovantes qui jouent sur l'exagération des volumes et des formes. A la surprise générale et pour le plus grand bonheur de tous, le duo parvient à traduire les créations haute couture de ses débuts spectaculaires sous forme de vêtements prêt-à-porter à la fois novateurs et portables, qu'ils présentent pour la première fois aux collections automne/hiver 2000. Revendiquant leur amour des rubans et des smokings aux coupes irréprochables, chaque défilé Viktor & Rolf est un événement absolument incontournable de la semaine du prêt-à-porter de Paris. En 2004, ils ont lancé leur premier parfum, Flowerbomb. Les années suivantes ont vu le duo atteindre de nouveaux sommets: ouverture de la boutique Viktor & Rolf sur la Via Sant'Andrea de Milan (2005), collaboration avec H&M (2006) et toute première exposition britannique au Barbican (2008). Aujourd'hui, ils vivent et travaillent toujours à Amsterdam.

JAMIE HUCKBODY

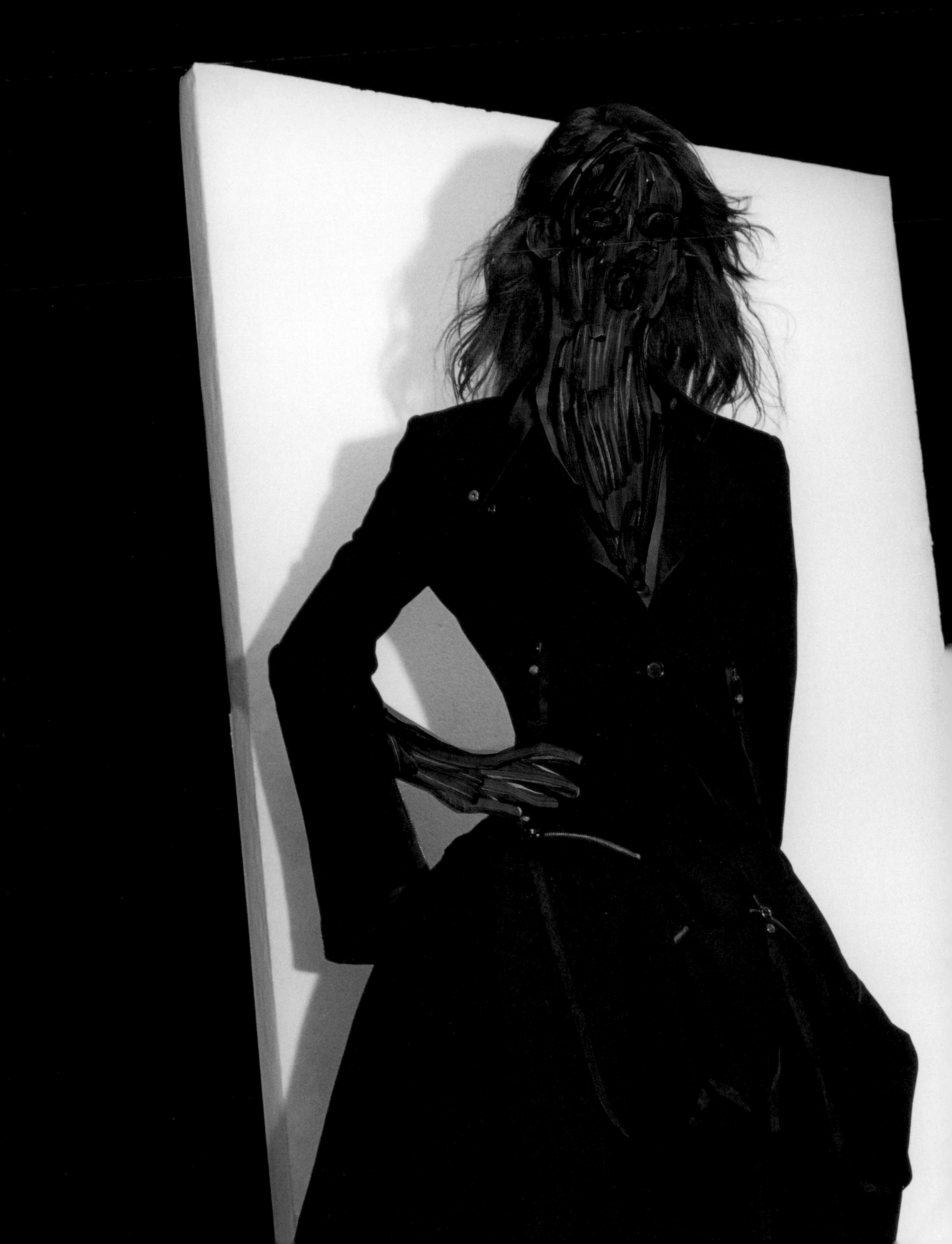

PRÊT-À-PORTER MODE, Gianni Versace, SPRING / SUMMER 1994

PHOTOGRAPHY DAVID LACHAPELLE. STYLING PATTI WILSON. MARCH 2002.

What are your signature designs? The ones that received the most attention. More important than the designs themselves is their capacity to communicate. Our signature designs are the designs that communicate best **What is your favourite piece from any of your collections?** The Babushka collection: the 'fashion dream' miniatures **How would you describe your work?** Difficult question **What's your ultimate goal?** "Wanna be famous, wanna be rich, wanna be a star" **What inspires you?** Fashion itself **Can fashion still have a political ambition?** Yes, fashion is a reflection of all aspects of life **Who do you have in mind when you design?** We have never designed with a specific person in mind, but always regarded our collections as autonomous: once the designs are finished, they are for whoever appreciates them. Recently, however, we have become more and more aware of the reality of the product we are creating. It was an inspiration to see our clothes worn by Tilda Swinton, who really brought them to life in a way we had imagined, but not yet seen in real life **Is the idea of creative collaboration important to you?** Collaborating is the essence of Viktor & Rolf. Working in tandem gives us an opportunity to go deeper. We have known each other for a long time and formed a very strong bond that is the basis of everything we do. Sometimes this can make it difficult to let other people in, but when they do succeed, it can feel like a breath of fresh air **Who has been the greatest influence on your career?** Inez van Lamsweerde and Vinoodh Matadin: they forced us to think in a more realistic way about fashion without being ashamed of it **How have your own experiences affected your work as designers?** Our work is always very personal. We try to translate our lives into our work. If we are down, we feel it is better to turn it into creative energy than to let it beat you. That is how the 'Black Hole' collection was born, for example **Which is more important in your work: the process or the product?** The result is the only thing that counts **Is designing difficult for you? If so, what drives you to continue?** Being a fashion designer is a challenging profession because it requires a variety of skills that go far beyond designing. Designing itself is very difficult, but the illusion that next time it might be perfect keeps us going **Have you ever been influenced or moved by the reaction to your designs?** We never take candy from strangers, however, if it's enough candy from an important stranger etc **What's your definition of beauty?** Originality **What's your philosophy?** Viktor and Rolf first **What's the most important lesson you've learned?** There are others, too.

"I design for men and women who value quality over quantity, and simplicity over decoration"
MARGARET HOWELL

Margaret Howell creates beautiful, understated clothes for everyday life. Taught to sew and knit by their mother, the Howells were a practical and creative tour de force, with mum making the kids clothes, and the kids indeed, following suit. They would while away many an hour rummaging through jumble sales, where Howell would find a shirt and be instantly attracted to the way it was made. Around this time, Howell was buying and adapting dressmaking patterns by Yves Saint Laurent into her own masculine style. Joseph had arrived in this country as a hairdresser, wanted to sell clothes in his shop and formed an easy alliance with Howell and stocked her burgeoning shirting collection in his store. Browns were next to place an order, as did Ralph Lauren and Paul Smith. Howell's take on the classic shirt shape was to remake it in a gentler, more casual fabric, instantly making it easier to wear. Joseph witnessed the business potential within Howell's easy aesthetic and offered her the chance to open a boutique to house her first complete range of menswear (1977). Howell realised the potential was there to cater for both sexes and downscaled the sizing, added some skirting and the women's range was launched (1980). Later parting company with Joseph, the company went independent and continued to grow. Now based in London's Wigmore Street, the store showcases her collection of fabulous knick knacks – like chopping boards and stationery – alongside the clothing collections, which often feature polka dots, shirting, double or single-breasted tuxedos, tweeds and cotton as the recurring theme. Echoing the peaceful time of Miss Marple, Darling Buds of May and a quintessential English summertime in full bloom, these clothes are for a modern world and perfect for times in which frivolity and lewd design features, such as logos and labelling, seem rather unnecessary.

Margaret Howell entwirft wunderbar schlichte Kleidung für den Alltag. Nähen und Stricken lernten die Kinder der Familie von ihrer Mutter, was eine praktische und zugleich kreative Herausforderung darstellte, denn die Mama fertigte die Kinderkleidung selbst an, und die Kids folgten postwendend ihrem Beispiel. Sie verbrachten Stunden mit dem Stöbern in Trödelläden, wo Howell ein Hemd entdeckte und sofort von seiner Machart begeistert war. Etwa um diese Zeit kaufte Howell auch Schnittmuster von Yves Saint Laurent und adaptierte sie gemäß ihrem eigenen maskulinen Stil. Joseph, der als Friseur ins Land gekommen war, wollte in seinem Laden auch Klamotten anbieten und ging bereitwillig einen Verbindung mit Howell ein, deren aufblühende Hemdenkollektion er fortan bei sich verkaufte. Browns gaben als erste eine Bestellung auf, gefolgt von Ralph Lauren und Paul Smith. Howells Version des klassischen Herrenhemds ist ein Remake aus weicherem, lässigerem Material, was den Tragekomfort ungemein steigert. Joseph erkannte das geschäftliche Potenzial in Howells unbeschwerter Ästhetik und bot ihr die Chance, eine Boutique zu

eröffnen, in der ihre erste komplette Herrenkollektion Platz fand (1977). Howell wiederum realisierte die Möglichkeit, für beide Geschlechter zu designen, verkleinerte die Größen, fügte ein paar Röcke hinzu, und fertig war die Damenkollektion (1980). Als die geschäftliche Verbindung zu Joseph endete, wurde Howells Firma unanhängig und expandierte weiter. Der Laden in der Londoner Wigmore Street präsentiert auch ihre Kollektion aus fabelhaftem Krimskrams – wie Schneidbrettern und Briefpapier – und dazu die Kleider-kollektionen, häufig mit Tupfenmuster, aus Hemden, Ein- und Zweireihern, Smokings, Tweed und Baumwolle. Das Ganze erinnert an die friedvollen Zeiten von ‚Miss Marple' und ‚Darling Buds of May' und an den typisch englischen Hochsommer. Trotzdem sind diese Kleider für eine moderne Welt gemacht und perfekt für Momente, in denen Oberflächlichkeit und anstößige Design-Features wie Logos und Etiketten eher überflüssig scheinen.

Margaret Howell crée des vêtements à la fois sobres et magnifiques pour le quotidien. La famille Howell représente un exploit pratique et créatif en soi, avec une mère qui confectionnait elle-même les habits de ses enfants et leur a appris à coudre et à tricoter, une tradition qu'ils ont d'ailleurs perpétuée. Alors qu'ils passent leur temps à chiner dans les ventes de charité, Margaret reste fascinée devant une chemise, instantanément attirée par son mode de construction. A cette époque, elle achète des patrons de couture Yves Saint Laurent et les inter-prète à sa façon dans un style masculin. Nouvellement immigré en Angleterre en tant que coiffeur, Joseph désire vendre des vêtements dans son salon et conclut un accord avec Margaret Howell pour distribuer sa jeune collection de chemises. Browns lui passe commande, ainsi que Ralph Lauren et Paul Smith. Sa vision de la chemise classique consiste alors à la refaçonner dans un tissu plus doux, plus décontracté et donc tout de suite plus facile à porter. Joseph, qui a flairé le poten-tiel commercial de cette esthétique, propose à Margaret d'ouvrir une boutique pour y vendre toutes ses créations pour homme (1977). Prenant conscience qu'elle peut créer pour les deux sexes, elle réduit ses proportions, ajoute quelques jupes et lance sa collection pour femme (1980). Son entreprise se sépare de Joseph pour devenir indépendante et poursuivre son développement. Désormais installée dans Wigmore Street à Londres, la boutique de Margaret Howell présente sa fabuleuse collection de gadgets – entre planches à découper et articles de papeterie – aux côtés de lignes de vêtements qui affichent souvent des pois, des tissus de chemise, des vestes droites ou croisées, des smokings, des tweeds et du coton comme thèmes récurrents. Faisant écho à l'époque paisible de «Miss Marple», de «The Darling Buds of May» et à la quintessence de l'été anglais en pleine floraison, ces vêtements conçus pour le monde d'aujourd'hui s'avèrent parfaitement adaptés en cette ère où la frivolité, les logos et les étiquettes sont autant d'inventions lubriques devenues plutôt inutiles. BEN REARDON

What are your signature designs? The shirt. The flat lace-up shoe. The raglan raincoat. Tailored jackets and trousers. Although designed for men and women, all are 'androgynous'. But also signature is a preference for natural-fibre fabric of the British Isles **How would you describe your work?** My clothes are functional and designed as individual pieces rather than part of an outfit or a pre-conceived, fixed look. Every detail is considered in order to achieve a style with a relaxed feel. The appropriateness of the fabric to the design is crucial as is both the quality of the cloth and the make **What inspires you?** People, places, things **Can fashion still have a political ambition?** For me, it is important that people should have active choice and self-expression while respecting the environment **Who do you have in mind when you design?** I design for men and women who value quality over quantity, and simplicity over decoration **Is the idea of creative collaboration important to you?** Yes. Technical and creative skill are a good combination. Working with specialists, taking inspiration from their work and adapting it, often produces very good results for me **Who has been the greatest influence on your career?** As far as lifestyle approach and values, my parents have been the most enduring influence. When I was at school in the '60s, I admired Yves Saint Laurent. More specific to my career was Sam Sugure, who believed in my designs and who established the brand throughout Japan in a considered and perceptive way **How have your own experiences affected your work as a designer?** Growing up in the post-war austerity years, we were encouraged to be creative and resourceful. We were always making things, including our own clothes, but we simply enjoyed it as well! Studying fine art at Goldsmiths taught me a lot about colour and proportion. Later still, facing adversity head on, I learnt about not giving up **Which is more important in your work: the process or the product?** Both. For me they are inseparable **Is designing difficult for you? If so, what drives you to continue?** Inspiration apart, it would seem wrong if it was easy. The struggle is part of the design process **Have you been influenced or moved by the reaction to your designs?** I have been surprised when people say how the clothes make them 'feel' different. I'm touched when people tell me they still have my clothes hanging in their wardrobe, even though they no longer fit them they can't throw them out **What's your philosophy?** I believe in 'less is more', and that form follows function.

"It's important for me that my clothes are not just an exercise in runway high jinks"
MARC JACOBS + LOUIS VUITTON

Season after season, Marc Jacobs (born 1963), manages to predict exactly what women all over the world want to wear, whether that be his super-flat 'mouse' pumps, Sergeant Pepper-style denim jackets or 'Venetia' handbags fitted with outsized silver buckles. Born in New York's Upper West Side to parents who both worked for the William Morris Agency, Jacobs was raised by his fashion-conscious grandmother. As a teenager, Jacobs immersed himself in club culture, observing the beautiful people at the Mudd Club, Studio 54 and Hurrah. Today, Jacobs' most fruitful source of inspiration is still the crowd of cool girls that surround him (including the stylist Venetia Scott, director Sofia Coppola and numerous art-house actresses). After high school, Jacobs completed a fashion degree at Parsons School of Design; his graduation collection (1984), which featured brightly coloured knits, caught the eye of Robert Duffy, an executive who remains Jacobs' business partner to this day. Together they launched the first Marc Jacobs collection (1986), winning a CFDA award the following year. In 1989, Jacobs was named head designer at Perry Ellis. His experience there was tempestuous and his infamous 'grunge' collection of 1992 – featuring satin Birkenstocks and silk plaid shirts – marked his exit from the company. By 1997, Jacobs' star was in the ascendant once again, when LVMH appointed him artistic director at Louis Vuitton. Jacobs has enhanced the luggage company's image – not least through his collaborations with artists Takashi Murakami and Stephen Sprouse on seasonal handbag designs – and repositioned it as a ready-to-wear fashion brand. Meanwhile LVMH have supported Jacobs' own company, which has now expanded to more than 100 stores worldwide. The company's impressive portfolio includes Marc Jacobs Collection ready-to-wear, Marc by Marc Jacobs womenswear, Men's Collection ready-to-wear, Marc by Marc Jacobs menswear, two shoe collections, two optical collections, two sunglass collections, one collection of watches, nine fragrances, the children's collection and the much-loved collection of special items.

Saison für Saison gelingt es dem 1963 geborenen Marc Jacobs, exakt vorherzusagen, was die Frauen überall auf der Welt tragen wollen – seien es superflache Mouse-Pumps, Jeansjacken im Sergeant-Pepper-Stil oder Venetia-Handtaschen mit überdimensionalen Silberschnallen. Der an der New Yorker Upper West Side als Kind von Eltern, die beide für die William Morris Agency tätig waren, geborene Jacobs wurde von einer modebewussten Großmutter aufgezogen. Als Teenager vertiefte er sich in die Clubkultur und studierte die Beautiful People der 1970er-Jahre im Mudd Club, im Studio 54 sowie im Hurrah. Noch heute ist Jacobs' fruchtbarste Inspirationsquelle die Truppe von coolen Girls, die ihn umgeben (darunter die Stylistin Venetia Scott, die Regisseurin Sofia Coppola und zahlreiche Art-House-Schauspielerinnen). Nach der Highschool machte Jacobs sein Modeexamen an der Parsons School of Design. 1984 erregte seine Abschlusskollektion mit leuchtend bunten Stricksachen die Aufmerksamkeit des Managers Robert Duffy, der bis heute sein Geschäftspartner ist. Gemeinsam brachten sie 1986 die erste Marc-Jacobs-Kollektion heraus und gewannen damit ein Jahr später ihren ersten CFDA-Preis. 1989 wurde Jacobs Chefdesigner bei Perry Ellis. Dort erlebte er ziemlich stürmische Zeiten und verabschiedete sich

mit seiner berüchtigten Grunge-Kollektion von 1992, zu der Birkenstocks aus Satin und Karohemden aus Seide gehörten. Ab 1997 war Jacobs' Stern wieder im Steigen begriffen, als ihn der LVMH-Konzern zum künstlerischen Direktor von Louis Vuitton ernannte. Jacobs verbesserte das Image des traditionellen Reisegepäck-Labels, nicht zuletzt durch seine Zusammenarbeit mit den Künstlern Takashi Murakami und Stephen Sprouse im saisonalen Handtaschendesign. Außerdem hat er die Prêt-à-porter-Mode des Hauses neu positioniert. Inzwischen unterstützt LVMH auch Jacobs' eigenes Unternehmen, das inzwischen auf über hundert Läden weltweit expandiert ist. Das eindrucksvolle Portfolio des Unternehmens umfasst die Prêt-à-porter Marc Jacobs Collection, die Damenlinie Marc by Marc Jacobs, die Prêt-à-porter Men's Collection, die Herrenlinie Marc by Marc Jacobs, zwei Schuhkollektionen, zwei Brillenkollektionen, zwei Sonnenbrillenkollektionen, eine Uhrenkollektion, neun Düfte, die Kinderkollektion und die überaus beliebte Kollektion besonderer Dinge.

Saison après saison, Marc Jacobs (né en 1963) réussit à prédire exactement ce que les femmes du monde entier auront envie de porter, qu'il s'agisse de ses ballerines «souris» ultraplates, de ses vestes en denim à la Sergeant Pepper ou des sacs à main Venetia ornés d'énormes boucles en argent. Né à New York dans l'Upper West Side de parents travaillant tous deux pour la William Morris Agency, Jacobs est élevé par sa grand-mère passionnée de mode. Adolescent, il s'immerge dans la culture club du milieu des années 70 et aime à observer les beautiful people qui se retrouvent au Mudd Club, au Studio 54 et au Hurrah. Aujourd'hui, la source d'inspiration la plus fructueuse de Jacobs réside dans la foule de filles branchées qui l'entoure (incluant la styliste Venetia Scott, la réalisatrice Sofia Coppola et de nombreuses actrices du cinéma indépendant). Après le lycée, Jacobs obtient un diplôme en mode de la Parsons School of Design; sa collection de fin d'études (1984), avec sa maille aux couleurs vives, attire l'attention de l'homme d'affaires Robert Duffy, qui reste son partenaire commercial à ce jour. Ensemble, ils lancent la première collection Marc Jacobs (1986), couronnée l'année suivante par un prix du CFDA. En 1989, Jacobs est nommé styliste principal de Perry Ellis. Son expérience est orageuse et sa scandaleuse collection «grunge» de 1992, avec ses Birkenstocks en satin et ses chemises en soie à carreaux écossais, signe ses adieux à la maison. En 1997, l'étoile de Marc Jacobs remonte au firmament quand LVMH le nomme directeur artistique de Louis Vuitton. Jacobs révolutionne l'image du fabricant de bagages, notamment grâce à des collaborations artistiques avec Takashi Murakami et Stephen Sprouse sur la création de sacs à main de saison, et repositionne Vuitton comme une marque de prêt-à-porter. Parallèlement, LVMH finance la griffe éponyme de Jacobs, qui compte désormais plus de 100 boutiques à travers le monde. L'impressionnant portefeuille de l'entreprise inclut Marc Jacobs Collection prêt-à-porter, Marc by Marc Jacobs pour femme, Men's Collection prêt-à-porter, Marc by Marc Jacobs pour homme, deux collections de chaussures, deux collections optiques, deux collections de lunettes de soleil, une collection de montres, neuf parfums, une collection pour enfant et une gamme d'articles spéciaux très appréciée.

SUSIE RUSHTON

PHOTOGRAPHY BY DAVID SIMS. FASHION EDITOR EDWARD ENNINFUL. MODEL SASHA PIVOVAROVA. MARCH 2006

PHOTOGRAPHY SØLVE SUNDSBØ. FASHION DIRECTOR EDWARD ENNINFUL. MODEL ALEK. MARCH 2009.

PHOTOGRAPHY DANIEL JACKSON STYLING MARIE CHAIX MODEL IRIS STRUBEGGER APRIL 2009

PHOTOGRAPHY PIERRE BAILLY. STYLING CATHY KASTERINE. MODEL CONSTANCE JABLONSKI. APRIL 2009.

PHOTOGRAPHY ALASDAIR MCLELLAN. STYLING OLIVIER RIZZO. MODEL ADAM. FEBRUARY 2004.

PHOTOGRAPH: SOLVE SUNDSBO. STYLING: HAVANA LAFFITTE. MODEL DARIA. MAY 2003.

PHOTO: ROB PAYNE AND LAUREN BAYS. MODEL: IRINA. SEPTEMBER 2006.

PHOTOGRAPH BEN JACQUES. STYLING HAVANA LAFFITTE. MODEL LINDSAY. MARCH 2005.

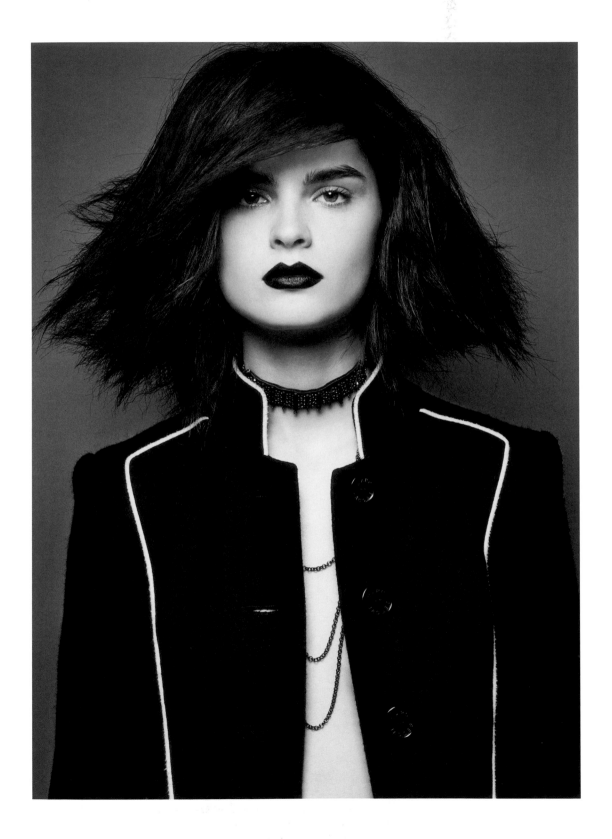

PHOTOGRAPHY GREG LOTUS. STYLING PATTI WILSON. MODEL ANOUCK LEPERE. JULY 2001.

MARC JACOBS

PHOTOGRAPHY SØLVE SUNDSBØ. FASHION DIRECTOR EDWARD ENNINFUL. MODEL SUSIE BICK. MARCH 2009.

PHOTOGRAPHY NICK HAYMES. STYLING HAVANA LAFFITTE. MODEL SIRI. MARCH 2008.

What's your favourite piece from any of your collections? Although there are pieces that I love, it's not only about the piece, but the piece on the right girl. What I really, truly love is the whole image **How would you describe your work?** I find it easy, perhaps too easy, to make things seem naughty or too – I hate this word – edgy. I find that all too easy. I quite like the idea of doing something more intelligent **What's your ultimate goal?** People say, 'Well, what's left?' All I want to do is what I'm doing today. And I would like to be able to do it tomorrow **What inspires you?** I do love rock 'n' roll music, I do love going out, I do love partying and having a good time. When it comes to fashion, I'm inspired by those things, but I try not to hold a mirror up to them and present a sort of clichéd, surface poseur version **What do you have in mind when you design?** I like to think that the clothes could have a life after the show is over. And that's important, because everything we make is some kind of fantasy; even if it's quite practical, it's still a heightened reality. But I like the believ-ability factor in clothes, so I like to think that a person I know, or some person I don't know who has an eclectic sense of style, could actually be walking down a street in one of those looks. It's important for me to think that it's not just an exercise in runway high jinks **Is the idea of creative collab-oration important to you?** I love working with people. Everybody brings something to the party **Who has been the greatest influence on your career?** I've always been very influenced by the mystique of the house of Saint Laurent. That's my fashion fantasy. But I guess I'm just influenced by people who are really, really passionate about their work. That could be musicians or artists or fashion designers, whoever, just somebody being so committed, and so truly connected, always inspires me **How have your own experiences affected your work as a designer?** I can imagine there were seasons when certain designers did such a good collection they must have felt like they were 'it' for the season. But I've never felt like 'it' and I don't think I ever will. I feel very outside. I'm comfortable acting within the fashion system. But I think I'm quite separate, in a way **Which is more important in your work: the process or the product?** You can't have one without the other **Is designing difficult for you? If so, what drives you to continue?** I define design as a series of creative choices. And there are so many choices that one can make. I don't know how it is with other people, but for me it is a very painful pro-cess because I feel like there has to be integrity and meaning in the choices. And I doubt myself a lot, I don't really have a lot of self-confidence. But I really, really enjoy being a part of this process and, even though it's painful for me sometimes, there's nothing else I'd rather be doing. I guess it's a gift to feel so passionate about something. What got us to this point is doing what we believe in our hearts is right **Have you ever been influenced or moved by the reaction to your designs?** Yeah, I have. I love it when I see strangers wearing my clothes, because there is such a vast amount of choice out there, and somebody choosing the work that we've done over somebody else's is a big thing **What is the most important lesson you've learned?** It has very little to do with fashion. The most important lesson I've learned is to just be present. Enjoy life today.

"My ultimate goal is always to improve on the last collection"
ROSSELLA JARDINI · MOSCHINO

The Italian fashion house Moschino owes much to Rossella Jardini who, since the untimely death of its founder Franco Moschino in 1994, has successfully held the reins of a brand which today still puts the kook into kooky. Moschino, having burst onto the scene in 1983, has grown up since its logo-mania '80s heyday (remember phrases like 'Ready To Where?' or 'This Is A Very Expensive Shirt' splashed onto garments?). But Jardini, as creative director of all Moschino product lines (sold through 22 shops worldwide), has steered this label in a contemporary direction while retaining its traditional wit. Since the millennium, we have seen Jardini and her team continue to tease the market through parody and stereotype, both of which are central to the original philosophy of the house. Rompish catwalk parades featuring housewives in curlers and sleeping masks, demure '50s ladies à la Chanel (one of Jardini's most important personal influences), over-the-top prints, trompe l'œil and swishy petticoats have all provided gleeful style moments. Born in Bergamo, Italy, in 1952, Jardini began her career selling clothes rather than designing them. Then, in 1976, she met Nicola Trussardi and began assisting with the development of that company's clothing and leather goods. Creating her own line in 1978 with two model friends, she soon made the acquaintance of Franco Moschino and in 1981 began assisting him. A stint designing accessories for Bottega Veneta followed, but by 1984 she had settled into a permanent role at Moschino. Ten years later, before his tragically early death, Franco Moschino made it quite clear he wished Jardini to take over the helm. She has been there ever since.

Das italienische Modehaus Moschino verdankt Rossella Jardini viel. Seit dem frühen Tod des Firmengründers Franco Moschino im Jahr 1994 steuert sie eine Marke, die man bis heute als verrückt im besten Sinne des Wortes bezeichnen kann. Moschino hatte 1983 sein Debüt in der Modeszene und ist erwachsen geworden, wenn man an die Logo-Manie im Boom der 1980er-Jahre denkt (wer erinnert sich nicht an auf Kleidungsstücken prangenden Sätze wie „Ready To Where?" oder „This Is A Very Expensive Shirt"?). Als Chefdesignerin aller Produktlinien des Hauses (die weltweit in 22 Läden verkauft werden) hat Jardini das Label in eine moderne Richtung gesteuert und dabei seinen traditionellen Witz bewahrt. Seit der Jahrtausendwende kann man wieder verstärkt beobachten, wie Jardini und ihr Team den Markt mit Parodien und Klischees necken, die beide von zentraler Bedeutung für die ursprüngliche Unternehmensphilosophie sind. So präsentierte man auf dem Catwalk schon Paraden von Hausfrauen mit Lockenwicklern und Schlafmasken, prüden Damen im 50er-Jahre-Stil von Chanel (einer der wichtigsten Einflüsse für Jardini), völlig verrückten Mustern,

Trompe l'œil und raschelnden Petticoats – was für jede Menge Ausgelassenheit sorgte. Die 1952 in Bergamo geborene Jardini begann ihre Karriere übrigens nicht mit dem Design, sondern mit dem Verkauf von Textilien. 1976 lernte sie Nicola Trussardi kennen und begann, ihm bei der Entwicklung des Textil- und Lederwarengeschäfts seiner Firma zu assistieren. Gemeinsam mit zwei befreundeten Models kreierte sie 1978 ihr eigenes Label und lernte bald darauf Franco Moschino kennen, dessen Assistentin sie ab 1981 war. Es gab noch ein kurzes Intermezzo als Designerin für Accessoires bei Bottega Veneta, bis sie 1984 ihre Dauerstellung bei Moschino einnahm. Zehn Jahre danach und kurz vor seinem tragischen frühen Tod ließ Franco Moschino keinen Zweifel an seinem Wunsch, Jardini das Ruder zu überlassen. Seither hat sie es nicht mehr aus der Hand gegeben.

La maison italienne Moschino doit beaucoup à Rossella Jardini, car depuis le décès prématuré de son fondateur Franco Moschino en 1994, elle tient avec succès les rênes d'une marque qui reste aujourd'hui fidèle à son côté fou et décalé. Apparue sur la scène de la mode en 1983, la griffe Moschino s'est depuis départie de la logomania qui a marqué son âge d'or dans les années 80 (qui aurait pu oublier les slogans « Ready To Where ? » ou « This Is A Very Expensive Shirt » ?). Mais Rossella Jardini, directrice de la création de toutes les lignes de produits Moschino (vendues dans 22 boutiques à travers le monde), a orienté la griffe vers un style plus contemporain tout en respectant l'état d'esprit qui a fait son succès. Depuis l'an 2000, Rossella Jardini et son équipe continuent à séduire le marché à travers la parodie et le stéréotype, deux piliers de la philosophie originelle de la maison. Défilés tapageurs où paradent des ménagères portant bigoudis et masques de nuit, discrètes dames années 50 à la Chanel (l'une des plus importantes contributions personnelles de Rossella Jardini), imprimés surchargés, effets trompe-l'œil et jupons précieux nous ont tous offert des moments de mode jubilatoires. Née en 1952 à Bergame, Rossella Jardini débute dans le métier par la vente et non par la création. En 1976, elle rencontre Nicola Trussardi et commence à l'assister dans le développement des vêtements et des articles de maroquinerie de sa marque. Elle crée sa propre ligne en 1978 avec deux amis mannequins, mais peu de temps après, elle fait la connaissance de Franco Moschino, dont elle devient l'assistante en 1981. Après un bref détour par Bottega Veneta, pour qui elle crée des accessoires, elle revient définitivement chez Moschino en 1984. Dix ans plus tard, avant sa mort tragique et précoce, Franco Moschino exprimera clairement son désir de voir Rossella Jardini reprendre le flambeau. Elle n'a plus jamais quitté la maison.   SIMON CHILVERS

PORTRAIT GRAZIELLA VIGO PHOTOGRAPHY PIERRE BAILLY STYLING CATHY KASTERINE MODEL CONSTANCE JABLONSKI APRIL 2009.

PHOTOGRAPHY TYRONE LEBON. STYLING JUDY BLAME. MODEL DUDLEY. JUNE 2009.

PHOTOGRAPHY GREG LOTUS. STYLING PATTI WILSON. MODEL BRUNO. JULY 2004.

What is your favourite piece from any of your collections? The lurex bouclé overcoat with mink coat collar from the Moschino autumn/winter 2004 collection **How would you describe your work?** My work is constant, at times it can be tiring and challenging, but always very satisfactory; anyway, a work that allows you to bet on yourself and try always to do your best **What's your ultimate goal?** To always improve upon the last collection **What inspires you?** I always start my work from the fabrics, from the fashion icons Claire McCardell, Diana Vreeland, Cecil Beaton. I also get my inspiration from clothes I see on passersby on the streets **Can fashion still have a political ambition?** In such difficult times, it seems unlikely to think of fashion as something 'political' **Who do you have in mind when you design?** Franco Moschino **Is the idea of creative collaboration important to you?** Definitely **Who has been the greatest influence on your career?** Franco Moschino **How have your own experiences affected your work as a designer?** My career and my private life have always been deeply entangled, so that it seems difficult for me to think about an influence **Which is more important in your work: the process or the product?** I think the product, now **Is designing difficult for you, if so, what drives you to continue?** At the beginning of every season, it seems to be very difficult, but as the work goes on, a kind of mechanism starts and continues by itself **Have you ever been influenced or moved by the reaction to your designs?** I am influenced by those clothes I love most **What's your definition of beauty?** All that is good becomes beautiful **What's your philosophy?** To work honestly, respecting the members of my staff **What is the most important lesson you've learned?** Humility.

"Trying hard to make it look easy"
WOLFGANG JOOP • WUNDERKIND

One of Germany's most recognised homegrown designers, Wolfgang Joop was born in Potsdam, Germany, on 18 November 1944. First tasting fame in the '80s with his JOOP! label, the brand rapidly expanded under a series of franchising deals. In 1998, Joop sold 95 per cent of his stake in the JOOP! GmbH to Wünsche AG and the remaining 5 per cent in 2001. Based in his hometown, the designer has been producing the label Wunderkind with his partner Edwin Lemberg since 2003. The collection is manufactured in Italy by Roscini, shown in Paris during Fashion Week and distributed exclusively in Wunderkind showrooms in Milan and Paris. Joop's passions stretch far beyond fashion. He has renovated two villas in his hometown of Potsdam, one of which, Villa Rumpf, was previously owned by the artist Fritz Rumpf and acted as a salon for the German Expressionists. The villas are home to an impressive collection of fine art, photography and antiques, which includes work by Jeff Koons, Tim Noble and Sue Webster and Alexandre Noll. Joop's own drawings and illustrations can be found in the permanent collections of several contemporary art museums and in 1995 the Kunstmuseum Wolfsburg held a retrospective of his graphic work. Joop is the author of several books, 'Hectic Cuisine', a satirical cookbook, 'The Little Heart', a children's fable and in 2003 he published a novel entitled 'In The Wolf's Coat'. Joop regularly writes articles on social issues for magazines and newspapers, including 'Der Spiegel', 'Stern' and 'Die Welt'. He is also a passionate supporter of the Dunkelziffer e.V. organisation for sexually abused children, and the Hamburg Leuchtfeuer organization for people with AIDS.

Der am 18. November 1944 in Potsdam geborene Wolfgang Joop gilt in Deutschland als einer der angesehensten inländischen Designer. Einen Vorgeschmack auf seine Prominenz erreichte er in den 80ern mit seinem Label JOOP!, das durch eine Reihe von Franchise-Geschäften rasch expandierte. 1998 verkaufte Joop 95% seiner Anteile an der JOOP! GmbH an die Wünsche AG, 2001 auch noch die verbleibenden 5%. Von seiner Heimatstadt aus produziert der Modemacher zusammen mit seinem Partner Edwin Lemberg seit 2003 das Label Wunderkind. Angefertigt wird die Kollektion bei Roscini in Italien, präsentiert bei der Fashion Week Paris und exklusiv vertrieben über die Wunderkind Showrooms in Mailand und Paris. Joops Leidenschaften beschränken sich allerdings nicht auf Mode allein. So hat er etwa zwei Villen in seiner Heimatstadt Potsdam renovieren lassen, von denen eine, die Villa Rumpf, früher dem Künstler Fritz Rumpf gehörte und als ein Salon der deutschen Expressionisten galt. Heute ist in den Villen eine eindrucksvolle Sammlung von Gemälden, Fotos und Antiquitäten untergebracht, unter anderem mit Werken von Jeff Koons, Tim Noble, Sue Webster und Alexandre Noll. Joops eigene Zeichnungen und Illustrationen findet man in den ständigen Ausstellungen einiger Museen für Gegenwartskunst. 1995 zeigte das Kunstmuseum Wolfsburg eine Retrospektive seiner grafischen Werke. Joop ist auch Autor mehrerer Bücher: „Hectic Cuisine" ist ein satirisches Kochbuch, „Das kleine Herz" eine Fabel für Kinder; 2003 veröffentliche er einen Roman mit dem Titel „Im Wolfspelz". Joop schreibt außerdem regelmäßig in Zeitschriften und Zeitungen, darunter Der Spiegel, Stern und Die Welt über gesellschaftlich relevante Themen. Er ist auch ein engagierter Förderer von Dunkelziffer e.V., einer Hilfsorganisation für sexuell missbrauchte Kinder, sowie dem Verein Hamburg Leuchtfeuer, der sich um Aidsinfizierte kümmert.

Considéré comme l'un des plus célèbres créateurs de mode formés sur le sol allemand, Wolfgang Joop est né à Potsdam le 18 novembre 1944. Après avoir goûté à la notoriété dans les années 80 avec sa griffe JOOP!, il diversifie rapidement ses activités à travers une série d'accords de licence. En 1998, il revend 95% de ses parts dans JOOP! GmbH à Wünsche AG, avant de céder ses 5% restants trois ans plus tard. Depuis 2003, Wolfgang Joop produit la marque Wunderkind dans sa ville natale avec son partenaire Edwin Lemberg. La collection est fabriquée en Italie par Roscini, présentée à Paris pendant la Semaine de la mode et distribuée exclusivement dans les showrooms Wunderkind de Milan et de Paris. Les passions de Wolfgang Joop ne se limitent pourtant pas à la mode. Il a rénové deux villas à Potsdam, dont l'une, la Villa Rumpf, appartenait autrefois à l'artiste Fritz Rumpf et servait de salon aux expressionnistes allemands. Ces villas accueillent d'impressionnantes collections d'art, de photos et d'antiquités, dont des œuvres de Jeff Koons, d'Alexandre Noll et de Tim Noble et Sue Webster. Les propres dessins et illustrations de Joop font partie des collections permanentes de plusieurs musées d'art contemporain. En 1995, le Kunstmuseum Wolfsburg a organisé une rétrospective de ses œuvres d'art graphique. Joop est aussi écrivain : il est l'auteur du livre de cuisine parodique «Hectic Cuisine», de la fable pour enfant «The Little Heart», et du roman «In The Wolf's Coat» publié en 2003, entre autres. Il écrit régulièrement des articles de société pour des magazines et des journaux tels que ‹Der Spiegel›, ‹Stern› et ‹Die Welt›. De plus, Wolfgang Joop est un fervent défenseur de Dunkelziffer e.V., une association qui vient au secours des enfants sexuellement maltraités, et de Hamburg Leuchtfeuer, une organisation de soutien aux personnes atteintes du sida.

MAX PEARMAIN

What are your signature designs? Constructed shoulders (summer 2006!) and deconstructed dresses. Sophisticated prints and sublime colours. Cross-fertilisation of sartorial and artistic influences **What is your favourite piece from any of your collections?** A white pagoda jacket (spring/summer 2006), which was customised in 1940 for my Tante Ulla. A dress from the autumn/winter 2009 collection in chiffon showing a black and white photo print of a deer framed by handpainted stripes. The idea is a mix of hyper-realism and constructivism **How would you describe your work?** Trying hard to make it look easy **What's your ultimate goal?** Having a goal! **What inspires you?** The smell of teenage spirit **Can fashion still have a political ambition?** The way we feel today or tomorrow has a political reason. Fashion's future is made out of the same stuff as fashion's history **Who do you have in mind when you design?** Human beings who do not have a certain 'event' in mind when they are in the mood for love or fashion. Ignoring winter or summer time to wear either fur or fringes **Is the idea of creative collaboration important to you?** As a painter, I can paint alone like a hermit. As a designer, I am as good as my team allows me to be **Who has been the greatest influence on your career?** Yves Saint Laurent and Tamara de Lempicka – and of course the revolutionary times I had the chance to grew up in **How have your own experiences affected your work as a designer?** My biography is a lecture of contradictions **Which is more important in your work: the process or the product?** The process is full of suspense and expectation. The end of a fashion show is for me a moment of depression and emptiness. The 'product' is a compliment to me if it's taken and owned **Is designing difficult for you? If so, what drives you to continue?** The spirits I am calling are always haunting me. They don't come one at a time, they come like an army. The force behind me is not to give up until the battle is over! Fashion is war! **Have you ever been influenced or moved by the reaction to your designs?** I always try to start with a commercial concept. But during my work, I forget it and just follow my instincts **What's your definition of beauty?** A balance between inner and outer beauty. Real and unique beauty demands us to keep distance! **What's your philosophy?** No one benefits your trying – and don't shed sweat-drops on stage if you want to be a ballet dancer! **What is the most important lesson you've learned?** Nice is the little sister of shit!

"I can find inspiration anywhere"
CHRISTOPHER KANE

Born 1982 in Glasgow, Christopher Kane's first taste of the fashion world was through Fashion TV, hosted by Jenny Baker. Growing up on a council estate until his father's business took off, Fashion TV introduced Kane to the world of Karl Lagerfeld, Gianni Versace, Thierry Mugler, Christian Lacroix and Helmut Lang. Straight after his 18th birthday, Kane applied to Central Saint Martins, going to London for the interview was the first time he came to the city. Winning a Lancôme Colour Award (2005) while at college proved a turning point; through the acquaintance of fashion journalist Sarah Mower, Kane went on to meet Anna Wintour and Donatella Versace. In September 2006 Kane was awarded the New Generation sponsorship from the British Fashion Council and held his first solo catwalk show. Kane's neon-coloured bandage dresses took the fashion press by storm, instantly sealing his name as the one to look forward to at every London catwalk season. Together with his sister, Tammy, who is his collaborator and business partner, each and every one of their collections has continued to surprise, impress and seduce. In November 2007 he was awarded the New Designer of the Year award at the British Fashion Awards.

Der 1982 in Glasgow geborene Christopher Kane kam erstmals durch die von Jenny Baker moderierte Sendung ‚Fashion TV' auf den Geschmack in Sachen Mode. Kane, der in einer Sozialwohnung aufwuchs, bis das Geschäft seines Vaters florierte, schenkte ‚Fashion TV' Einblick in die Welt von Karl Lagerfeld, Gianni Versace, Thierry Mugler, Christian Lacroix und Helmut Lang. Gleich nach seinem 18. Geburtstag bewarb Kane sich am Central Saint Martins – und die Reise zum Aufnahmegespräch war sein erster Ausflug in die Hauptstadt. Als er noch als Student einen Lancôme Colour Award (2005) gewann, war das der Wendepunkt für ihn. Über die Bekanntschaft mit der Modejournalistin Sarah Mower lernte Kane Anna Wintour und Donatella Versace kennen. Im September

2006 gewann er das New-Generation-Stipendium des British Fashion Council und veranstaltete seine erste Solo-Schau auf dem Catwalk. Kanes neonfarbene Bandagenkleider eroberten die Modepresse im Sturm und sorgten unverzüglich dafür, dass man sich seither in jeder Londoner Catwalk-Saison auf seinen Namen freut. Gemeinsam mit seiner Schwester Tammy, die als Mitarbeiterin und Geschäftspartnerin zugleich fungiert, ist es ihm gelungen, wirklich all seine Kollektionen überraschend, eindrucksvoll und verführerisch zu gestalten. Im November 2007 wurde er bei den British Fashion Awards als New Designer of the Year ausgezeichnet.

Né à Glasgow en 1982, Christopher Kane a découvert la mode sur ‹Fashion TV› grâce à l'animatrice Jenny Baker. Jusqu'à ce que l'entreprise de son père décolle, il grandit dans des logements sociaux et regarde cette chaîne de télévision qui l'introduit au monde de Karl Lagerfeld, Gianni Versace, Thierry Mugler, Christian Lacroix et Helmut Lang. Juste après son 18e anniversaire, Kane postule à Central Saint Martins : son entretien de candidature lui donne l'opportunité de venir à Londres pour la première fois. Le Lancôme Colour Award (2005) qu'il remporte pendant ses études s'avère décisif ; ami avec la journaliste de mode Sarah Mower, Kane finit par rencontrer Anna Wintour et Donatella Versace. En septembre 2006, il décroche la bourse New Generation du British Fashion Council et donne son tout premier défilé en solo. Ses robes « bandage » fluorescentes prennent la presse spécialisée par surprise et font immédiatement de lui le nouveau talent à suivre à chaque édition de la London Fashion Week. Avec sa sœur Tammy, à la fois sa collaboratrice et son associée, il présente des collections qui ne se lassent pas de surprendre, d'impressionner et de séduire. En novembre 2007, les British Fashion Awards le consacrent New Designer of the Year. KAREN LEONG

PHOTOGRAPHY DANIEL JACKSON STYLING MARIE CHAIX MODEL HELENA SOPAR SEPTEMBER 2007

PHOTOGRAPHY SØLVE SUNDSBØ. FASHION DIRECTOR EDWARD ENNINFUL. MODEL ELIZA CUMMINGS. MARCH 2009.

What is your favourite piece from any of your collections? I will always love my sequin palette pants from Fall/Winter 2008 worn with the metal cashmere sweater, it is such a strong look besides my graduation show work **How would you describe your work?** Who cares what I think of my work, I want other people to think. If pushed I would describe it as covetable and desirable, with integrity. **What's your ultimate goal?** I love my job and I am very passionate about fashion and art. I want to be in the industry for a long time. That is my goal, to be successful and keep producing work that makes me feel happy and fulfilled **What inspires you?** Things that people find non-inspiring. I like to dig around to discover things that people would say are ugly or non-fashion and then create something beautiful from them. We go back to our childhood a lot for references, whether it be characters from where we used to live or films. I can find inspiration anywhere **Can fashion still have a political ambition?** Of course, thinking back to Vivienne Westwood's punk era, they shocked and excited people. I guess it just depends on the designer and your objective for the season **Is the idea of creative collaboration important to you?** I have collaborated with my sister Tammy for the past 8 years. I am lucky that I have someone so strong to work with. I like to keep it close knit and have very little opinion except myself and Tammy's **Who has been the greatest influence on your career?** Tammy, Louise Wilson whilst studying for my MA at college and Sarah Mower for introducing me to Anna Wintour and Donatella Versace **How have your own experiences affected your work as a designer?** I think the older you become, the wiser you become. Working with Donatella Versace on Versus has definitely opened my eyes to what can be achieved by a proper atelier **Which is more important in your work: the process or the product?** Both are very important, it's the same thing to me. I never really think of anything that I do as a product until I see it on a shop floor then I immediately hate it **Is designing difficult for you? If so, what drives you to continue?** To design can be both easy and hard, it depends on the workload, pressure and how you're feeling at the time. I am sure all designers, artists or writers suffer from creative block. That can be frustrating, but I know it will always come back **What's your philosophy?** To work hard at creating new and exciting fashion **What is the most important lesson you've learned?** Be discreet and be careful who you trust. This business is tough and cut-throat.

"I never see one woman when I design, it's always a universe of women"
DONNA KARAN

While she was still a student at the Parsons School of Design in New York, Long Island native Donna Karan was offered a summer job assisting Anne Klein. After three years as associate designer, Karan was named as Klein's successor and, following her mentor's death in 1974, Karan became head of the company. After a decade at Anne Klein, where she established a reputation for practical luxury sportswear separates, typically in stretch fabrics and dark hues, Karan founded her own company in 1984 with her late husband, Stephan Weiss. A year later, her highly acclaimed Donna Karan New York Collection, based on the concept of 'seven easy pieces', unveiled the bodysuit that was to become her trademark. Karan's emphasis on simple yet sophisticated designs, including everything from wrap skirts to corseted eveningwear, captured the popular mood of 'body consciousness' that swept Hollywood in the '80s. By 1989, she had expanded this philosophy to the street-smart diffusion line DKNY. In 1992, inspired by the desire to dress her husband, a menswear line was launched, with a DKNY Men emerging a year later. Since then, Donna Karan International has continued to diversify and expand to cover every age and lifestyle, including a children's range, eyewear, fragrances and home furnishings. She has been honoured with an unprecedented seven CFDA awards, including 2004's Lifetime Achievement Award to coincide with her 20th anniversary. The company became a publicly traded enterprise in 1996 and was acquired by French luxury conglomerate LVMH in 2001 for a reported $643 million. Karan remains the chief designer. Today Donna Karan International boasts over 100 company-owned, licensed, free-standing Donna Karan collection, DKNY and DKNY Jeans stores worldwide. In 2007, she launched The Urban Zen Foundation, a non-profit organisation inspired by her global travels. The Foundation includes The Urban Zen store and Urban Zen fashion line, proceeds of which go towards raising awareness in areas of well being, empowering children and preserving cultures.

Noch während ihres Studiums an der New Yorker Parsons School of Design bekam die aus Long Island stammenden Donna Karan einen Ferienjob als Assistentin von Anne Klein angeboten. Nach drei Jahren als Associate Designer wurde sie schließlich Kleins Nachfolgerin und übernahm nach dem Tod ihrer Mentorin 1974 die Firmenleitung. Nach einem Jahrzehnt bei Anne Klein, in dem sie den Ruf des Modehauses als erste Adresse für praktische, aber zugleich luxuriöse Sportswear-Separates – üblicherweise aus Stretchmaterialien und in dunklen Farbtönen – etabliert hatte, erfolgte 1984 die Gründung der eigenen Firma, zusammen mit Stephan Weiss, ihrem späteren Ehemann. Ein Jahr später wurde die viel gelobte Donna Karan New York Collection präsentiert, die auf dem Konzept von „sieben einfachen Teilen" basierte. Dazu zählte auch der schwarze Body, der ihr Markenzeichen werden sollte. Karans Faible für schlichte und doch raffinierte Entwürfe, egal ob Wickelröcke oder Abendkleider mit Corsage, entsprach ganz dem Trend zu mehr Körperbewusstsein, der im Hollywood der 1980er-Jahre so verbreitet war. 1989 wandte Karan diese Philosophie auch auf die street-smarte Nebenlinie DKNY an. Inspiriert von dem Wunsch, den eigenen Mann einzukleiden, entstand 1992 eine Linie für Herrenmode. Seit damals

diversifiziert und expandiert Donna Karan International weiter und bedient inzwischen jedes Alter und diverse Lebensstile, u. a. mit Kindermode, Brillen, Düften und Wohnaccessoires. Bislang unerreicht sind ihre sieben Auszeichnungen durch die CFDA, darunter 2004 ein Lifetime Achievement Award, der mit ihrem 20-jährigen Berufsjubiläum zusammenfiel. Zum börsennotierten Unternehmen wurde die Firma 1996. Im Jahr 2001 kaufte sie schließlich der französische Luxuswarenkonzern LVMH für angeblich 643 Millionen Dollar auf. Heute hat Donna Karan International über 100 firmeneigene, lizenzierte, aber eigenständige Filialen von Donna Karan Collection, DKNY und DKNY Jeans weltweit vorzuweisen. 2007 rief Karan The Urban Zen Foundation ins Leben, eine Non-Profit-Organisation, zu der ihre Reisen in alle Welt sie inspiriert haben. Die Foundation umfasst auch einen Laden namens The Urban Zen und eine gleichnamige Modelinie. Ziele dieses Projekts sind ein verbessertes Gesundheitsbewusstsein, Stärkung von Kinderrechten sowie der Schutz bedrohter Völker.

Alors qu'elle est encore étudiante à la Parsons School of Design de New York, la jeune Donna Karan, originaire de Long Island, se voit proposer un job d'été comme assistante d'Anne Klein. Après trois années au poste de styliste associée, elle est nommée à la succession d'Anne Klein et, à la mort de son mentor en 1974, reprend la direction de l'entreprise. Après une décennie passée chez Anne Klein, où elle se forge une solide réputation en créant des séparés sportswear luxueux et faciles à porter généralement coupés dans des tissus stretch aux couleurs sombres, Donna Karan fonde sa propre griffe en 1984 avec son mari Stephan Weiss, aujourd'hui décédé. Un an plus tard, sa collection à succès Donna Karan New York articulée autour du concept des « seven easy pieces » dévoile le bodysuit qui devait devenir sa signature. Sa prédilection pour les pièces simples mais sophistiquées, de la jupe portefeuille aux tenues de soirée corsetées, capture tout l'esprit de la tendance au « body consciousness » qui déferle sur Hollywood dans les années 80. En 1989, elle étend cette philosophie à sa ligne de diffusion DKNY. Inspirée par l'envie d'habiller son mari, elle lance une ligne pour homme en 1992. Depuis, la société Donna Karan International ne cesse de se diversifier et de se développer pour couvrir toutes les tranches d'âge et styles de vie, notamment avec une gamme pour enfant, des lunettes, des parfums et des meubles. Elle a reçu sept prix du CFDA, un record sans précédent, notamment un Lifetime Achievement Award couronnant sa carrière en 2004, une année où elle célèbre également le 20e anniversaire de sa société. Introduite en bourse en 1996, son entreprise a été rachetée par le groupe de luxe français LVMH en 2001 pour un montant estimé à 643 millions de dollars. Aujourd'hui, Donna Karan International possède plus de 100 boutiques indépendantes distribuant les collections Donna Karan, DKNY et DKNY Jeans dans le monde entier. En 2007, Donna Karan crée The Urban Zen Foundation, une association à but non lucratif inspirée par ses voyages autour du monde. Au sein même de la fondation, la boutique The Urban Zen vend, entre autres, la collection de vêtements du même nom et réinvestit ses bénéfices dans la sensibilisation du public aux questions du bien-être, de l'émancipation des enfants et de la sauvegarde des cultures.

MARK HOOPER

PORTRAIT JENNIFER LIVINGSTON. PHOTOGRAPHY SATOSHI SAIKUSA. STYLING HAVANA LAFFITTE. MODEL DARIA. MAY 2004.

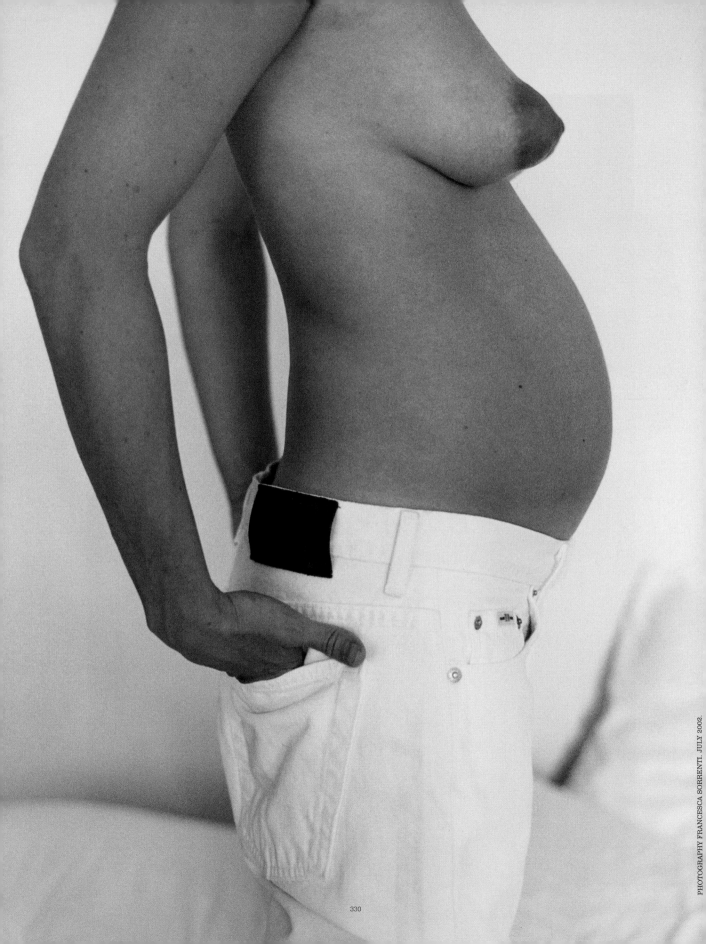

PHOTOGRAPHY FRANCESCA SORRENTI. JULY 2002.

What are your signature pieces? My seven easy pieces wardrobe. It's a simple, sophisticated system of dressing that takes a woman from day into evening, weekday to weekend **How would you describe your work?** Sensual, urban and body-conscious **What's your ultimate goal?** Professionally, it's always what I haven't done that excites me. But my ultimate goal in life is to find peace and happiness **What inspires you?** Any- and everything. Passion. Sensuality. Nature – the textures of the beach, the melding colours of water, the electricity of the night **Can fashion still have a political ambition?** Absolutely. When you're creating something, you must be sensitive to what people want and the times

they live in. However innovative it is, what you create must be relevant and reflect the here and now **Who do you have in mind when you design?** I never see one woman when I design, it's always a universe of women. Strong passionate women, women who are true to themselves and their visions. I see clothes as a canvas to their individuality. The woman is the first thing you see, not the clothes **Is the idea of creative collaboration important to you?** You are only as good as the people behind you. It can't be done alone **Who has been the greatest influence on your career?** Anne Klein – her passing pushed me into becoming a designer. It wasn't something I was sure I wanted to do **How have your**

own experiences affected your work as a designer? My own personal needs – what works and doesn't work – affect my work. The fact that I'm a woman and, like all women, want to be taller, thinner and look sophisticated without a lot of effort. Everything I create works to that end **Which is more important in your work: the process or the product?** When all becomes one. When the product fulfils the dream of inspiration **Is designing difficult for you? If so, what drives you to continue?** The challenge of creation. I try to stay open to new things. To live is to move forward, to discover new means of expression **Have you ever been influenced or moved by the reaction to your designs?** Yes – I have to

think twice about the way people react. People's reactions can motivate me to another level **What's your definition of beauty?** Beauty is about individuality. There is nothing more attractive than a woman who values her uniqueness. She has the confidence to express herself, to say something new, to create from within **What's your philosophy?** Never stop challenging yourself. When I design, I'm always looking for a balance between purpose and expression **What is the most important lesson you've learned?** No matter how bad or good it is, it will always change. Everything is in constant motion.

"The same spirit runs through everything I do"
REI KAWAKUBO · COMME DES GARÇONS

Rei Kawakubo established Comme des Garçons in Tokyo in 1973. A designer who has dispensed with the rule book, who cuts and constructs in such a way that her clothes have skirted art, Kawakubo's readiness to challenge conventions – to produce uniform-like clothes that are neither obviously for men nor for women, that distort rather than enhance the female form, that use unusual fabrics and deconstruct them sometimes to the point of destruction – has nevertheless created a global concern. She launched Comme des Garçons to the West in 1981, when she showed her first collection in Paris and was among the avant-garde Japanese to introduce black as an everyday fashion staple – unthinkingly dubbed 'Hiroshima Chic' by some critics. Then as now, it bewildered as much as it excited. The self-taught, multiple award-winning Kawakubo (born in Tokyo in 1942) did not, however, follow the standard route into the fashion industry. She began her career by reading literature at Tokyo's Keio University and, on graduation in 1964, joined the Ashai Kasei chemical and textiles company, working in its advertising department. Unable to find the garments she wanted for herself, she started to design them. She launched menswear in 1978, and a furniture line in 1982. Comme remains progressive: the label's fragrances, for instance, have played with tar, rubber and nail polish odours. Retail projects have included short-term 'guerrilla' stores in the backwater areas of, for the fashion world, unexpected cities, through to London's monolithic Dover Street Market, in which the company, which she co-runs with British husband Adrian Joffe, also rents space to like-minded designers. Recent collaborations include a capsule collection for H&M and a bag collaboration with Louis Vuitton to celebrate 30 years of Louis Vuitton in Japan.

Rei Kawakubo gründete Comme des Garçons 1973 in Tokio. Sie ist eine Designerin, die alle Regeln bricht und so zuschneidet und konstruiert, dass ihre Kleider geschneiderte Kunstwerke sind. Kawakubo war bereit, Konventionen in Frage zu stellen, indem sie uniformähnliche Teile produzierte, die weder eindeutig als Herren- noch als Damenmode identifizierbar waren, die weibliche Formen eher verzerrten als unterstrichen und die aus ungewöhnlichen, oft bis zur Zerstörung dekonstruierten Materialien gefertigt waren – und schuf trotzdem einen weltweit agierenden Konzern. Im Westen wurde Comme des Garçons erstmals 1981 lanciert, als Kawakubo ihre erste Kollektion in Paris zeigte. Damals gehörte sie zu den avantgardistischen Japanern, die Schwarz in der Alltagsmode etablierten – was einige Kritiker gedankenlos als „Hiroshima Chic" geißelten. Damals wie heute ruft diese Mode ebenso viel Verwirrung wie Interesse hervor. Die 1942 in Tokio geborene und mit zahlreichen Auszeichnungen überhäufte Autodidaktin kam übrigens nicht auf dem klassischen Pfad in die Modeindustrie. Vielmehr begann sie ihre Berufslaufbahn mit einem Literaturstudium an der Keio Universität von Tokio. Nach ihrem Abschluss 1964 trat sie in die Werbeabteilung des Chemie- und Textilunternehmens Ashai Kasei ein. Weil sie keine

Kleidung fand, die ihr gefiel, begann sie, diese selbst zu entwerfen. Ihre erste Herrenkollektion präsentierte sie dann 1978, eine Möbellinie kam 1982 hinzu. Das Label bleibt progressiv: So experimentierte man etwa bei Comme-des-Garçons-Düften mit Teer, Gummi und dem Geruch von Nagellack. Alternative Vertriebsprojekte waren u. a. die zeitlich begrenzten Guerilla Stores in rückständigen Gegenden von – zumindest für die Modewelt – unbedeutenden Städten. Nicht zu vergessen der gigantische Dover Street Market in London, wo das Unternehmen, das Kawakubo gemeinsam mit ihrem britischen Ehemann Adrian Joffe führt, auch anderen gleichgesinnten Designern Raum bietet. Jüngste Kooperationen waren eine einmalige Kollektion für H&M und eine Taschenkollektion bei Louis Vuitton anlässlich des 30-jährigen Jubiläums von Louis Vuitton in Japan.

Rei Kawakubo a créée Comme des Garçons à Tokyo en 1973. Tournant le dos aux règles établies, Rei Kawakubo taille et construit des vêtements qui ressemblent plus à des œuvres d'art qu'à des créations de mode. Son enthousiasme à défier les conventions attire l'attention du monde entier avec des vêtements confinant à l'uniforme – dont on n'arrive pas vraiment à savoir s'ils ont été conçus pour les hommes ou les femmes, qui déplacent la forme du corps féminin plutôt que de la souligner, qui utilisent des tissus atypiques et les déconstruisent parfois jusqu'au point de non retour. En 1981, elle lance Comme des Garçons en Occident lors de son premier défilé parisien et s'impose alors à l'avant-garde de la mode japonaise, qui introduit le noir comme un basique de la mode : un style que certains critiques peu inspirés surnommeront le « Hiroshima Chic ». A l'époque comme aujourd'hui, sa mode déroute autant qu'elle ravit. Autodidacte maintes fois primée, Rei Kawakubo (née en 1942 à Tokyo) est arrivée dans l'univers de la mode par des chemins détournés. Elle étudie d'abord la littérature à l'université Keio de Tokyo. En 1964, après l'obtention de son diplôme, elle travaille pour le département publicité d'Ashai Kasei, un fabricant de produits chimiques et textiles. Comme elle n'arrive pas à trouver dans le commerce les vêtements qu'elle a envie de porter, elle apprend à les confectionner elle-même. Elle lance une ligne pour homme en 1978, puis une collection de meubles en 1982. Comme des Garçons reste une griffe progressiste : par exemple, les parfums Comme des Garçons jouent sur d'étonnantes notes de goudron, de caoutchouc ou de vernis à ongles. Parmi ses projets les plus récents, elle a installé des boutiques-concepts éphémères dans des quartiers peu fréquentés de villes inattendues dans l'univers de la mode. Et dans le monolithique Dover Street Market de Londres, l'entreprise qu'elle dirige avec son mari anglais Adrian Joffe loue également des ateliers à d'autres créateurs partageant le même état d'esprit. Ses dernières collaborations en date incluent une mini-collection pour H&M et la création de sacs Louis Vuitton pour célébrer les 30 ans de présence de la marque au Japon.

JOSH SIMS

PORTRAIT TIMOTHY GREENFIELD. PHOTOGRAPHY RICHARD BURBRIDGE. FASHION DIRECTOR EDWARD ENNINFUL. MODEL MISSY RAYDER. JUNE 2004.

PHOTOGRAPHY WILLY VANDERPERRE. STYLING OLIVIER RIZZO. MODEL JEREMY. FEBRUARY 2005.

REI KAWAKUBO

PHOTOGRAPHY RICHARD BURBRIDGE FASHION DIRECTOR EDWARD ENNINFUL MARCH 2001.

PHOTOGRAPHY NICK HAYMES. STYLING HAVANA LAFFITTE. MODEL NATALIA CHABANENKO. APRIL, 2009.

PHOTOGRAPHY EMMA SUMMERTON. FASHION DIRECTOR EDWARD ENNINFUL. MODEL SASHA PIVOVAROVA. JULY 2008.

Tass appeal

Wednesday 3rd June 06 at approx
50pm a Man was assaulted
side Marden Squ. Drummond rd.
urton

Thinking of you

Did you see or hear anything?
an you help?
In the strictest confidence Telephone
220 7232 684
ce call at local police Stn
or call crime Stoppers
on 0800 555 111

What are your signature designs? There are no signature designs as such. But the same spirit runs through everything I do **What is your favourite piece from any of your collections?** I have none **How would you describe your work?** My job, my responsibility, it's what I do **What's your ultimate goal?** I have none. I want to carry on having a free and independent company **What inspires you?** Many, many things. Strength and beauty **Can fashion still have a political ambition?** Not for me **Who do you have in mind when you design?** Depends on each collection. Every time it is different **Is the idea of creative collaboration important to you?** I find it interesting **Who has been the greatest influence on your career?** No one **How have your own experiences affected your work as a designer?** No one is not affected by their own experiences. My experiences made me **Which is more important in your work: the process or the product?** Both **Is designing difficult for you? If so, what drives you to continue?** It is very difficult, but I have a responsibility to my company **Have you ever been influenced or moved by the reaction to your designs?** Never **What's your definition of beauty?** Beauty is whatever anyone thinks is beautiful **What's your philosophy?** Freedom **What is the most important lesson you've learned?** Every lesson is important. I don't believe in a hit parade of lessons.

What are your signature designs? Jumpsuits, handmade suits and sportswear all made in Italy. As well as worker cottons for tailoring and soft fabrics that look rough **What is your favourite piece from any of your collections?** The classic jumpsuit from autumn/winter 2005, which was inspired by the worker mentality of the mid-century studio artist **How would you describe your work?** I tell a story every season, which captures a feeling from the past and lets that aesthetic resonate with my contemporaries. Menswear should feel familiar to the man who wears it. Incorporating silhouettes and fabrics that evoke that sense of classic, individual style makes the clothing more effortless and real. I don't mind making more avant-garde pieces, as long as it's rooted in a classic masculine context **What's your ultimate goal?** To keep creating forever **What inspires you?** Movements in American culture, specifically art and their immediate subcultures **Can fashion still have a political ambition?** A designer's values come out through the clothes and should remain in the clothes **Who do you have in mind when you design?** My fellow New York contemporaries **Is the idea of creative collaboration important to you?** Yes, I'm a big believer in honouring the work of others and, in many ways, each collection is a collaboration with artists and creators past and present. Most recently, I made a record of the autumn/winter 2009 collection with the help of legendary artist and photographer Gerard Malanga, who recreated his iconic Warhol screen tests with contemporary New York artists wearing the clothes **Who has been the greatest influence on your career?** My brother, Alexei Hay **How have your own experiences affected your work as a designer?** My experiences when researching a particular time or scene greatly affects my work. So much of what I ultimately produce comes from very real experiences in the research stage **Which is more important in your work: the process or the product?** Both. I enjoy the process of finding an inspiration and translating that into a collection, but I think the product is what really matters in the end **Is designing difficult for you? If so, what drives you to continue?** It's not difficult. I think humans like doing what they are good at and they are good at what they like doing **Have you ever been influenced or moved by the reaction to your designs?** Feedback is always making me a better designer. The upside of working in fashion, you're in constant dialogue with your audience – at least you are twice a year **What's your definition of beauty?** Beauty is human personality and freedom to express anything you want **What's your philosophy?** I've always tried to keep my work between the poles of the literal and the conceptual **What is the most important lesson you've learned?** Stick to your guns.

"My aim is always to hit a chord"
SOPHIA KOKOSALAKI

Sophia Kokosalaki has never gone about things the usual way. Instead, she relies on single-minded individualism. Born in Athens in 1972, Kokosalaki's first love was literature, studying Greek and English at the University of Athens. She went to London in 1996 and completed a womenswear MA at Central Saint Martins. For her graduation show, she worked with Abigail Lane to produce the video installation 'Never Never Mind' and her graduate collection was snapped up by the (now defunct) London boutique Pellicano. Kokosalaki set up her own label in 1999 and quickly established a trademark style, dipping into the rich heritage of ancient Greek drapery, a '70s folk aesthetic and complex leatherwork. It wasn't long before others wanted a piece of the action. In June 1999, Kokosalaki worked on a knitwear line for Joseph. By 2000, after just three solo collections, she was invited to work as a guest designer for Italian leather goods label Ruffo Research. She also entertained the more accessible end of the fashion market, producing two capsule collections for Topshop's TS label. In 2004, she was chosen to design the costumes for the Athens Olympic Games, the highlight of which was a vast marine-blue dress worn by Björk. Despite such demanding extracurricular activities, her day job has flourished. A menswear line was set up in 2000 and a shoe collection was added in 2003. The recipient of many awards, Kokosalaki's notable gongs include the first ever Art Foundation Award given to a fashion designer. Kokosalaki constantly develops her themes, and dedicated fans return every season as she evolves – rather than rethinks – her signatures. Spring/summer 2005 saw ruched pastels for a delicate seaside feel and a somewhat strategic move to the Paris schedule. Both cerebral and fun-loving, Kokosalaki is never complacent.

Sophia Kokosalaki ist die Dinge noch nie auf herkömmliche Weise angegangen. Stattdessen setzt sie auf zielstrebigen Individualismus. Die erste Liebe der 1972 in Athen geborenen Designerin galt der Literatur, weshalb sie zunächst Griechisch und Englisch an der Universität ihrer Heimatstadt studierte. 1996 ging sie nach London, wo sie einen Master in Damenmode am Central Saint Martins erwarb. Für ihre Abschlusskollektion tat sie sich mit Abigail Lane zusammen und produzierte die Videoinstallation „Never Never Mind". Die Kollektion selbst sicherte sich die inzwischen nicht mehr existierende Londoner Boutique Pellicano. 1999 gründete Kokosalaki ihr eigenes Label und etablierte schnell einen unverwechselbaren Stil. Dazu nahm sie Anleihen bei den im antiken Griechenland üblichen Drapierungen sowie der Folk-Ästhetik der 1970er-Jahre und kombinierte beides mit aufwändigen Lederarbeiten. Schon bald waren ihre Entwürfe extrem begehrt. Kokosalaki kreierte im Juni 1999 eine Strickkollektion für Joseph. Und bereits im Jahr 2000, nach nur drei Solokollektionen, wurde sie als Gastdesignerin vom italienischen Lederwarenhersteller Ruffo Research eingeladen. Sie bediente aber auch das erschwinglichere Ende des Modemarktes mit zwei Minikollektionen für das Label TS bei Topshop. 2004 bekam sie den Auftrag für die Kostüme zu den Olympischen Spielen von Athen. Das Highlight dieser Kollektion war das aufwändige marineblaue Kleid für die Sängerin Björk. Trotz solch anspruchsvoller Nebentätigkeiten ist die Designerin auch in ihrem Hauptberuf produktiv. Im Jahr 2000 wurde eine Herrenlinie ins Leben gerufen, eine Schuhkollektion kam 2003 hinzu. Unter ihren zahlreichen Auszeichnungen verdient der erste je für Modedesign verliehene Art Foundation Award besondere Beachtung. Kokosalaki entwickelt ihre Themen ständig weiter, und so kehren pflichtbewusste Fans in jeder Saison zu ihr zurück, um zu sehen, wie sie ihre Charakteristika mehr aus- als umarbeitet. Für Frühjahr/Sommer 2005 erzeugten pastellfarbene Rüschen ein Flair von Ferien am Meer, und die Designerin passte sich vermutlich aus strategischen Gründen dem Pariser Show-Kalender an. Kokosalaki ist nachdenklich und lebenslustig zugleich, aber niemals selbstgefällig.

Privilégiant son farouche individualisme, Sophia Kokosalaki ne fait jamais rien comme tout le monde. Née en 1972 à Athènes, elle se passionne d'abord pour la littérature et étudie le grec et l'anglais à l'université d'Athènes. Elle s'installe à Londres en 1996, où elle décroche un Master en mode féminine à Central Saint Martins. Pour sa présentation de fin d'études, elle collabore avec Abigail Lane sur l'installation vidéo « Never Never Mind », une collection sur laquelle se jette la boutique londonienne Pellicano (fermée depuis). Sophia Kokosalaki crée sa propre griffe en 1999 et impose rapidement son style caractéristique, inspiré par le riche héritage des drapés grecs antiques, une esthétique folk très années 70 et un travail élaboré du cuir. Son travail ne tarde pas à attirer l'attention d'autres créateurs. En juin 1999, Sophia Kokosalaki conçoit une ligne en maille pour Joseph. En l'an 2000, après seulement trois collections en solo, le maroquinier italien Ruffo Research lui commande également des collections. Elle a aussi travaillé pour le marché plus accessible de la grande consommation en produisant deux mini-collections pour la griffe TS de Topshop. En 2004, on lui confie la création des costumes des Jeux olympiques d'Athènes, dont personne n'oubliera jamais la volumineuse robe bleu marine portée par Björk. En dépit de ses nombreuses activités annexes, sa propre griffe prospère. Elle a lancé une ligne pour homme en l'an 2000 et une collection de chaussures en 2003. Couronnée de nombreux prix, elle a notamment reçu le premier Art Foundation Award jamais remis à un couturier. Sophia Kokosalaki n'a de cesse de développer ses propres thématiques et ses fans lui restent fidèles chaque saison, quand elle propose une évolution plutôt qu'une réinterprétation de ses looks signature. Pour la saison printemps/été 2005, elle présente des couleurs pastel et des ruchés au style balnéaire délicat, et défile désormais à Paris, une décision quelque peu stratégique. A la fois cérébrale et insouciante, Sophia Kokosalaki ne fait jamais dans la complaisance.

LAUREN COCHRANE

PORTRAIT WILLIAM SELDEN. PHOTOGRAPHY REBECCA PIERCE. STYLING MARCUS ROSS. MODEL RINA. OCTOBER 2004.

PHOTOGRAPHY RICHARD BUSH. STYLING JANE HOW. APRIL 2002.

What are your signature designs? A signature design would have to involve elaborate handwork, traditional or military elements and an alternative or Teutonic silhouette **What's your favourite piece from any of your collections?** A draped patchwork leather and jersey dress from my spring/summer 2000 collection, as it was one of my first experiments **How would you describe your work?** Complex and labour-intensive, but also light and contemporary **What's your ultimate goal?** Achieving a perfect balance between life and work **What inspires you?** It is usually a combination of elements and situations **Can fashion still have a political ambition?** No, but it can have an emotional feel **Who do you have in mind when you design?** Nobody specific **Is the idea of creative collaboration important to you?** Yes, dialogue with people that share a similar aesthetic can be unexpectedly conclusive and productive **What has been the greatest influence on your career?** The need to be independent was the one thing that controlled my career **How have your own experiences affected your work as a designer?** In a decisive way because experiences define your personality and my personality interferes with my work a lot **Which is more important in your work: the process or the product?** Both **Is designing difficult for you? If so, what drives you to continue?** Designing is never difficult but the technical complexities can be a challenge **Have you ever been influenced or moved by the reaction to your designs?** Of course, because with my work, my aim is always to hit a chord **What's your definition of beauty?** It changes constantly, but a slight imperfection always adds more allure **What's your philosophy?** It's never as hard as it seems **What is the most important lesson you've learned?** You can never start working early enough.

"There's no point in design for design's sake.
Everything I believe in is about getting women dressed"
MICHAEL KORS

Michael Kors designs pure American opulence: luxurious perfectly tailored sportswear in contrasting textures of leather and cashmere with a cheeky flash of pelt. Growing up in deepest suburbia, Kors (born Long Island) always had a healthy focus on fashion and the city of New York. After studying design at the Fashion Institute of Technology, New York, by the age of 19, he was designing and merchandising for Lothar's boutique. The attention this received by the fashion press led him to launch the Michael Kors label in 1981. The Kors Michael Kors bridge line followed in 1995. After launching a capsule menswear collection in 1997, Kors was named the first women's ready-to-wear designer for the house of Céline. By February 1999, he had become creative director of the luxury label, overseeing all women's products. 1999 marked the beginning of a remarkable period for Kors: he was awarded the CFDA Award for Womenswear Designer of the Year, followed by the Menswear Designer of the Year award in 2003. His contribution to the world of accessories was also recognised, with Kors being nominated five years in a row (2001–05) for the prestigious Accessories Designer of the Year award. He has also had success in the fragrance world, launching his signature scent in 2000, a cologne Michael for Men in 2001, and the Fifi award-winning Island Michael Kors scent in 2005. While 2004 saw Kors make his TV debut as one of the judges on the Emmy-nominated reality TV show 'Project Runway', a role that he continues to hold for the programme's five series. With celebrity fans including Jennifer Lopez, Charlize Theron, Liv Tyler, Gwyneth Paltrow, Anjelica Huston and Madonna, Kors continues to design to a sophisticated ethic, a sexy American Dream.

Michael Kors entwirft amerikanische Opulenz in Reinkultur: luxuriöse, perfekt geschnittene Freizeitmode aus Leder und Kaschmir als Materialien mit kontrastierender Textur, dazu frech aufblitzender Pelz. Aufgewachsen ist der auf Long Island geborene Kors in der Vorstadt, doch hatte er bereits dort die Mode und New York City genau im Blick. Nach dem Studium am New Yorker Fashion Institute of Technology entwarf er schon mit 19 erfolgreich für Lothar's Boutique. Nachdem er damit bereits die Aufmerksamkeit der Modepresse auf sich gezogen hatte, wagte er sich 1981 an die Gründung eines eigenen Labels mit seinem Namen. Die preiswertere Nebenlinie Kors Michael Kors folgte 1995. Nach der Präsentation einer kleinen Herrenkollektion im Jahr 1997 wurde Kors erster Designer für die Prêt-à-Porter-Damenmode im Hause Céline. Bis Februar 1999 war er zum Creative Director des Luxuslabels aufgestiegen und fortan für alle Damenprodukte zuständig. 1999 war aber auch in anderer Hinsicht ein bemerkenswertes Jahr für Kors: Das CFDA ernannte ihn zum Womenswear Designer of the Year. 2003 folgte die Auszeichnung als Menswear Designer of the Year. Seine Leistungen im Bereich Accessoires wurden ebenfalls honoriert, denn Kors war von 2001 bis 2005 fünfmal in Folge für den renom-mierten Titel Accessories Designer of the Year nominiert. Auch in der Welt der Düfte kann Kors Erfolge verzeichnen: Im Jahr 2000 brachte er ein Parfüm mit seinem Namen heraus, 2001 Michael for Men, 2005 folgte der mit dem Fifi ausgezeichnete Duft Island Michael Kors. 2004 gab Kors sein TV-Debüt als einer der Juroren in der für die Emmys nominierten Reality-Show „Project Runway". Diese Rolle übernimmt er seit nunmehr fünf Staffeln der Sendung. Mit promi-nenten Fans wie Jennifer Lopez, Charlize Theron, Liv Tyler, Gwyneth Paltrow, Anjelica Huston und Madonna setzt Kors seine Arbeit am Design eines sexy American Dream fort.

Michael Kors crée dans la plus pure tradition de l'opulence américaine : sportswear luxueux aux coupes impeccables, taillé dans des matières constrastées de cuir et de cachemire, avec quelques touches audacieuses de peau çà et là. Né à Long Island et élevé en banlieue, Kors a toujours eu une vision plutôt saine de la mode et de la ville de New York. Après des études de design au Fashion Institute of Technology, dès l'âge de 19 ans il commence à dessiner pour la boutique Lothar's. Encouragé par l'intérêt de la presse spécialisée, il crée la griffe Michael Kors en 1981, suivie en 1995 par la ligne de vêtements plus abordables Kors Michael Kors. Après le lancement d'une collection capsule pour homme en 1997, Kors est nommé styliste principal du prêt-à-porter féminin de la maison Céline. En février 1999, il devient directeur de la création de la griffe de luxe et supervise tous les produits pour femme. 1999 est une année en or pour Kors : le CFDA le consacre Womenswear Designer of the Year, puis Menswear Designer of the Year en 2003. Sa contribution dans le domaine des accessoires est également distinguée par cinq nominations consécutives (2001–2005) au prestigieux Accessories Designer of the Year Award. Il remporte tout autant de succès côté parfums : il lance sa fragrance éponyme en l'an 2000, le parfum masculin Michael for Men en 2001 et Island Michael Kors en 2005, couronné d'un Fifi Award. En 2004, Kors fait ses débuts à la télévision dans le jury de l'émission de télé-réalité « Project Runway », nommée aux Emmy Awards, un rôle qu'il continue d'assumer pour la cinquième saison du programme. Avec des fans aussi célèbres que Jennifer Lopez, Charlize Theron, Liv Tyler, Gwyneth Paltrow, Anjelica Huston et Madonna, Kors conserve toutefois une éthique sophistiquée, à l'image d'un sexy American Dream.

PHOTOGRAPHY HIROSHI KUTOMI. STYLING RACHAEL ZILLI. OCTOBER 2002.

What are your signature designs? The mix of something glamorous with something casual **What are your favourite pieces from any of your collections?** I always have a great white shirt, camel coat, trench, grey flannel trousers, the perfect cashmere pullover, brown croc slingbacks and a black sheath as part of my collections in one way or another… it's not necessarily about 'favourite', just pieces that should be part of every woman's wardrobe **How would you describe your work?** Chic, sexy, luxurious American sportswear **What's your ultimate goal?** To have more free time **What inspires you?** Women and their ever-changing moods and needs **Can fashion still have a political ambition?** I think fashion has a sociological impact rather than political **Who do you have in mind when you design?** I don't necessarily have a 'muse' or one woman in mind, rather it's about a group of women who constantly inspire me. Everyone from clients, to celebrities, to the women who work with me, to my mom **Is the idea of creative collaboration important to you?** I surround myself with people who have a strong opinion and I love the collaborative dialogue that takes place in my office on a daily basis, even if it is exhausting at times. Also, working with people in related fields is always inspiring, like Fabien Baron, who works with me on all of our creative materials, and Daniel Rowen, our architect **Who or what has been the greatest influence on your career?** Pop culture – everything from film and theatre to television and music – and my mother and grandmother **How have your own experiences affected your work as a designer?** I think that who I am and everything that I do comes out in my work. Whether it be a destination I'm dreaming of going to that inspires a collection, or the colour of water at my beach house that might inspire a palette for the season… it's all intertwined in my mind **Which is more important in your work: the process or the product?** Definitely the product…there's no point in design for design's sake. Everything I believe in is about getting women dressed. It has to be somewhat practical: I might love something throughout the process, but if a woman can't get into it because it has no zipper, or can't walk because it has no slit, then what's the point? **Is designing difficult for you?** If it was, I wouldn't still be doing this after 20-plus years **What's your definition of beauty?** Confidence and a great sense of humour **What's your philosophy?** Glamour combined with comfort is the only modern answer **What is the most important lesson you've learned?** Listen to your gut instinct and always remain open and curious.

"Creation never ends, once you start you can't stop"
TAO KURIHARA

PORTRAIT COURTESY STUDIO HARCOURT. PHOTOGRAPHY SØLVE SUNDSBØ. FASHION DIRECTOR EDWARD ENNINFUL. MODEL LILY COLE. MARCH 2009.

Comme des Garçons protégée Tao Kurihara is one of the most exciting young Japanese designers working today. Born in Tokyo in 1973, Kurihara moved to London when she finished school to study fashion at Central Saint Martins. In 1998, one year after graduating, she began work at Comme des Garçons, and in 2002 was appointed designer of the Tricot Comme des Garçons line. She spent the next eight years working closely with Junya Watanabe, before launching her own label under the Comme umbrella in 2005. Kurihara rose to the challenge, presenting her debut collection 'Tao' for spring/summer 2006 to instant critical acclaim. Working with knitwear, lace and lingerie, the small, concentrated collection of coquettish corsets, shorts and baby-doll dresses notched up more editorial than other new designers could hope to achieve in a lifetime. Always true to her own vision, Kurihara fiercely pursues her own path, claiming she doesn't make clothes she thinks people will like, but rather clothes she likes herself. In just a short number of years, she has risen up the ranks from showing off-schedule to being one of the most hyped and talked about shows on the catwalk schedule, with journalists and buyers falling over themselves to gain attendance. From her wedding dress collection to her vast twisting and voluminous silhouettes, Kurihara's clothes continue to challenge the imagination as much as she challenges the zeitgeist.

Tao Kurihara, Protégée von Comme des Garçons, ist wohl eine der aufregendsten japanischen Designerinnen der Gegenwart. 1973 in Tokio geboren, zog sie am Ende ihrer Schulzeit nach London, um am Central Saint Martins Mode zu studieren. Ein Jahr nach ihrem Studienabschluss (1998), begann sie bei Comme des Garçons, wo man sie 2002 zur Designerin der Tricot-Linie ernannte. In den folgenden acht Jahren arbeitete sie eng mit Junya Watanabe zusammen, bevor sie 2005 ihr eigenes Label unter dem Schirm von Comme gründete. Kurihara stellte sich der Herausforderung und präsentierte ihre Debüt-Kollektion „Tao" für Frühjahr/Sommer 2006, die bei den Kritikern auf Anhieb Zustimmung fand. Ihre Arbeiten aus Strick, Spitze und Dessous im Rahmen dieser kleinen, konzentrierten Kollektion aus koketten Corsagen, Shorts und Baby-Doll-Kleidern erzielte mehr Medienecho, als andere Jungdesigner in ihrem ganzen Leben bekommen. Kurihara bleibt stets ihrer eigenen Vision treu, verfolgt ihren Weg konsequent und behauptet von sich, keine Kleider zu machen, von denen sie glaubt, sie könnten den Leuten gefallen, sondern vielmehr Kleidung, die ihr selbst gefällt. In nur wenigen Jahren hat sie den Sprung von den Off-Präsentationen zu einem der meist gehypten und besprochenen Events im offiziellen Catwalk-Kalender vollbracht. Journalisten wie Einkäufer überschlagen sich fast, um daran teilnehmen zu können. Ob mit ihren Hochzeitskleidern oder den riesigen verwundenen und voluminösen Silhouetten – Kuriharas Kleider fordern nach wie vor die Phatansie ebenso heraus wie sie selbst den Zeitgeist.

Petite protégée de Comme des Garçons, Tao Kurihara est l'une des jeunes créatrices japonaises les plus prometteuses du moment. Née à Tokyo en 1973, Tao s'installe à Londres après ses études secondaires pour suivre le cursus en mode du Central Saint Martins. En 1998, un an après l'obtention de son diplôme, elle commence à travailler chez Comme des Garçons, où elle est nommée styliste de la ligne Tricot Comme des Garçons en 2002. Elle collabore étroitement avec Junya Watanabe pendant huit ans avant de lancer sa propre griffe sous la houlette de Comme des Garçons en 2005, un défi que Tao Kurihara relève sans problème : la première collection baptisée « Tao » qu'elle présente pour le printemps/été 2006 est immédiatement plébiscitée par la critique. Marquée par la maille, la dentelle et la lingerie, cette petite collection concentrée sur les corsets aguichants, les shorts et les robes baby-doll fait l'objet de plus d'articles de presse que tout autre jeune créateur n'espère en obtenir dans sa vie. Toujours fidèle à son approche personnelle, Tao Kurihara poursuit son chemin avec acharnement, affirmant qu'elle ne crée pas des vêtements pour qu'ils plaisent aux gens, mais pour qu'ils lui plaisent à elle. En quelques années seulement, elle a quitté le calendrier « off » pour s'imposer parmi les noms dont on parle le plus dans l'agenda des défilés officiels, les journalistes et les acheteurs faisant des pieds et des mains pour y assister. De sa collection de robes de mariée à ses nombreux modèles tordus et volumineux, les collections de Tao Kurihara ne cessent de défier l'imagination tout comme la créatrice défie l'esprit du temps.

HOLLY SHACKLETON

PHOTOGRAPHY KERRY HALLIHAN. STYLING ALASTAIR MCKIMM. MODEL MARIACARLA BOSCONO. NOVEMBER 2007.

How would you describe your work? The business of creation **What's your ultimate goal?** Near future goal: to continue and to become bigger in both the creative and business side **What inspires you?** Anything from my every day life **Is the idea of creative collaboration important to you?** In a way, I do collaborate creatively with my team and factory **Who has been the greatest influence on your career?** Comme des Garçons creation and power (Kawakubo and Watanabe) **Which is more important in your work: the process or the product?** Process equals products and products equals process **Is designing difficult for you? If so, what drives you to continue?** Creation never ends, once you start you can't stop **What's your definition of beauty?** Beauty makes people's hearts beat **What's your philosophy?** To feel or sense anything in everyday life from happiness to anger. Creation occurs from it **What is the most important lesson you've learned?** Never compromise.

© 2013 TASCHEN GMBH
HOHENZOLLERNRING 53, D-50672 KÖLN
WWW.TASCHEN.COM

EDITOR: TERRY JONES
DESIGN: MATTHEW HAWKER
FASHION DIRECTOR: EDWARD ENNINFUL
FASHION EDITOR: ERIKA KURIHARA
MANAGING EDITOR: KAREN HODKINSON
EDITORIAL ASSISTANCE: BEN REARDON, HOLLY SHACKLETON
DESIGN ASSISTANCE: KEVIN WONG
PROJECT ASSISTANCE: DOMINIQUE FENN, BEN KEI
EXECUTIVE DIRECTOR: TRICIA JONES

WRITERS:
JAMES ANDERSON
LEE CARTER
SIMON CHILVERS
LAUREN COCHRANE
PETER DE POTTER
AIMEE FARRELL
JO-ANN FURNISS
LIZ HANCOCK
MARK HOOPER
JAMIE HUCKBODY
TERRY JONES
DAVID LAMB
KAREN LEONG
AVRIL MAIR
TERRY NEWMAN
MAX PEARMAIN
BEN REARDON
MARCUS ROSS
SUSIE RUSHTON
HOLLY SHACKLETON
SKYE SHERWIN
JAMES SHERWOOD
JOSH SIMS
DAVID VASCOTT
GLENN WALDRON
NANCY WATERS

EDITORIAL COORDINATION: SIMONE PHILIPPI, COLOGNE
PRODUCTION COORDINATION: UTE WACHENDORF, COLOGNE
GERMAN TRANSLATION: HENRIETTE ZELTNER, MUNICH
FRENCH TRANSLATION: CLAIRE LE BRETON, PARIS

PRINTED IN CHINA
ISBN 978-3-8365-4892-2